Officer Survival

for

Probation & Parole Officers

Scott Kirshner, M.Ed.

Neither the author nor the publisher assumes any responsibility for the use or misuse of information contained in this book.

Copyright © 2014 Scott Kirshner, M.Ed.

All rights reserved.

ISBN-10: 1495391922
ISBN-13: 978-1495391927

DEDICATION

Officer Survival for Probation and Parole Officers is foremost dedicated to those officers who have perished in the line of duty. Your sacrifice will never be forgotten.

This book is also dedicated to those who have been seriously injured protecting the community.

I also would like to thank all the community corrections officers who work ethically and diligently oftentimes for little pay, long hours, with huge caseloads, and poor training. The majority of civilians have no idea of the sacrifice you make on a daily basis to keep our communities safe.
Thank you.

Last, I would like to thank all those who have been involved in my training and growth as an instructor. Along the journey there have been many people who have influenced me. Sometimes I learn improved ways to teach a skill or facilitate an important topic while other times I learn what not to do which is equally important. All of these experiences have made me a better instructor.

Table of Contents

Acknowledgments i
Preface iii
Chapter 1: Introduction to Community Corrections 1
Chapter 2: Combat Mindset 45
Chapter 3: Survival Fundamentals 123
Chapter 4: Use of Force 171
Chapter 5: Office Safety 263
Chapter 6: Field Safety 311
Chapter 7: Probation – Parole Searches 355
Chapter 8: Self-Aid / Buddy-Aid 403
About The Author 447
References 449

Acknowledgments

There have been many individuals who have helped me to bring this book to completion. Some have involved long conversations while others were brief exchanges. Yet, all have been tremendously helpful. I would like to thank my wife Stacy who has had to hear about this book for years. A special thank you goes to Brian Kohler who has always provided excellent advice and direction but most of all he has been a great friend for many years.

I thank Jason Wuestenberg, Edrid Tirado, Dave "Buck Savage" Smith, Ken Good, Chris Heben, Chris Sajnog, Herschel Bento Davis, Michael T. Rayburn and Loren Christensen.

A special thanks to R.T. who is a current member of the U.S. Air Force Special Operations Pararescue.

A special thank you to Chris Cosgriff from the Officer Down Memorial Page.

Preface

This book is dedicated to all probation and parole officers who diligently work to make our communities safer. Oftentimes you are overworked and underpaid. You supervise offenders who have committed a wide variety of crimes from minor to extremely violent. Many of the offenders you supervise have multiple needs to be addressed during their community supervision grant. These include: substance abuse issues, mental health problems, lack of job skills, minimal education, lack of a steady residence, poor communication skills, transportation problems, health issues, and a host of other factors that impact your ability to supervise the offender so that he or she becomes a law abiding and productive member of society. Additionally, every offender you supervise is capable of causing you harm. Man or woman, juvenile or adult, healthy or frail, first time offender or career criminal, each offender that you supervise is a potential threat to your safety and well-being. You must maintain situational awareness at all times to prevent or respond to violence while the offender only needs to find one opportunity that you are not alert to cause you harm. On a daily basis you are faced with a multitude of challenges to include: Non-compliant offenders, safety issues, lack of funding, training requirements, old equipment, limited resources, limited time, busy family life, health issues, etc. The department you work for also faces challenges that can directly impact your safety.

Many departments are currently facing severe budgetary and fiscal challenges where scarcity of funds has to be allocated accordingly. Difficult decisions must be made regarding where to spend a limited amount of dollars. Unfortunately, officer safety training and acquisition of new safety tools is often sacrificed. Many times this is justified by saying that officers rarely get injured or killed in the line of duty. Yet, when this does occur the price paid is far too high. It is never acceptable for departments to sacrifice officer safety. Officers are burdened with high caseloads, often work nights and weekends, and typically go well above and beyond what is required. At minimum, departments must provide officers with safety training that is ongoing, dynamic, performance based, and realistic. Departments must issue officers with safety equipment that will provide the best chance of prevailing in a violent encounter. Too many times I have heard both officers and administrators complain that officer safety equipment such as OC spray, handcuffs, expandable batons, and firearms will negatively impact the way offenders view officers or will make officers act like police officers. These fears are inaccurate, not worthy of debate, and detract from the real issue of officer safety. They are excuses without justification or merit. I have been with two large departments that went from very limited officer safety training to providing significant training followed by the issuing of safety equipment to include firearms. Overwhelmingly officers acted professionally. They knew that their job functions and duties did not change because they received officer survival training and equipment. And, they did not act like police officers. In fact, the majority of officers performed their jobs as they always have prior to being issued safety equipment. Yes, every now and then there will be an officer who doesn't follow the rules but these officers can be addressed individually to resolve the issue. Offenders did not view officers differently and in the majority of cases nothing changed at all...except that officers now had survival training and tools.

My goals with writing this book include the following:

1. Officers will take officer safety much more seriously in the course of their job duties. Officers cannot afford to become complacent which happens far too often. Complacency is an insidious outcome of routine that fools officers into believing that you will always be safe from harm because nothing harmful has happened in the past. You can never allow this line of thought to be acceptable. From the moment an officer leaves his or her residence the goal is to be in Condition Yellow and maintain situational awareness until you are back home in the safety and security of your residence.

2. Officers will train officer survival skills even if it means training on your own time and at your own expense. Survival skills in defensive tactics and firearms are perishable skills meaning that these skills degrade over time if you do not regularly practice. Training once a quarter or less is not enough. Training must be consistent, ongoing, dynamic, and realistic. Some departments conduct an initial defensive tactics training academy but never require that officers attend refresher training. Other departments require refresher training annually. Realistically, you must train on a consistent basis in order to build the necessary confidence and skill set to prevail in the **worst case scenario**. If you only practice the minimum of what is required by your department then do not expect a great result when it comes time to perform these skills under less than ideal circumstances where the psychological and

physiological reactions to stress may work against you. You must take some responsibility and ownership to train. After all, it is you that will suffer the consequences if you fail to train.

3. Encourage officers, when possible, to work with a partner. It is well understood that working with a partner significantly increases your level of safety. The caveat is that you must choose a partner who is safety conscious and has the skills to actually back you up should an offender contact turn violent. You want more than just a warm body backing you up. You want a competent officer with skills to cover your six. I understand that it is often challenging to work with a partner due to caseload size, work load issues, department size, and a host of other factors. It is advantageous for you to find solutions to such problems. At a minimum, use a competent partner on all first residential contacts or anytime that you suspect trouble may occur.

4. To make officer safety a priority for administrators and decision makers. When tough fiscal challenges hit, and they always do, department leaders cannot automatically cut safety training or equipment from the budget. It sends a clear message to officers that officer safety is not a priority. Leaders must find other places to cut funding but never allow officers to work in an environment where they are not provided the best safety training and equipment. I would like to see departments become proactive instead of reactive.

Rarely does a community corrections officer hear the words "thank you." I thank you for your dedication to a profession that does not get enough recognition for the hard work you conduct. Many citizens fail to understand how you positively impact the community. They only hear about the times when an offender on probation or parole commits a high-profile crime. Yet, there are hundreds if not thousands of offenders that you have supervised and positively impacted who are now active, productive, and law abiding members of society. Be safe today so that you can be successful tomorrow.

Stay safe,

Scott Kirshner

November 14, 2014

Chapter 1: Introduction to Community Corrections

It takes only one act of violence to dramatically change your world for the worse. Generally, you don't get to choose the time, location, or circumstances. It matters not that you are tired, sick, injured, or distracted. You are either prepared to respond appropriately or you are not. There tends not to be a middle ground when violence is directed at you.

Scott Kirshner

Introduction and Overview of Community Corrections

Community Corrections refers to the field of corrections, which encompasses probation and parole officers, who supervise offenders in the community and provide services outside jail or prison. Community Corrections can also include home confinement, electronic or GPS monitoring, day reporting centers, work release, halfway houses, curfews, and community-based correctional facilities. Community Corrections can be applicable to both adult and juvenile offenders who are placed on either probation or parole.

As a Probation or Parole Officer you have the opportunity to enter into a very rewarding and challenging career that will allow you to supervise varying types of offenders and work in a variety of assignments. You may be assigned to supervise sex offenders, domestic violence offenders, violent offenders, white collar criminals, drug addicts, alcoholics, seriously mentally ill offenders or more likely a combination thereof. You may work with adults or juveniles. You can be assigned to a standard caseload, intensive probation supervision caseload, presentence investigations, court liaison, Drug Court, DUI Court, mental health caseload or the Fugitive Apprehension Unit (warrants) among others. For the sake of consistency I will utilize the title of 'officer' throughout this book in reference to community corrections officers which includes both probation and parole officers.

What is the difference: Probation and Parole

Many people outside the criminal justice system are confused with the difference between probation and parole.

<u>Probation</u> is a suspended sentence in which an offender agrees to comply with certain conditions imposed by the Court in lieu of a jail or prison sentence. After the offender has been found guilty of a criminal offense, he/she is granted

a "suspension" of punishment and is placed under the supervision of the Court via the Probation Department. Probation can include a term of jail, treatment, counseling, restitution, fines, and other special terms of probation.

Parole is the release from prison after serving a portion of the imposed sentence. It is a conditional release from prison granted by the Board of Executive Clemency. The offender will be under the supervision of a parole officer. Parole can be revoked if the offender fails to observe the terms and conditions of parole. Failure to follow these may result in the parolee being returned to prison to complete his prison sentence. Parolees will sometimes state that they would rather "kill their number" meaning they would rather serve out their complete prison sentence instead of being placed on parole.

Essentially, probation is community supervision *before* the offender is sentenced to prison with the goal that the offender will not have to be incarcerated in prison. Parole is a form of community supervision *after* the inmate has served a portion of his prison term.

What is the difference: Jail and Prison

Another area of confusion is the difference between jail and prison. Typically, a jail sentence is imposed when a defendant is incarcerated for a period of less than one year. Jails are normally run by the county. Prison is typically for offenders sentenced to the Department of Corrections who commit felonies and have a sentence of longer than one year. Prisons are run by the state. Media outlets typically use the terms jail and prison incorrectly. For example, you may hear a news report that a man was sentenced to 35 years jail for sexual assault. This would be incorrect as he would be sentenced to prison, not jail.

Probation in More Detail

Probation is a suspended sentence in which an offender agrees to comply with certain court conditions imposed by the court rather than being sentenced to jail or prison. After the offender has been found guilty of a criminal offense, he is granted a "suspension" of punishment and is placed under the supervision of the court via the probation department. Probation can include jail time, treatment, restitution, and other special terms & conditions. Probation is subject to supervision from a probation officer and the probationer must follow conditions of probation. It is a substitute for a jail or prison term, which is contingent upon good behavior. Probation is a suspended sentence in which the judge will allow a defendant to remain in the community while being supervised by a probation officer. When an offender is sentenced to probation, depending on your style or the policy of your agency, they may be called: probationer, defendant, offender, or client. The defendant will be required to follow conditions of probation which are court ordered rules that must be followed to be successful. Typically they will include:

- Obey all laws,
- Report to your probation officer as directed
- Pay fines, fees and restitution,
- Attend and successfully complete required treatment, i.e. substance abuse treatment, sex offender treatment, anger management, domestic violence treatment, etc.
- Do not use any drugs or alcohol
- Not have any contact with the victim without prior written approval from the probation officer
- Do not move residence without prior written approval from your probation officer
- Do not possess any weapons
- Maintain legal employment or be enrolled in school

Failure to follow conditions of probation may result in the

judge imposing a sentence which can lead to a term of jail or prison. Oftentimes when an offender is non-compliant and in violation of probation the probation officer will file paperwork with the court requesting the defendant return to court to see a judge. Typically, this is done through a process called probation revocation. The probation officer may utilize a summons, warrant, or an arrest to take the defendant back to court.

Method	Procedure	Type of Offender
Summons	Defendant is provided written notification of the date, time, and location to appear in court. A summons must be delivered to the defendant and contain his signature to be valid. Failure to appear will result in the issuance of a warrant.	Low risk, non-violent offenders who have a high probability of appearing in court
Warrant	A warrant can be utilized when the defendant has absconded and his location is unknown.	Use with absconders
Arrest	An arrest is utilized on defendants that pose a risk to the community or are a flight risk. Can be executed in the office or in the field.	High risk, violent, flight risk

Once the defendant appears in court he will have a Revocation Arraignment Hearing where he can admit or enter a denial to the PV allegations. If he admits the, judge will reinstate or revoke probation. The judge will utilize information provided by the probation officer that was written in a probation revocation report which typically includes a disposition recommendation. If the defendant enters a denial he will be scheduled for another court date for a witness violation hearing where the state must prove by preponderance of the evidence that the defendant has violated one or more of his conditions of probation. A preponderance of the evidence means that the state must prove by at least 51% that the defendant is in violation of probation. If the prosecution does not meet the preponderance of evidence the defendant will then remain on probation as before. If found guilty of violating probation the judge may reinstate the defendant back to his original probation grant. If the defendant was on a standard probation caseload the judge may increase his sanction and put him on an Intensive Probation Supervision (IPS) caseload which has more stringent requirements and different contact standards. The judge may also revoke the defendant's probation and sentence the offender to prison. Whatever jail time the defendant has served as part of his probation violation process will be credited as time served for his prison sentence. For example, if the defendant was in jail for 30 days during his probation revocation proceeding and he was found in violation of probation and sentenced to prison for 3.5 years, the sentence would be reduced by 30 days for time already served.

Community Corrections Officers: Same Title Different Job

When one thinks of a police officer we instantly know what that officer's job entails regardless of where in the country they work. There will always be some variations but for the most part a police officer's job duties and functions are the same whether they work in Washington, Michigan, New York, Kansas, Florida or Arizona. The same cannot be said of community corrections officers where for example some have peace officer status and others do not. The job duties, functions, and even authority of a probation/parole officer can vary dramatically from state to state. In addition, defendants can be sentenced to probation from different court systems. There is federal probation, county probation, municipal probation and some agencies are responsible for both probation and parole at the state level. Each of these jurisdictions may have different rules, policies, and levels of authority. When probation and parole officers gather at such events such as the American Probation and Parole Association (APPA) institute it will not take long to see that officers with the same job title have different levels of authority and responsibility.

Examples of job differences include (Not indicative of all departments):

Peace Officer Status	Non Peace Officer Status
Authority to conduct arrests	Not authorized to conduct arrests
Authority to conduct probation searches	Not authorized to conduct probation searches
Conducts field contacts to residence, employment, and treatment providers	Job is strictly office work; field contacts are not required
Receive officer survival training to include defensive tactics and/or firearms training	Safety training is limited to verbal de-escalation skills
Authority to utilize sanctions as deemed necessary for non-compliant behavior	Reports non-compliant behavior to court
Has units consisting of specialized caseloads to include sex offenders, domestic violence offenders, seriously mentally ill offenders, white collar crimes, etc.	No specialized caseloads. Officers supervise a variety of defendants. Officers do not specialize in a specific type of offender or offense.

When we mention the job title of Community Corrections Officer whether it be Probation Officer or Parole Officer it can have a very different meaning depending on your location, state/federal laws, and the policies and procedures of the department. All community corrections officers are not the same.

Probation and Parole Populations

According to the Bureau of Justice Statistics, Correctional Populations in the United States, 2009[i], there were 5,018,900 adults on community supervision with 4,203,967 on probation and 819,308 on parole[ii].

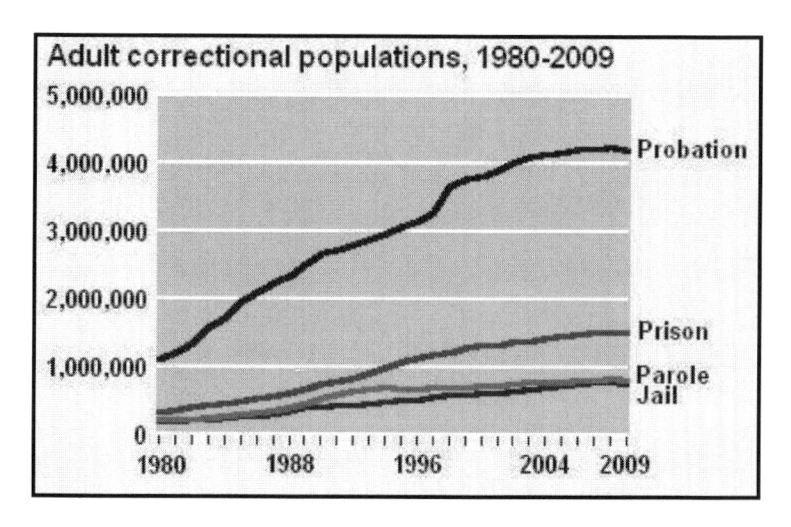

Probation and Parole Populations in the U.S. [iii]

[Chart: Adult correctional populations, 1980-2009, showing Probation, Prison, Parole, and Jail lines from 1980 to 2009]

Of the 4,203,967 adults on probation the following lists some of the more serious offenses[iv]:

# of Reported Offenses	Type of Violent Offense
277,698	Violent Offenses not specified
81,535	Domestic Violence
67,114	Sex Offense
426,347	Total Reported Violent Offenses

Of the 819,308 on parole the following lists some of the more serious offenses[v]:

# of Reported Offenses	Type of Violent Offense
134,073	Violent Offenses not specified
58,546	Sex Offense
192,619	Total Reported Violent Offenses

In 2010, an estimated 491,100 delinquency cases resulted in a term of juvenile probation.[vi]

Juvenile Probation 1985-2009

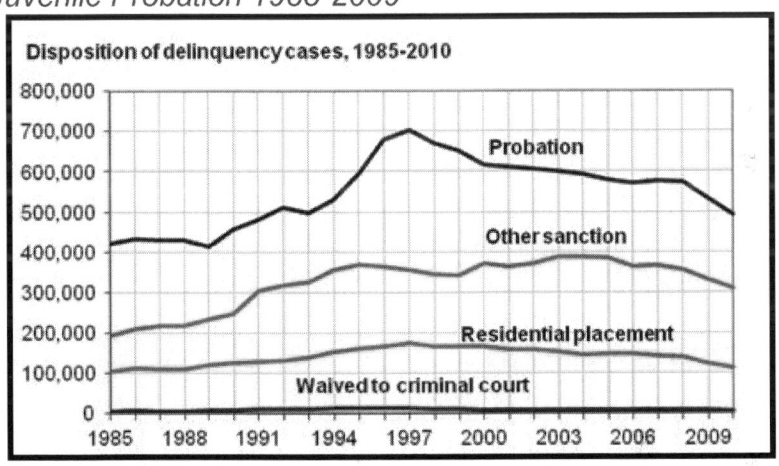

Disposition of delinquency cases, 1985-2010

With such a large population of both adult and juvenile offenders being supervised in the community for serious and violent offenses it becomes apparent that these offenders can pose a serious risk to you. Now the majority of offenders you supervise have no intention of harming you but you rarely have the luxury of knowing which ones have such intentions. During your career you will, at some point, supervise a violent offender who is more concerned with their freedom rather than your safety. It is imperative that you never lose sight of this point.

Being an officer means that offenders can view you as a threat to their freedom regardless of what actual authority you are granted to limit such freedom. The offender's perception may be that you have the authority to arrest or take them back to court or prison. Even if you lack such authority the offender's perception becomes reality in their mind. You are perceived as the gatekeeper or roadblock to the offender's freedom. It is critically important to understand this truth up front and realize that anyone on your caseload can view you not as an officer who is fair, just, and wants to help but as an officer who wants to limit freedom. Offenders often act in unpredictable ways when their freedom and liberty is at stake.

Mission of Community Supervision

When discussing the primary mission of community supervision one of the main priorities is <u>public safety</u>. This can be accomplished through a variety of methods:

1. Using validated assessment tools to accurately measure offender risk and needs in order to help guide court decisions and supervision strategies by applying the appropriate level of services; periodic reassessments must be completed to measure progress or regress of the offender, and case management plans must be updated to reflect current needs;
2. Managing offender risk by enforcing court orders, affording opportunities for pro-social change, and expecting law-abiding behavior and personal accountability;
3. Working in partnerships with community based providers who utilize research based prevention and intervention services;
4. Working in a collaborative manner with other law enforcement agencies;
5. Facilitating victim involvement and restorative justice services;

6. Recognizing and rewarding staff performance and achievement;
7. Providing exceptional training opportunities to enhance professional skills and build leadership;
8. Providing staff with current and necessary equipment to successfully carry out all job duties, functions, and responsibilities.

If community supervision is viewed as ineffective the courts, community, and victims will lose confidence and trust in your ability to effectively and efficiently carry out the mission. This can result in negative public attention which has dire consequences on funding, hiring, training, equipment purchases, etc. There will always be situations of high profile crimes committed by offenders on community supervision. In such cases it is necessary to ensure that the supervising officer was following all policies, procedures, and supervision strategies correctly to mitigate negative consequences to the officer and department.

The profession of community corrections is in a continuous state of flux with opinions varying on the most effective manner to supervise offenders. The pendulum swings between the extremes of "lock them up" or "hug them" depending on the political climate and public opinion. Despite the current climate, which you have little control over, you must always believe that offenders have the ability to change. That is, to become law abiding and productive members of society. If you do not have this belief then you are doomed to fail as your thought process will be that all offenders are incapable of change or being productive members of society.

Supervision Styles: Cop vs. Counselor

The profession of community corrections is the ultimate balancing act between being a "cop" and being a "counselor" as a style when supervising offenders. The best officers are the ones that know when to wear the appropriate hat. An officer that is at either extreme of these supervision styles will never be a good community corrections officer because they lack flexibility in adapting to different situations.

Supervision Style Comparison	
"Cop"	**"Counselor"**
Very "black and white" approach	Tends to be very "grey"
Compliance focused	Treatment focused
Holds offenders accountable to unrealistic expectations & conditions	Fails to hold offenders accountable for non-compliant behavior
Exaggerates non-compliance	Minimizes non-compliance
Directive communication style	Communicates with advice and guidance
Can be viewed as a dictator	Viewed as supportive and understanding
Focus is on "public safety"	Focus is on "supporting" the offender

The most effective community supervision officers are those who utilize a balanced approach. They adjust their supervision style based upon the circumstances of the offender while taking into account the big picture. Your supervision style will impact how offenders view you as their supervising officer. Let's examine these two styles in more detail.

If you are the "cop" who sees everything as black and white you will be seen as a strict disciplinarian who is not able to take into account situations that arise. You will be viewed as an officer who wants to send the offender back to jail or prison at the first opportunity. Offenders who believe that you are treating them unfairly may potentially take out their frustration on you through violence.

Officer Survival for Probation and Parole Officers

Following is a hypothetical scenario:

1. You have an offender who is reporting to the probation/parole office but shows up five minutes late. You immediately write him up with a violation warning followed by a ten minute lecture on the importance of being on time. During your berating of the offender you keep stating how busy you are and how much work you have to complete today. Never once do you ask the offender why he was late which in this case was due to traffic from a fatal auto accident; a situation that the offender has no control. In fact, the offender states he left you a voicemail on your phone explaining that he would be a few minutes late but you didn't answer your phone and you haven't checked your voicemail yet. Your response to the offender is that he should always plan for the unexpected! The offender just keeps his mouth shut because he knows he isn't going to win this battle.

   If this situation is a typical scenario on how you treat offenders it is be easy to see how those under your supervision may become frustrated over time. How this offender reacts over the long haul can be unpredictable and possibly lead to violence.

If your supervision style is that of the "counselor" you tend to allow frequent instances of non-compliance with few to no sanctions or consequences. The offender quickly realizes they can get away with a lot of non-compliant behavior. When they get caught doing something wrong, they use manipulation to get you to utilize therapeutic techniques instead of negative consequences. The offender will convincingly beg for *"one more opportunity"* to comply and state *"this will not happen again."* But, because of your inconsistency in holding offenders accountable the offender will continue to test your limits. The "counselor" supervision style can be a safety hazard because you tend to not want to see or believe the bad intentions of many offenders.

It is vitally important to be flexible with your supervision style and strategies that you use to obtain both offender compliance and behavioral change. Offenders should be held accountable in a way that is both fair and equitable. Supervising at the extremes of being too harsh or too lenient is not a good strategy and can have safety implications.

Officer Survival

The focus of this book is geared toward a narrow, yet critical, component of your job which is officer survival. Community corrections officers have varying levels of authority, wear many hats, and are required to have a variety of job skills. Yet, none is more important than those skills that can protect your life or another officer's life from harm by a dedicated threat who wants to cause serious bodily injury or death. The risks are real but you rarely hear of officers getting injured or killed on the job. One reason for this is that there is no centralized depository of information that gathers statistics on probation or parole officer injuries. Police officer injuries and deaths are tracked through the Federal Bureau of Investigation with the Uniform Crime Report which is produced annually from data provided by nearly 17,000 law enforcement agencies across the United States. The FBI publishes *Law Enforcement Officers Killed and Assaulted* each year to provide information about the police officers who were killed, feloniously or accidentally, and those police officers who were assaulted while performing their duties. The FBI collects this data through the Uniform Crime Reporting (UCR) Program.

In September 2005, The American Probation and Parole Association (APPA) urged the Director of the Federal Bureau of Investigation to require the National Incident Based Reporting System to include uniform reporting of state data of probation, parole and community supervision officers killed or assaulted while on duty. So far this process has failed to move forward and information relating to probation and parole injuries and deaths is not tracked by any central depository. Because there is no central resource to track such information it is very difficult to obtain detailed and accurate data on injuries or deaths that occur in probation and parole. Until there is a similar accounting for community corrections officers we will truly not know the extent of injuries, assaults or deaths to probation and parole officers. Making matters worse is that many departments do a poor job internally of tracking officer statistics related to injuries or critical incidents.

Below are basic details of the thirteen probation and parole officers killed in the line of duty.[vii]

Name	Age	Years of Service	Cause of Death	Wpn	Location
David Burns	Unk	Unk.	Gunfire	Handgun	Field - Transporting Prisoner
David McReynolds	60	Unk.	Gunfire	Handgun	Field Contact
Paul Weber	26	Unk.	Stabbed	Knife	Field Contact
Barry Sutherland	32	4	Gunfire	Handgun	Field Contact to conduct a planned arrest on a warrant
Pauline Stewart	58	7	Stabbed	Knife	Field Contact
Bjorn Svenson	33	10	Gunfire	Handgun	Office – ambushed in parking lot
Brian Rooney	35	4	Gunfire	Unknown Firearm	Field Contact – contract attack
Mary Fine	42	Unk.	Sexually Assaulted, Strangulation	Physical Assault	Field Contact
Thomas Gahl	38	11	Gunfire	Shotgun	Field Contact
Gerald Moberly	44	6	Gunfire	Handgun	Field Contact to conduct a planned arrest on a warrant
Donald Knepple	48	12	Gunfire	Handgun	Field - ambushed at counseling center
Louise Pargeter	34	3	Strangulation	Rope	Field Contact
Jeffrey McCoy	32	7	Gunfire	Handgun	Field Contact

The above list is comprised exclusively of officers killed in the line of duty by violent means and is not necessarily a complete list of all officers killed in the line of duty. Some officers were not included due to lack of available information and scarcity of details. Again, a National Incident Based Reporting System would allow more information to be assessable and afford an accurate and detailed picture of injuries and deaths to community corrections officers.

Based upon the previous list we can determine the following:

    40.2: Average Officer Age
    7.8: Average Years of Service

Cause of death:

    61.5%: Handgun
    15.4%: Knife
    15.4%: Strangulation
    7.7%: Shotgun

Location of Incident:

    92.3%: Field
    7.7%: Office

Circumstances of Incident:

    46.2%: Residential contact[viii] (Webber, Stewart, Fine, Gahl, Pargeter, McCoy)
    23.1%: Ambushed (Svenson, Rooney, Knepple)
    15.4%: Homicide occurred during a planned arrest (Sutherland, Moberly)
    7.7%: Transporting prisoner (Burns)

It should be noted that there are other probation, parole, and correctional staff, who are not officers, that were killed in the line of duty. Their ultimate sacrifice is no less meaningful.

And while not the focus of this book officers are more likely to be killed in the line of duty from an auto accident than by violence.

    Let's now examine a few of the above homicides and look at some safety procedures to consider and, when applicable, discuss common myths that are often told about certain types of offenders that are not necessarily true. In looking at these cases I am focusing on the big picture and not all the details or minutia of the homicide. The points that I discuss are not intended as a comprehensive analysis; they are designed to make officers think about potential hazards so that these situations can be avoided in the future. I would also like to stress that none of the information discussed is to pick out flaws or faults that may have occurred. This is not about Monday morning quarterbacking or hindsight bias with the benefit of knowing what has already occurred to these officers who have made the ultimate sacrifice.

Officer Survival for Probation and Parole Officers

Parole Officer Barry N. Sutherland

New York State Division of Parole
End of Watch: December 13, 1976
Age: 32
Years of Service: 4.5
Cause of Death: Gunfire from a .32 caliber firearm
Circumstance: Planned field arrest

Summary:

Officer Sutherland along with two other parole officers were attempting to arrest a parole violator who had a parole violation warrant. The offender was placed on parole after serving a prison sentence for criminal possession of a firearm. Sutherland and two other parole officers were waiting for the parolee in the crowded lobby of a building. When the suspect entered the lobby he immediately recognized the parole officers and ran to affect his escape. The parolee then drew a .32 caliber handgun and began firing which resulted in the death of Officer Sutherland and wounding of a civilian who was caught in the line of fire. The other parole officers restrained from firing their weapons due to the presence of civilians and the possibility of injuring or killing an innocent person. The parole officers courageously tackled the suspect and initiated an arrest.

The parolee was convicted of 2nd Degree Murder in the homicide of Officer Sutherland and sentenced to life in prison. He later escaped from prison and on June 20, 1978, was shot and killed in a shootout with police officers in Brooklyn, New York.

Discussion:

This case drives home the level of danger involved when

arresting an offender. Sutherland used excellent judgment in having two other parole officers with him to arrest the parolee. Except for certain situations which generally would be out of your control you should never attempt to arrest an offender by yourself. It is critical to always have backup. This case demonstrates that things can go horribly bad even with multiple officers available.

Items to consider when planning an arrest of a violator:

1. What is the offense that the offender was convicted?

   In this case we know the parolee had a history of weapons violations which significantly raises the risks and dangerousness of this arrest. It is a good practice to consider anyone that you are going to arrest as being armed with a weapon until proven otherwise.

2. How many officers will be needed to execute the arrest as safely as possible that will minimize injuries to officers, civilians, and the arrestee?

   Generally, a minimum of three officers would be recommended to carry out an arrest. If there are specific indicators or prior history of violence, weapons, or suicidal thoughts then more officers would be required. Having too many officers on hand is better than not having enough.

3. Will the assistance of police be needed?

   Utilization of your local police department or sheriff's office is a good idea. Police officers, due to the nature of their jobs, generally have more experience with arrests and typically have a higher level of training and tactics than probation or parole officers.

4. What is the safest location to conduct the arrest that will minimize potential escape or injury to officers and civilians?

   When deciding on a safe location to conduct an arrest it is a good practice to have the offender at a location that does not have civilians around to reduce the possibility of injuring innocent people or having them taken hostage which then requires an immediate police response. It is also good tactics to have all potential avenues of escape covered by armed officers should the offender attempt to escape.

5. What is your medical plan should an officer, civilian, or arrestee become injured during the arrest?

   It is always a good idea to have a medical plan and know the location of the nearest hospital should an injury occur. Common sense and good judgment will dictate which method is appropriate depending on the situation.

   Potential options include:

   - Call 9-1-1 for an emergency response and render aid until medical help arrives. The scene must be safe with no active threats.
   - Depending on the severity of the injury and the location of appropriate medical care you may decide to transport the injured person in your vehicle.
   - You may also consider having an ambulance and/or the fire department on standby if your jurisdiction allows. If you have an ambulance or fire department on standby you will need to notify them of a safe location to stage until needed or until they are released from service.

Again, these items are not meant to judge the officers in the Sutherland case but to get you to think about possibilities and contingencies in order to effectively and safely plan and execute an arrest.

Parole Officer Pauline Stewart

West Virginia Division of Corrections
End of Watch: August 1, 1977
Age: 58
Years of Service: 7
Cause of Death: Knife, Stabbed to death
Circumstance: Residential field contact

Summary:

Officer Stewart was conducting a field contact at the home of 79 year old parolee Freeman Collins who she had supervised for a period of just less than 5 years. Collins contacted Officer Stewart about an injury he received in a car accident for which she had planned to drive him to the doctor the following day. Collins called Officer Stewart the evening before she planned to take him to the doctor stating that he was getting worse. This prompted Officer Stewart to go to his residence at approximately 6:00PM to check on the situation. After arriving Officer Stewart and parolee Collins got into an argument reportedly because she wasn't going to take Collins to the hospital that evening and would wait until the following day. Collins grabbed a butcher knife and repeatedly stabbed Officer Stewart resulting in her death within minutes. Neighbors heard Officer Stewart screaming and called the police. Upon police arrival parolee Collins was simply sitting in a chair very calm.

Freeman Collins served 42 years in prison for a murder in 1930 where he killed an individual with an ax. He was sentenced to life in prison but received parole in September

1972. While on parole Collins had issues with alcohol for which his parole could have been revoked but Officer Stewart chose to work with him rather than violate his parole.

Collins was convicted of 1st Degree Murder for the homicide of Officer Stewart and he was sentenced to life in prison. Due to his age and poor health he was eventually transferred to a nursing home and died at the age of 96.

Discussion:

The brutal homicide of Officer Stewart imparts the lesson that an offender's age or medical conditions does not mean that an offender is not capable of inflicting extreme violence. Collins, despite being 79 years old and complaining of medical problems was still able to viciously stab Officer Stewart to death.

Officer Stewart supervised this offender for almost five years which can give officers a sense that they "know" the offender which is never the case. In fact, the longer you supervise the same offender the easier it becomes to become complacent and lax with safety and security procedures. The result of complacency can be fatal!

Myth:

All too often I have heard officers make statements referring to an offender's age that they could not possibly pose a threat to their safety. This belief is simply not true and causes a false sense of security. Even worse, officer's then let their guard down and become lax in their safety procedures and tactics which they would not do with other offenders.

You must never assume that offenders under your supervision are not capable of causing serious bodily injury or death. You must avoid feeling safer due to an offender's age, either young or old, or reported medical condition. Proper safety procedures must be used all the time with all offenders. It is extremely important to be consistent in your safety practices.

Parole Supervisor Bjorn Svenson

> Florida Probation and Parole Commission
> End of Watch: August 31, 1982
> Age: 33
> Years of Service: 10
> Cause of Death: Gunfire
> Circumstance: Ambushed in the probation and parole office parking lot

Summary:

Supervisor Svenson was gunned down by parolee Harry Phillips in the probation and parole office parking lot while placing items in the trash. Phillips shot Svenson multiple times in the chest, back, and head even taking time to reload his weapon. After being shot Svenson tried to run but one of the bullets struck his spine causing him to collapse shortly thereafter. Phillips then reloaded and emptied the gun into Svenson. This case should be considered a planned execution. Phillips had a violent history with a prior conviction of armed robbery.

Svenson was the supervisor of probation officers who were responsible for supervising Phillips. Svenson had repeated problems, over an extended period of time, with Phillips having unauthorized contact, due to an imagined crush, with his female probation officer. Phillips was directed to stay away from the probation and parole office unless he had an authorized reason to report. Eventually Phillips's parole was revoked for technical violations due to continued incidents and he was returned to prison.

After being placed back on parole Phillips began appearing at places attempting to contact persons who had been involved in his revocation and there were issues with veiled threats. Phillips was observed several times by his parked vehicle at the routes that several of the officers involved in the case used to travel to their homes after work. Phillips became increasingly agitated at meetings where parole rules were addressed.

A week prior to Supervisor Svenson's murder there was an incident in which an unknown suspect fired several shots into the home of a probation officer who was dating Phillips' probation officer. Fortunately, the shots did not hit or injure these officers. Phillips was the prime suspect but there was no evidence linking him to the crime.

Harry Phillips was sentenced to death for the homicide of Svenson and is currently on death row in Florida.

Discussion:

The murder of Supervisor Svenson reiterates the importance of addressing non-compliant and threatening behavior in an appropriate manner and having a plan of action if the noncompliant behavior continues. The longer an offender gets away with non-compliant behavior the more embolden they can become in their actions. Even when officers and supervisors take all appropriate actions the outcome can still result in tragedy as evidenced in the Svenson homicide.

All threats whether veiled or direct are to be taken seriously. In cases of non-compliant behavior or threats it is important to factually and thoroughly document the threat to include exactly what the offender said or implied. All threats must be taken seriously and reported to a supervisor and up the chain of command for possible further action. All departments should have a process in place to address threats to include a threat assessment instrument and measures to take that ensure staff remains safe.

When there is improper behavior from the offender, consider transferring the offender to a different officer's caseload to be supervised. Also consider having the offender report to a completely different probation/parole office if possible. Offenders must know that threats of any kind will immediately and appropriately be addressed.

It is also important to change your routine and not become complacent with your activities. Harry Phillips had knowledge of where officers lived and the routes they traveled. People tend to be creatures of habit and it is good practice to vary work schedules and travel routes.

Parole Officer Brian Rooney

New York State Division of Parole
End of Watch: October 10, 1985
Age: 35
Years of Service: 4
Cause of Death: Gunfire
Circumstance: Ambushed while in vehicle

Summary:

Officer Rooney was ambushed while sitting in his vehicle when another vehicle pulled up next to him and begin shooting. Officer Rooney's murder was a contract execution planned by Lorenzo Nichols who was considered a drug kingpin with an extensive criminal history. The motive for the homicide was revenge because Officer Rooney revoked Nichols parole. Nichols alleges that he only wanted to hurt Officer Rooney and that he never intended him to be killed.

Discussion:

The murder of Officer Rooney stresses the point that we never know how an offender will react when their freedom is taken away. The authority to arrest an offender is an awesome responsibility bestowed upon officers and it is difficult to predict how the offender will respond to their loss of freedom. This is one reason why conducting arrests are so dangerous. But we must also realize that the danger can be just as real while the offender sits in jail or prison plotting his revenge, not to mention what they are capable of upon their release from custody. Even when an offender is incarcerated they still have the ability to plan violence against officers who have been perceived as doing them wrong.

Juvenile Probation Officer Mary Fine

Detroit, Michigan
End of Watch: August 28, 1986
Age: 42
Years of Service: Unknown
Cause of Death: Strangulation
Circumstance: Residential Field Contact

Summary:

Officer Fine was conducting a residential contact at the home of 16 year old Terrell Banks who was on juvenile probation for truancy. Officer Fine's body was found by neighbors of Banks. She was beaten, sexually assaulted, and strangled to death. Banks was convicted as an adult for 2nd Degree Murder and is serving a prison sentence of 75-130 years in Michigan Department of Corrections.

Discussion:

The brutal murder of Officer Fine is a reminder that juveniles can be extremely unpredictable, dangerous, and violent. The juvenile brain is not fully developed and youth lack cognitive skills or the ability to understand that there are consequences for their actions.

Myth:

I cannot tell you how many times I have heard juvenile probation and parole officers make statements such as, "*I know the kids on my caseload*" or "*My kids would never do that.*" Such comments are completely inappropriate and clearly reveal the mindset that the supervising officer has when dealing with juveniles. The use of such vernacular by officers not only shows an extreme level of complacency; it is dangerous. When an officer refers to a juvenile that they supervise as "*my kid*" they are personalizing this juvenile as if this offender is part of their family. This thought process should never occur. When I have discussed this issue with officers they routinely say they can separate their "caseload kids" from their family but this can still be problematic. Having been the lead instructor for many Defensive Tactics Academy's this is an issue that I have discussed many times with juvenile probation and parole officers. Some officers have thanked me for clarifying their perspective while others think I am going overboard and claim they can separate "their kids" meaning that there is a clear and distinct delineation of their real family and their offender caseload. The problem becomes real when you become involved in a violent encounter with "my kid" and instead of responding immediately to the situation you freeze long enough for the juvenile to injure or kill you. Remember, it only takes one incident for your life to be forever changed. If your mindset categorized juvenile offenders in a way that you either personalized the youth or incorporated them, even tangentially, as part of your family this is not a safe practice and the consequence can be high.

Let's look at the following hypothetical example.

Suppose you have been supervising a 17 year old juvenile on your caseload for 2 years. He is on juvenile probation for burglary, possession of dangerous drugs, and underage drinking. Not an uncommon scenario. There is no history of violence or use of weapons. This juvenile has had his share of substance abuse problems for which you, as the officer, have always gone the extra mile to help. You have chosen to help this troubled youth with the appropriate use of sanctions, rewards, and consequences instead of a violation. You feel good about going the extra mile to help this youthful offender. This is why you got into this profession, to help those in need and to turn troubled lives around to more positive and productive endeavors.

During the past three months this juvenile offender has been repeatedly testing positive for drug use for which you have the option of issuing a violation. Instead you directed him to enter a relapse prevention plan, institute a more restrictive curfew, and increase residential contacts. At times you feel that you are working harder for the offender's compliance than he is but you are willing to work with him a bit more. During the majority of the last two years this juvenile has been mostly compliant and seems to have hit a difficult "phase" as many juveniles do.

While in your office you get a fax indicating his fourth positive drug test. You call the juvenile and schedule him to come into the office to discuss his continued drug use. You are not ready to issue a violation yet and want to work just a little longer to gain compliance. He reports with his parents and the office visit was very positive and productive. The juvenile is dressed very nice and states he will try harder with his sobriety, that he is attending treatment, and getting good grades in school. You talk to his parents who feel that things are going better and that they see positive progress. The parents report that the juvenile is a bit moody lately but think it is due to a busy schedule with treatment, school, newly instituted home chores, and a restrictive curfew. You feel positive about the progress this juvenile has made, despite his positive drug tests, and you are happy with the decision you made to make the effort to work this juvenile towards compliance as opposed to issuing a violation.

A week later you decide to conduct a random home contact by yourself to see how the offender is doing. You knock on the door, the offender answers and is very cordial. In fact, the offender looks surprisingly happy to see you. The juvenile invites you in just as he has 15-20 other times during random and unscheduled contacts. As you enter the residence he states his parents went to the grocery store to go shopping for food. You feel relaxed and confident that he is doing better. Now that you entered the residence you realize the juvenile is high on drugs and pissed off at you for constantly riding him over his drug use and imposing sanctions such as a curfew. In a split second he goes from cordial to extremely agitated and irate…at you! This juvenile offender wants to harm you and aggressively comes toward you with pure evil in his eyes.

Now you, as the officer, are like a deer in headlights. You did not foresee or anticipate such anger or rage. There has never been a problem with this juvenile offender before this incident; you have gone above and beyond what you need to do to help this troubled youth and your thinking, *"my kid would not harm me."* But tonight his intentions are to harm you and while you will say that you can separate "my caseload kids" from "my kids at home" tonight this flux has caused you to hesitate long enough for this juvenile offender to do you harm.

The reality is that such a mindset and how you verbalize offenders that you supervise, i.e., "my kids," can cause you to either:

- Freeze and not react to the sudden, violent encounter that you suddenly find yourself engaged in
- Attempt to process the current situation which causes you to pause instead of immediately and appropriately respond to the threat, or
- Deny what is currently happening and you are victimized.

None of the above responses are appropriate and all can result in potential injury to the officer due to failure to respond appropriately and immediately to an imminent attack. Having a proper mindset and perspective is critical. A few seconds can truly be the difference between life and death. Please, do not refer to juveniles on your caseload as "my kid" or any similar phrasing. You obtain no benefit from referring to any offender that you supervise as "my kid" and the consequences of doing so can be devastating for you and your family. They are simply offenders assigned to your caseload and do not warrant any personalization. Some will gasp and say that such a viewpoint is cold and impersonal. This is not to say that you will not provide the best supervision possible; you just will not do or say anything to make it a personal relationship as opposed to a purely professional relationship.

Federal Probation Officer Thomas Gahl

United States Courts Probation and Pretrial Services
End of Watch: September 22, 1986
Age: 38
Years of Service: 11
Cause of Death: Gunfire, Shotgun
Circumstance: Residential Field Contact

Scott Kirshner

Summary:

Michael Jackson was on probation for a firearms offense and had a history of mental illness, violence, substance abuse, and criminal activity. A mental competency evaluation determined that Jackson's psychiatric diagnoses were paranoid schizophrenia and antisocial personality disorder. At the time of the homicide Jackson was not taking his prescription psychiatric medication as directed. Officer Gahl was conducting a home contact in order to obtain a urine specimen because Jackson was suspected of using drugs. As officer Gahl approached the residence Jackson opened the door and fired a shotgun three times in an unprovoked attack. Jackson then went on a ten day crime spree killing two more people, injuring a police officer, and kidnapping several people. On October 2, 1986, prior to being apprehended by the police Jackson committed suicide. An autopsy of Jackson failed to find evidence of drugs in his system. The shotgun used in the killing of Officer Gahl was purchased by Jackson in a pawn shop just ten days prior to the homicide.

Discussion:

The murder of Officer Gahl is truly troubling in that this extreme act of violence by Jackson was random and unprovoked. With violence of this nature the lesson to learn is that situations can go bad for no rational reason and without warning. Unfortunately there are situations when an officer can do everything correctly when it comes to safety and still have a bad outcome. It is important not to get too focused on situations that are outside of our control and instead focus on safety practices that are in our control.

Things to consider:

Jackson had a history of mental illness which begs the question: Does being mentally ill make an individual more prone to violence than individuals who are not mentally ill? Many studies have been conducted on this topic and most professionals agree that mentally ill individuals are not more violent than the general population. An officer should be more concerned with an offender who has a prior history of violence especially with a substance abuse problem or in conjunction with a mental health diagnosis such as antisocial personality disorder.

Also, it is a safer practice to obtain urine samples in the probation/parole office as opposed to an offender's home. Another option is the use of a private company who will conduct drug screenings of offenders and provide the results to you.

Parole Officer Gerald Moberly

Louisiana Department of Corrections
End of Watch: October 23, 1990
Age: 44
Years of Service: 6
Cause of Death: Gunfire, .22 caliber
Circumstance: Planned field arrest

Summary:

Officer Moberly and a police officer went to serve a warrant on a parolee. Officer Moberly escorted the parolee to his room to obtain clothes but instead of getting clothes the parolee grabbed a .22 caliber handgun and shot officer Moberly multiple times. A gunfight broke out between the parolee and police officer with both men receiving minor wounds. The wounded police officer transported officer Moberly to a hospital where he died from the gunshot wounds.

Discussion:

Officer Moberly used excellent judgment in having the back up of a police officer while serving the warrant. Serving a warrant is always a high risk task that requires the utmost caution and utilization of appropriate safety procedures and tactics. Anytime that an offender is going to be arrested whether it is for an outstanding warrant, an office arrest, or an unplanned field arrest it is critical to immediately handcuff the offender and conduct a thorough search for weapons and contraband. The offender is to be ***immediately*** handcuffed even if they appear to be compliant and non-threatening. Again, when a person is going to lose their freedom you do not know how they will respond. An offender who is not handcuffed may decide to escape or fight at any time which is a risk that should never be taken. If the offender wants to get something before being taken into custody he must first be handcuffed and searched and then escorted at all times. The officer must be alert to potential weapons in the environment. Arrests are dangerous situations that must be treated seriously.

Probation Officer Donald Knepple

Allen County Adult Probation Department
End of Watch: April 28, 1997
Age: 48
Years of Service: 12
Cause of Death: Gunfire, 9mm handgun
Circumstance: Ambushed at a counseling center

Summary:

Officer Knepple was supervising Gary Wright a convicted child molester. Wright, who had been non-compliant with his probation requirements, arranged a meeting with his counselor, Steven Tielker, and officer

Knepple with the intent of murdering both men. During the meeting Wright pulled out a 9mm handgun and shot both men in the head resulting in their deaths. Wright fled to another part of the building where he committed suicide.

Discussion:

This is another incident where an officer was ambushed and executed. This time the incident was committed by non-compliant sex offender. Anytime you deal with an offender who is non-compliant there is always risk involved because the offender knows that their freedom is in jeopardy which can lead to unpredictable and violent behavior.

Myth:

When referring to sex offenders there is a pervasive myth that "*sex offenders are not violent.*" I have seen many officers who supervise a specialized caseload of sex offenders make such claims repeatedly. The sex offenders are often labeled as liars, manipulative, deceitful, sly, tricky, cowardly, and cunning but not violent. This myth needs to stop as sex offenders, like any other offender, has the potential for violent behavior. Sex offenders should not be summarily dismissed or labeled as not violent. In fact, when talking about sexual related homicides we are talking about sex offenders who use the ultimate level of violence by murdering their victims. Offenders who sexually assault often use violence to control their victims.

Parole Officer Louise Pargeter

Correctional Service of Canada, Yellowknife, NT
End of Watch: October 6, 2004
Age: 34
Years of Service: 3
Cause of Death: Strangulation

Scott Kirshner

Circumstance: Field contact

Summary:

Officer Pargeter was murdered by violent sex offender, Eli Ulayuk, because she previously revoked his parole for which he had unresolved resentment. Officer Pargeter was re-assigned Ulayuk's case and was conducting a scheduled residential contact but failed to return to the office. The Royal Canadian Mounted Police were notified and found her body in the offender's apartment. Officer Pargeter was struck multiple times from behind with a hammer. After assaulting her with the hammer Ulayuk took twine and strangled her to death. He then removed her clothing and had sexual intercourse with her lifeless body. The homicide of Officer Pargeter was violent, brutal, and horrific.

On August 19, 1988, Ulayuk, age 20, killed 23 year old Martha Ammaq by stabbing her seven times and then strangling her to death with a belt. Ulayuk said he had an urge to have sex with the victim's dead body and killed her for that purpose but claims that he changed his mind after killing the victim and that he did not have sex with the body. Psychological tests revealed that Ulayuk has the paraphilia of necrophilia which is an obsession with and erotic interest with a corpse. Ulayuk denies being a sex offender because he didn't have sex with the victim's body yet his offense was sexually motivated. He was resistant to sex offender treatment and did not begin treatment until 1995 which is seven years after the murder of Ammaq.

He was originally found guilty of 2nd Degree Murder and sentenced to life imprisonment with parole eligibility in 15 years. His case was appealed on technical grounds and to avoid a new trial he plead guilty to a lesser charge of manslaughter. For the manslaughter charge he was sentenced to the maximum which is life in prison but he was soon eligible for parole.

The judge who sentenced Ulayuk stated[ix]:

> "Of the many cases of manslaughter to come before this court in the last 35 years, I cannot help but class this as the worst in terms of its extraordinarily horrible facts."

In another statement the judge states:

> "Of the many offenders who have come before the courts of the Northwest Territories over the past 30 or more years, there are very few whom I remember to have been potentially as dangerous to the public as Mr. Ulayuk."

Despite his level of dangerousness and brutal crime Ulayuk was granted day parole in August 1993 and full parole in August 1995.

Discussion:

The murder of Officer Pargeter, similar to that of officer Rooney, was revenge for having revoked the offender's parole. And similar to the Officer Knepple case the perpetrator was a sex offender. In situations where an offender fails to take ownership of their probation/parole non-compliance which results in a revocation back to jail or prison it is important for officers to understand that the offender may harbor resentment. In such cases it would be a good practice to utilize a partner when conducting any type of field contact. Even if your department does not foster a culture where conducting field work with a partner is acceptable it is you that will pay the price if things turn violent. Working with a safety conscious and knowledgeable partner is always a good practice.

Probation/Parole Officer Jeffrey McCoy

Oklahoma Department of Corrections
End of Watch: May 18, 2012
Age: 32
Years of Service: 7
Cause of Death: Gunfire from the officers own weapon
Circumstance: Field contact

Summary:

Officer McCoy was conducting a pre-release supervision check at a home. Answering the door was 21 year old Lester Kinchion when a struggle ensued. According to an eyewitness Kinchion beat McCoy until he was unconscious obtained his service weapon and shot him in the head. Kinchion was the roommate of the offender that Officer McCoy came to contact at the residence. Kinchion was sentenced to life without parole for the murder of McCoy. Officer McCoy leaves behind a wife, 7 year old son, and a 4 year old daughter.

Discussion:

Without knowing specific details of this incident it is a reminder that officers must always maintain situational awareness and be highly proficient in defensive tactics skills to include weapons retention and disarming. Violence can be random, unpredictable, and occur very quickly with little to no advance warning. Officers must be trained for the worst case scenario.

A Note on Redundancy

As you read this book you will notice that many topics and subjects are repeatedly covered throughout the book. This is intentionally and purposely done by design to reinforce critical and important learning points, concepts, or skills that need constant reinforcement. As an officer survival instructor I have researched, developed, written, implemented, and taught numerous training curriculums on officer survival. I have instructed classes on the subjects of: use of force, safety policies, defensive tactics academy, firearms academy, low light shooting, officer awareness and the tactical mindset, applied defensive tactics, force-on-force, verbal de-escalation, etc. In teaching these classes I have learned that critical information must redundant to foster learning, mastery and, more important, application of the subject matter. It is not enough to just "know" the material; you must be able to "apply" your knowledge under stress and on demand.

It is my goal that the remainder of this book will provide officers with a solid foundation to begin utilizing officer survival practices that will keep you safe so that you can return home at the end of your shift with the same physical and mental capacities that you had when you began your shift.

Stay safe.

Self-Assessment

The purpose of this brief assessment is to quickly identify areas that may be problematic requiring further training or lifestyle changes. There are many lifestyle habits that can severely and negatively diminish your ability to respond at peak performance during a crisis.

None of the questions are designed to trick you. Answer in an open and honest manner without the temptation to make yourself look good.

1. Does the possibility exist that you can be assaulted or attacked in the course of your job duties?

    _____ Yes,   ___ No

2. How would you rate the possibility of being assaulted?

    _____ High   ___ Medium
    _____ Low   ___ Not Possible

3. Are you *mentally* prepared to respond to an assault?

    _____ Yes,   ___ No

4. Do you regularly practice visualization or imagery techniques to help improve your performance relating to a crisis situation?

    _____ Yes,   ___ No

5. Are you *physically* prepared to respond to an assault?

    _____ Yes,   ___ No

Officer Survival for Probation and Parole Officers

6. Are you confident in your ability to respond to a physical confrontation?

    ____ Yes,   ____ No

7. Do you have a difficult time staying focused during a crisis?

    ____ Yes,   ____ No

8. Are you current on all department policies regarding the *use of force?*

    ____ Yes,   ____ No

9. Do you completely understand the *use of force continuum* that is used by your department?

    ____ Yes,   ____ No

10. Do you regularly practice defensive tactics skills?

    ____ Yes,   ____ No

11. Do you regularly practice firearms skills?

    ____ Yes,   ____ No   ____ N/A, not armed

12. Do you exercise for at least 30 minutes at a time, 3 days per week?

    ____ Yes,   ____ No

13. Can you run one mile in 10 minutes?

    ____ Yes,   ____ No

14. Do you eat at least two healthy meals per day?

    _____ Yes,   _____ No

15. Do you drink more than three caffeinated beverages per day?

    _____ Yes,   _____ No

16. Do you get at least seven hours of sleep per night?

    _____ Yes,   _____ No

17. Do you drink more than 5 alcoholic drinks per week?

    _____ Yes,   _____ No

18. Do you use tobacco products such as cigarettes or chewing tobacco?

    _____ Yes,   _____ No

19. Do you abuse prescription medication or use medications in a manner that differ from the directions in which they were prescribed?

    _____ Yes,   _____ No

20. Do you use goal setting as a way to plan accomplishing your written goals?

    _____ Yes,   _____ No

Officer Survival for Probation and Parole Officers

Once you have completed this assessment go back and review your answers. Based upon your answers:

1. Do you have the proper mindset, knowledge, and understanding of policies, mental skills, and physical skills to successfully resolve a crisis?

2. Are your lifestyle choices relating to sleep, exercise, and use of alcohol, tobacco, caffeine or prescription medication preventing you from performing at an effective level to respond appropriately to a crisis?

3. Do you have clearly defined written goals relating to fitness, lifestyle or skills along with a clear action plan to accomplish your goals?

Once you have identified problematic answers develop an action plan and, if necessary, training regimen to improve deficient areas. The reality is that we cannot perform at a peak level in a crisis, especially a life or death crisis, without proper:

- Mindset
- Mental skills
- Physical skills
- Working knowledge of department policies and procedures
- Healthy lifestyle that includes a healthy diet, exercise, and stress management skills

You owe it to yourself, family, friends, and those who love you to have the knowledge, skills, and ability to function at a peak performance during a crisis. The goal is not just to go home at the end of your day but to go home healthy and unharmed.

Before proceeding any further I urge you to make a commitment to yourself that you will "**commit to win**" by developing an action plan to improve any deficient areas that you have identified. Failure is not an option.

1. Will you commit right now to correcting any noted deficiencies?

    _____ Yes,   ____ No

Chapter 2: Combat Mindset

Never Give Up

Never Give In

Commit to Survival

Commit to Win

Combat Mindset

When a person has the ability, opportunity, and intent on causing you serious bodily injury or death you are in a combat situation. How you respond, or fail to respond, can have lifelong consequences for you, family members, friends, and fellow officers in your department. As a community corrections officer you will not like this situation and you may have done everything in your power to avoid this potentially lethal confrontation but nonetheless you must defend yourself or risk being injured or killed. This requires having a combat mindset to not only win but prevail in such an encounter. Many community corrections managers and administrators do not like the term 'combat' and cringe at its implications. They believe that the phrase "combat mindset" is too militaristic or geared toward police officers. After all isn't combat reserved only for those who job tasks them with running toward the sound of gunfire such as police officers or members of the military? Having a combat mindset could not possibly fit into the profession of community corrections! A warrior engages in combat during a war. A police officer engages in combat during an active shooter situation in the local high school or college. Community corrections officers do not engage in combat. Or do they?

The reality is that anyone who is attacked and is forced to fight for their life or the lives of others is engaged in combat. Combat is not restricted to a job title. When violence is directed at you job titles and job descriptions become irrelevant. You will have interactions with probationers, parolees, their family members, spouses, significant others, etc. who may think that you are cause of the offenders problems. These individuals might view you as a threat to their freedom or lifestyle. Think back to chapter one and the probation and parole officers who were killed in the line of duty. The reality is that if someone is intent on causing you harm you must realize that you are in combat and this requires a combat mindset to neutralize the threat(s). You cannot sugar coat this truth or wordsmith this into a phrase that is more user friendly or politically correct. Failure to "get in the fight" can lead to you, fellow officers or civilians being seriously injured or killed because you did not recognize the seriousness of the situation. The most effective definition I have seen for combat mindset comes from Paul Howe[x]:

An aggressive combat mind-set is possessed by people who can screen out distractions while under great stress to focus on the mission and are willing to go into harm's way, against great odds if necessary.

Generally, in community corrections we avoid confrontation and attempt to remove ourselves from potential use of force situations. This is one significant difference from our role as probation/parole officers compared to police officers who have a duty to respond. We do not "go into harm's way" voluntarily; we are forced into this situation by the actions of the aggressor and a lack of escape from his or her actions.

The idea behind developing a combat mindset is so that you will decisively win and prevail when engaged in a potentially life threatening situation against a dedicated threat. A **"Dedicated Threat"** is a person or persons whose main goal, desire, and motivation is to severely injure or kill you by any means necessary. This is the proverbial *worst case scenario*. When engaged in a physical confrontation you must never give up. Surviving an attack depends on your ability to focus on the task at hand, outlast your attacker(s), and respond appropriately. You are never going to give up and as long as you are alive and breathing you will do everything within your power to be the victor in this violent engagement. This is why attending ongoing, realistic, and scenario based training is so critically important. You must not only be trained for such worst case scenarios but you must actively participate in ongoing training to maintain and improve a high level of skill that will ensure peak performance on demand. If your current training classes are not dealing with the *worst case scenario* against a *dedicated threat* then your training is failing you.

Probation Related Statistics on Assaults

Again, I will mention that due to the absence of a National Incident Based Reporting System for probation and parole officers it is difficult to obtain a complete and accurate picture of assaults that occur in the community corrections environment. Some of the studies that have been completed are now dated yet they still provide a partial picture of community corrections assaults.

Years of service and assaults[xi]:

- 0-5 Years   16%
- 5-9 Years   37%
- 9+ Years   47%

Based upon the above data, your chances of being assaulted actually increase as you continue your career and become more experienced. We will discuss why the experienced officer gets assaulted more often when we talk about complacency.

Officers are Assaulted by[xii]:

- Probationer   41.3%
- Probationer's Friend   31.2%
- Anonymous   19.5%
- Probationer's Family   8.0%

Assaults occurred at the following locations[xiii]:

- Field   50%
- Office   25.5%
- Other   18%
- Court   6.5%

Officer Survival for Probation and Parole Officers

> **Analysis of the statistics:**
>
> It is the **experienced officer** who is more likely to be assaulted by a **probationer** while working in the **field**.

Now let's examine some statistics of law enforcement officers, specifically police officers, killed and assaulted in 2011[xiv].

Police officers Killed in the Line of Duty, 2011:

Number of police officers killed in the line of duty:	72
-Male	69
-Female	3
Average age of the officer	38
Average length of service in years	12
Number killed with firearm[xv]:	63
-Handgun	50
-Rifle	7
-Shotgun	6
Number of officers killed with their own weapon	3 (4.2%)
Number of officer deaths at a distance of 0-5 feet from offender	21 (29%)
Number of officers wearing body armor	51 (71%)

Profile of known assailants:

Number of offenders responsible for the 72 officer deaths	77
Average age of the offender	32
Sex of the offender:	
-Male	72
-Female	2
Average height and weight of offender	5'9" 181 pounds
Number of assailants with prior criminal records	64 (83%)
Number of assailants under judicial supervision	17 (22%)

Officers <u>Assaulted</u> in the Line of Duty, 2011:

Number of police officers assaulted in the line of duty:	54,774
Weapons Percent of officers assaulted with the following weapons:	
-Personal Weapons (i.e., hands, fists, knees, elbows, or feet)	79.9%
-Firearms	4.0%
-Knives or other edged weapons	1.8%
-Other dangerous weapons	14.3%
Circumstances:	
Percent of officer assaults while responding to disturbance calls	33.3%
Percent of officers assaulted while attempting arrests	14.7%
Percent of officers assaulted while handling or transporting prisoners	12.6%

Comparison between Probation/Parole Officer's and Police Officer's Killed in the Line of Duty:

	Probation/Parole Officer's	Police[xvi] Officer's
Average Age of Officer	41	39[xvii]
Average Years of Service	12	11[xviii]
Weapon Used:		
-Handgun	58.3%	66.6%
-Rifle	0%	17.5%
-Shotgun	8.3%	7.1%
-Vehicle	0%	7.1%
-Knife/Edged Weapon	16.7%	0.6%
-Bomb	0%	0.4%
-Personal Weapon	16.7%	0.2%
-Blunt Instrument	0%	0.2%

Probation and Parole Officers Feloniously Killed by Type of Weapon:

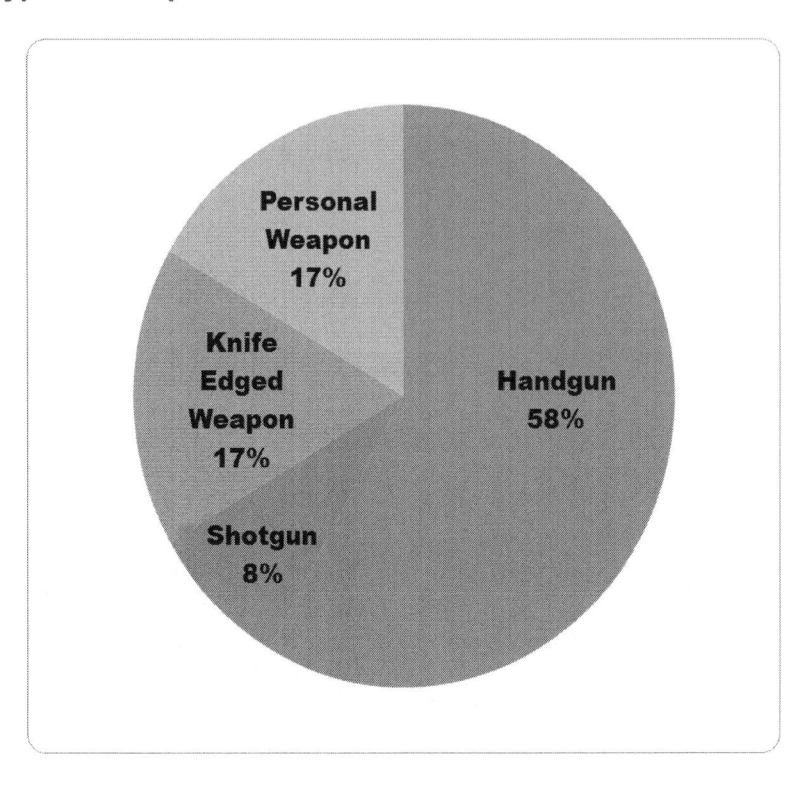

- Handgun 58%
- Personal Weapon 17%
- Knife Edged Weapon 17%
- Shotgun 8%

Officer Survival for Probation and Parole Officers

Police Officers Feloniously Killed by Type of Weapon; 2000-2009[xix]:

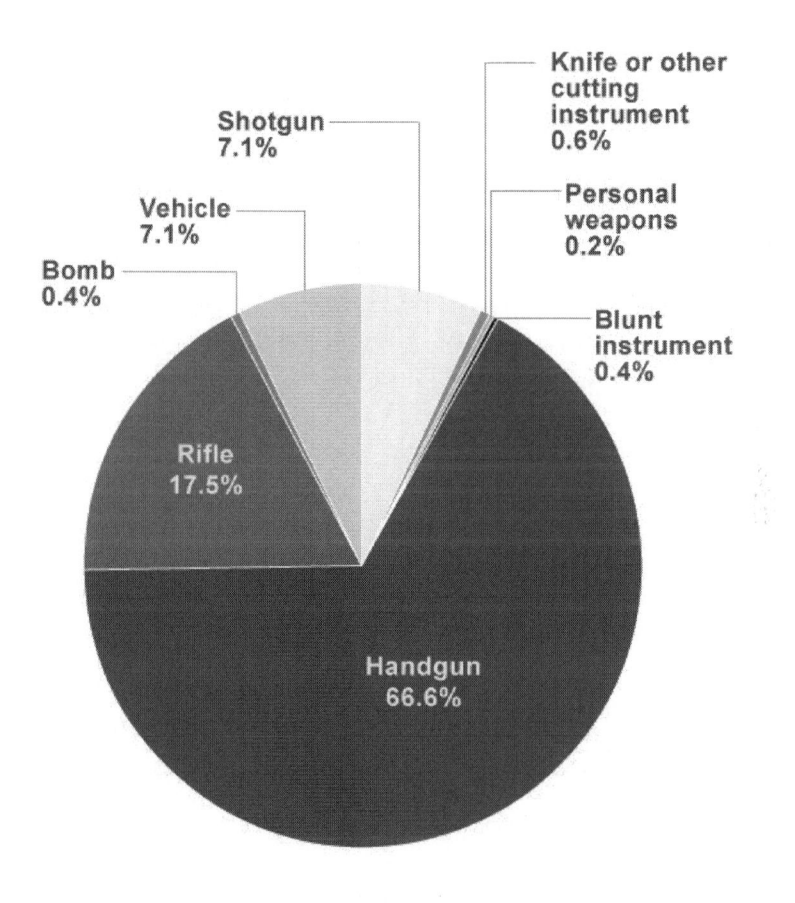

- Knife or other cutting instrument 0.6%
- Shotgun 7.1%
- Personal weapons 0.2%
- Vehicle 7.1%
- Bomb 0.4%
- Blunt instrument 0.4%
- Rifle 17.5%
- Handgun 66.6%

What this Information Means to Community Corrections Officers

In some respects the task of comparing a probation/parole officer with that of a police officer is not a completely accurate comparison. While both are professional law enforcement officers they are tasked with a different mission and have different job duties. Police officers are considered first responders who have an obligation to respond to emergencies while probation/parole officers would rarely be a first responder. Police officers tend to run toward the direction of gunfire while probation/parole officers try to avoid such incidents. Despite the differences there is some beneficial and applicable information that can be relevant to community corrections officers.

- In relation to probation/parole officers and police officers killed in the line of duty there is a significant similarity in both the <u>age of the officer</u> and <u>years of service</u>.

- Handguns are the prevalent weapon of choice used to kill these law enforcement officers. It is critical that community corrections officers are proficient with weapon disarming skills and for officers who are armed as part of their job they must be proficient with weapon retention skills.

- 83% of the assailants who assaulted police officers had a prior criminal record and 22% of the assailants were under judicial supervision. There are two important points for community corrections officers to understand relating to this information:

    1. If an offender is willing to assault a police officer there is a good probability that they would be willing to assault a community corrections officer.

2. The 22% of assailants that were under judicial supervision are the same offenders on your caseloads that you supervise in the community! Do not become victim to a thought process where you believe that these could not possibly be the same offenders that you supervise.

- The "average" assailant responsible for police officer deaths in 2011 was a male, 32 years old, 5'9" tall and weighs 181 pounds. Are you mentally and physically prepared to deal with this "average" person who is on your caseload wants to injure or kill you?

- In 2011, 29% of the officer's deaths were at a *distance of 0-5 feet from offender*. Is your training preparing you to defend yourself at such an extremely close distance? Even if you carry a firearm you may not have the time or opportunity to draw your weapon at such a close range. Are you prepared to use other force options to neutralize the threat? Does your training cover close quarter battle?

- In 2011, 71% of the officer's killed were wearing body armor. While body armor is a necessary piece of equipment that I highly recommend all officers use, this statistic shows that body armor does not eliminate the need to use proper safety tactics and techniques.

Faulty Assumptions

As an officer survival instructor I have talked with many community corrections officers about officer safety and survival as well as use of force incidents. I have found an alarming number of officers who think and act like they have an imaginary safety bubble around them that will protect them from harm. In reality, they subscribe to a laundry list of faulty assumptions that gives them a false sense of security. Not only is this belief foolish; it can be deadly. Following is a list of actual statements officers have made rationalizing why offenders they supervise could not possibly be a threat to their safety or security:

- I know the offenders on my caseload and they would never hurt me.

- I'm helping my offenders. They have no reason to harm me.

- I don't supervise high-risk offenders so I'm sure that I'm safe.

- I treat offenders with respect so they have no reason to want to hurt me.

- I've been on the job for 15 years and nothing has ever happened so there is no chance that anything is going to happen in the future.

- Some of my defendants' talk big and put on an act but they would never follow through. They are just trying to scare me. All talk and no action. They know that I'm the boss.

- I supervise a standard caseload of drug offenders, DUI's, and common criminals. These are low-risk offenders who have no history of violence so I have nothing to be concerned about.

- I'm just doing my job and they (the offender) have to understand that it is not my fault that they get in trouble.

- I'm a law enforcement officer and they have to respect my position.

- I can talk my way out of any situation.

- If the situation gets out of control I will just call 9-1-1 on my cell phone.

- When I'm conducting field contacts I always have my radio which has an emergency button. If I need help I will just activate the emergency button and help will arrive.

- I carry a firearm while on duty so I have all the tools I need.

Many times officers get trapped into making assumptions based upon past experiences. Typically these past experiences are usually non-eventful which leads to complacency. It is easy for your thought process regarding officer survival to become:

- I go to work everyday
- Nothing ever happens at work
- I will go to work today and nothing will happen
- I will go to work tomorrow and nothing will happen
- I am safe at work and nothing will happen to me because nothing ever happens

Once you begin thinking nothing bad will happen to you it is time to realize that you are caught in the grip of complacency. The good news is that you can break out of this inaccurate mindset.

Complacency

    Complacency evolves over time and sneaks up on you slowly day by day. With each passing day that is uneventful you get caught up more and more into the belief that nothing bad is going to happen, nothing is going to go wrong, and that you will remain safe as you have been in the past. For you complacency has now become routine due to a lack of incidents. You actually start believing that not only are you safe but there is no possibility that anything is going to happen. You begin taking unsafe shortcuts on safety policies, procedures, tactics, and techniques. You are now "that" complacent officer. Avoiding complacency is a daily task that begins with the belief that: **Today may be the day that violence will be directed toward you.** You must take all safety precautions to avoid becoming a victim or a statistic. You must believe that complacency is your greatest enemy. You must believe that routine leads to complacency and complacency can lead to serious bodily injury or death.

Steps to avoid complacency:

- Acknowledge that complacency is real and that it is your enemy
- Understand that routine leads to complacency
- Have the belief that today there is possibility, however remote, that your safety and survival may be at risk
- Develop a daily routine aimed at battling complacency as it is always better to be proactive than reactive
- Continue to develop a winning mindset so that you will prevail in a violent encounter

It is important to develop a routine against complacency that does not involve paranoia. The reality is that being a community corrections officer is a relatively safe occupation and the chance of being injured or killed in the line of duty is remote. However, there is always the possibility that such an incident may occur. This is why it is critical to your safety that you are mentally, physically, and emotionally prepared to respond to such an incident.

Following is the routine that I used to fight complacency:

1. Before leaving for work I would examine and inspect all of my safety equipment to include: firearm, holster, duty belt, magazines, ammunition, body armor, baton, OC spray, handcuffs, handcuff keys, and flashlights. After confirming that all my equipment is accounted for and functioning properly I would put on all of my safety gear.

2. I then would read an officer survival creed that I wrote down on a note card:

    - I will not allow routine to lead to complacency.
    - I will remain in Condition Yellow.
    - I have trained for the worst case scenario; oftentimes at my own expense.
    - I will never give up and winning is not enough; <u>I WILL prevail.</u>
    - I owe it to myself, my family, my friends, my co-workers, and my department to not only survive but prevail.
    - I am prepared to respond to any act of violence that is directed toward me or a fellow officer.
    - I know and understand department policies relating to the use of force.
    - I am confident in my officer survival knowledge, skills, and abilities that I honed and I have trained hard to prevail in a violent encounter.

- I will use lethal force if necessary and understand that if I am forced to take a life today it is because the adversary left me no other option.
- I am confident and prepared.

I start each sentence with an "I" statement as a way to take ownership over the words that I have written. I use the word "prevail" often because winning is not enough. I know that when I leave my residence my mindset is "locked in" and that I am prepared to begin my day. You can tape this creed to your bathroom mirror, put it in a dresser drawer that you use on a daily basis, put a copy in your personal wallet, put a copy with your badge and credentials, or place it in a location that is easily assessable to you. Shortly we will do an exercise where you create your own officer survival creed.

3. My next step is to conduct dry fire drills with my firearm. I would unload my firearm and remove all of my ammunition and magazines from my gear. I then go to a room that I have designated specifically for dry fire practice and again confirm that no magazines or ammunition are in this area. This "dry fire room" never has any firearms or ammunition in it so that I know it is a safe location to dry fire. I check my firearm one more time to confirm that it is unloaded, that I have no ammunition on me or in the room and that I have no loaded magazines. This ensures that it is safe for me to begin my dry fire practice session. I then conduct 10 perfect dry firing drills drawing my firearm from the holster which is concealed. As part of my drill I include scanning after each shot. Before holstering I mentally ask myself the following questions:

    I. Is the threat neutralized? If not, do I need to re-engage?
    II. Are there other threats that need to be addressed?

    III. To break the possibility of tunnel vision I tell myself: Scan left, scan right.
    IV. Is it now safe for me to holster my firearm?

After answering these questions I would holster my firearm and repeat this drill for a total of 10 repetitions. I would remain focused and strive for perfect technique and execution. I never rush this process and I never rush to holster my weapon. It is imperative that I not cheat or hurry through this practice drill. I would do this dry fire practice both before AND after work. This would ensure that I completed 20 dry fire drills per day for a total of 100 per week. These drills do not take a lot of time to complete, instill proper technique, and during the course of a year this practice really adds up.

Upon completion of the dry fire drill I return to the location of the magazines and ammunition. I load my firearm, conduct a function check to confirm that a round is in the chamber, and then holster my weapon. All of my safety equipment is now accounted for, functional, and ready for use should the need arise.

Once I complete steps 1 – 3, I am mentally prepared and almost ready to leave the relative safety of my home for work. But, before I leave the last thing I do is say to myself:

"I'm on duty now and I will remain in condition yellow."

I am now in the proper mental state to leave for work.

Above is the routine that I used on a daily basis to combat complacency. This routine not only fights complacency it gets me mentally prepared for the day, provides me with 20 perfect dry fire practice sessions and verifies that all my equipment is accounted for and that it is functional.

I believe that complacency is a significant contributing

factor why experienced officers get injured or killed in the line of duty. With an average of 12 years of service for community corrections officers and 11 years for police officers (2000-2009), these officers may have allowed routine to lead to complacency. Experienced officers must remain vigilant, on a daily basis, to battle against complacency. Developing an effective action plan to complacency is critical.

Officer Survival for Probation and Parole Officers

Exercise 1: Develop a list of 10 things that you can proactively do to avoid becoming complacent. If you can't come up with 10 ideas then come up with as many as you can.

1. _____

2. _____

3. _____

4. _____

5. _____

6. _____

7. _____

8. _____

9. _____

10. _____

Exercise 2: Write down your own "Officer Survival Creed":

Exercise 3: Develop a routine that you can use before you leave for work each day to get you in the right mindset that will guarantee you from falling into the complacency trap. It is important to be specific and detailed: _____

_____

_____

_____

_____

_____

_____

_____

_____

_____

_____

_____

_____

_____

_____

_____

Motivation

Having just reviewed the statistics on violence directed at law enforcement officers, to include probation and parole officers, along with contributing factors such as routine and complacency it is important to discuss your motivation to train for mitigating your chances of becoming a statistic. Unfortunately, there is no way to completely eliminate risk even if you do everything correctly but this is a reality that is out of our control. There is no benefit to worrying about things that you cannot control.

There are many people who have devoted their lives to helping motivate others to achieve their goals. Motivation is a huge business with big profits. There are books, DVD's, seminars, webcasts, websites, Internet blogs, infomercials, etc. all selling the concept of motivation dealing with a wide variety of topics. Whether you need motivation to increase sales, reach your fitness goals, stop smoking, or to plan for an early retirement there is someone out there willing to provide you with advice and guidance. But there is a big difference between increasing sales goals or obtaining a perfect beach body verses surviving a lethal force encounter. The difference is that a failure to reach sales goals or having a great physique will not result in your death. Law enforcement officers who lack motivation to train their mind and body can, and do, result in job related deaths. This is often the "white elephant" in the minds of many officers. They intrinsically know that they should train but often lack the motivation to put in the time, effort, and consistency required especially if they have to pay for the training at their own expense. When you talk with these officers the one consistent item you will get as to why they don't work on their officer survival skills is excuses.

Short List of Excuses:

- I don't have time
- I don't have money
- I work too many hours
- I'm too old to attend training classes
- I have a bad back, knee, pulled muscle, etc.
- It is too hot, cold, rainy, windy, humid, etc.
- I'm not using personal time outside of work to train
- I'm not using my own money to attend outside training classes
- The department already mandates that I attend yearly training
- Why train for something that is never going to happen
- Training makes you paranoid
- There are never any good training classes available
- I'm afraid that I will look stupid if I don't do things correctly
- I'm too embarrassed to put myself in a challenging situation
- Other officers don't take training seriously; why should I?
- I'm worried that I will get injured during training
- I can't find anyone else to go with me
- Trainers have out of control egos and try to make students look stupid

This is just a small sample of excuses that people use to avoid training. Following are three realities for those who use excuses:

1. Excuses are equivalent to negative self-talk and provide an unacceptable platform to keep you stagnant.
2. Excuses and success are mutually exclusive since excuses are what prevent you from moving forward, improving, and accomplishing goals.
3. Excuses are a negative defense mechanism that allows you to accept failure and foster mediocrity as the norm. This should not be acceptable to you.

Do you see excuses on the previous list that you have used? If yes, are you okay with using excuses or do you want to make some positive changes?

Motivation that leads to action and goal attainment is the ultimate anti-excuse. Individuals who are motivated rarely use excuses and remain goal oriented. Motivation is a process that allows you to initiate, guide and maintain goal oriented behaviors. Motivation is frequently described as being either intrinsic or extrinsic.

Intrinsic motivations: Are those that arise from within the individual such as personal gratification of completing your personal best in an activity.

Extrinsic motivations: Are those that arise from outside of the individual and often involve rewards such as recognition, praise, awards, trophies, or money.

Intrinsic motivation is longer lasting and more self-directive than extrinsic motivation which must be repeatedly reinforced by praise or rewards. When it comes to your motivation to train officer survival skills you are best served if your motivation is intrinsic.

The question in relation to officer survival is:

What is your motivation to be a survival oriented officer?

Officers who are serious about officer survival will instantly be able to identify a host of valid reasons why their safety and survival is important. They are able to clearly articulate responses that go beyond the often repeated one liner: *"I go home at the end of my shift."* That saying seems to be the knee jerk response that many officers parrot when asked what officer safety means. These officers have heard other officers say the same line over and over again. When you ask them to clarify what that saying means they tend to repeat it verbatim with no added insight; only added emphasis. They change their posture to a more official stance with head up, chest out, forward leaning, deep voice, beady eyes, grinding teeth, contorted face, and clenched fist: I GO HOME AT THE END OF MY SHIFT. Yet, there is no added clarity or insight. And when you press them for a more in-depth response all too often they rarely have one. Sometimes the depth of the clarification becomes, *"I go home; the bad guy doesn't."* This scene is repeated in departments all over the country and it is not limited to probation or parole officers. I have heard this from police officers, corrections officers, detention officers, and court security officers. This shows that officers are able to repeat an often used phrase but fail to really understand its implication. Next, I want you to do the following exercise with the goal that you will understand why you should be motivated to train all of your officer survival skills to include verbal de-escalation, defensive tactics, firearms, mindset, and physical fitness.

Generally, I prefer to conduct exercises that are positive and focused on constructive outcomes. This time you will do an exercise that is focused on negative outcomes with the goal being that you will change your perspective on the need to train and these negative factors will motivate you to take action. In fact, your response to this exercise should not only be negative but disturbing to you. The benefit is that it can be powerful in helping you realize what your motivation is to be a survival oriented officer who goes home at the end of your shift AND knows why this is important!

Exercise 4: Write a specific list of all the negative outcomes that may result if you were to get injured or killed in the line of duty:

1. _____

2. _____

3. _____

4. _____

5. _____

6. _____

7. _____

8. _____

9. _____

10. _____

If you come up with more than 10 items get a separate piece of paper and continue to create your list.

Negative outcomes resulting from serious injury or death that you may have included on your list:

- If I am killed in the line of duty I do not know how my family will make ends meet
- My children will grow up without a mother/father
- I may not/will not be able to provide for my family
- I may end up with a career ending injury
- If I am able to return back to work what will my confidence level be? How will I treat offenders? How will co-workers treat me? Will I become paranoid and think that a violent act is going to happen again?
- I might end up with Post Traumatic Stress Disorder (PTSD) and have to relive this nightmare again and again
- I could lose passion or interest in my job
- How will I adjust to all the life changes if I am seriously injured?
- I will be a burden to my family
- How will my spouse/significant other respond to my injury? Will they leave me?
- How will my children treat me if I can't play with them anymore due to an injury?
- I could not deal with losing my vision, hearing, use of a limb, etc.

When you are done with your list put them in order of what is most disturbing to you. Keep this list and use it as a motivator to train. Also, think about how intrinsic and extrinsic motivation plays a role in your willingness to train. No item on your list should be acceptable to you.

Now having gone through this exercise it is important to note that things can still go wrong even when you do everything correct. If you are in this situation it is important to not to second guess yourself. Unfortunately very bad things happen to very good people. In such situations seek out all the services you need to get to the best possible quality of life. This is where family, friends, a strong support system, and faith will be invaluable in your recovery and progress forward.

Now that we have discussed motivation let's focus on mental preparation to create a solid mindset.

Mental Preparation

Mental Preparation consists of learning, practicing and application of psychological skills that will enhance ones commitment to not only win but prevail when involved in a confrontation, especially a violent confrontation. This process will provide you with skills so that you can control your thoughts, feelings, and perception of the situation to react appropriately when faced with violence. If you are mentally weak it will not matter how physically strong your body is, how much endurance you have, or the physical skill set that you have attained through training.

> *Nothing can stop the man with the right mental attitude from achieving his goal; nothing on earth can help the man with the wrong mental attitude.*
>
> *Thomas Jefferson*

Officer Survival for Probation and Parole Officers

Let's look at two examples of a community corrections officer during a residential contact who find themselves in an imminent use of force situation. The goal is to emphasize the importance of being mentally prepared and having a combat mindset.

Officer Derek:

Derek realizes that this residential contact went from "routine" to problematic within a few seconds. Derek has used excellent verbal de-escalation skills but they have not been effective. To make matters worse Derek does not have an avenue of escape and knows that a fight is just seconds away. Derek regularly works out and is in good physical condition. He takes a deep breath to calm himself as he gets into a defensive posture. He reminds himself of his hard work practicing defensive tactics skills. Derek is focused on this offender and is telling himself to "*stay calm, relax, and rely on all of your hard training.*" His focus is on using whatever force is necessary and reasonable based on the actions of the offender. Derek knows what he needs to do to remain safe.

Officer Josh:

Josh realizes that this residential contact went from "routine" to problematic within a few seconds. Josh has used excellent verbal de-escalation skills but they have not been effective. To make matters worse Josh does not have an avenue of escape and knows that a fight is just seconds away. Josh regularly works out and is in good physical condition. He takes a deep breath to calm himself as he realizes that he is beginning to breathe heavy and shake uncontrollably. He questions whether he trained his defensive tactics skills enough. Josh is worried and his internal self-talk is saying, "*I don't know if I can do this, I am going to get hurt, I don't want to be here.*" His mind is racing a mile a minute. Josh is so anxious that he cannot focus on what he needs to do to neutralize the threat.

In comparing Derek and Josh, it seems that both officers are physically in shape and well-conditioned. They have trained hard and their bodies are physically prepared for combat. Are both officers going to be able to protect themselves from an imminent violent encounter? Not a chance! While Derek is both physically and mentally prepared for violence, Josh is not mentally prepared, is experiencing fear, and more than likely will not perform at a level needed for a positive outcome. Your body will not carry you through a violent encounter if you are not mentally prepared and committed to win.

According to the now classic officer survival book The Tactical Edge[xx]:

If you approach high-risk situations without the proper mental preparation, the strongest force in deciding your destiny is going to be luck. In fact, after studying dozens of shootings, one trainer has assigned this relative weighting to the factors that tend to determine whether <u>UN</u>prepared officers survive:

Mental Skill	5%
Physical Skill	5%
Shooting Skill	15%
LUCK	75%

What truly prepared officers can depend on for winning violent clashes is this:

Mental Skill	75%
Shooting Skill	15%
Physical Skill	5%
LUCK	5%

A lot of research has been conducted since the writing of The Tactical Edge in 1986 but even back then it was known how important a role mental skills plays in officer survival. Mental skills remain a key and relevant factor in officer survival. On the other hand if you choose to depend on luck then you better be lucky all the time. The offender only has to be luck one time…the moment that he attacks you!

Depending on luck for your survival is nothing more than depending on the incompetence of your assailant. This is not survival strategy.

Let's discuss steps that officers can take to ensure a proper mindset leading to peak performance. This will be the basis of your mental toughness or psychological body armor. Think of mental conditioning as defensive tactics for your mind. It means that you are mentally prepared to take action in a given situation. Remaining calm, staying focused, and performing under stress will be much easier if you have proper mental conditioning.

Goal Setting

One of the first steps in developing a mental conditioning program is the development of goals detailing exactly what it is that you are striving to achieve relating to officer survival skills. It is easy to know where you are now and where you want to be at a certain point in time. But, in order to reach your goals you will need a detailed plan that outlines your step by step process of goal attainment. Think of your plan as a roadmap with specific points of accomplishment along the way to measure progress and a method that provides feedback in case you need to adjust or modify your plan. An effective way to create goals is using a technique called S.M.A.R.T. Goals. The acronym S.M.A.R.T. stands for the following:

S.M.A.R.T. Goals	Meaning
Specific	Goal must be specific and detailed (who, what, where, when, why)
Measurable	Establishment of criteria to measure progress
Attainable	You have to have the ability to accomplish the goal
Realistic	You must be willing and able to strive toward your objective
Time-Lined	Having timeframes to reach milestones and ultimately the goal

Example: Suppose you lack confidence when dealing with confrontational offenders. In these situations you instantly become nervous, your breathing increases, your heart is pounding, your hands become sweaty, you begin to shake, you don't know what to say, and you easily lose focus. You feel like the offender can easily sense your nervousness which makes you feel even worse about your reactions. Even in scenario based training classes you have the same non-productive reaction. Based upon advice from an officer survival instructor you decide to use imagery as a tool to improve your confidence level so that you can more effectively respond to a confrontational offender.

Following is an example of a goal using the S.M.A.R.T. approach:

Specific:

I will use imagery techniques a minimum of three times per week to increase my confidence level and decrease negative physiological reactions of stress so that I have a more effective response when dealing with confrontational offenders.

Measurable:

I will register for one scenario based training classes each month for the next two months where I will be put into confrontational situations and see if and how much my responses improve without negative physiological reactions.

Attainable: Yes

Realistic: Yes

Time-Lined: Two Months

Now that we have broken the goal down into its individual S.M.A.R.T. components we can write out the goal in a paragraph format.

S.M.A.R.T. Goal:

Over the next two months I will use imagery techniques a minimum of three times per week at home to increase my confidence level and decrease negative physiological reactions of stress so that my response when dealing with confrontational offenders is effective and appropriate. I will register for one scenario based training class each month for the next two months to measure my progress and level of improvement.

It is important to note that you still need to work on complimentary skills in conjunction with your goal in order to successfully accomplish your goal. For example, if you lack verbal de-escalation skills or communication skills to deal with confrontational offenders then the use of imagery alone will not be effective.

You will notice that the above goal is specific and detailed. Based upon the written goal lets re-examine the S.M.A.R.T. components.

Specific:

Who?	You the officer
What?	Will use imagery techniques
Where?	At home
When?	A minimum of three times per week after work
Why?	To increase your level of confidence and decrease negative physiological reactions to stress

Measurable:

I will register for one scenario based training class each month for the next two months to measure my progress and level of improvement

Attainable: Yes, through practice

Realistic: Yes, you are willing and able to strive toward your objective

Time-Lined: Two months

Now that you have a very specific and detailed goal it is important to be able to modify the goal based upon your measurable outcome. Using the previous goal as an example let's suppose that at the end of the second month you register for a scenario based training class and perform poorly despite practicing imagery three times a week for the past eight weeks. Now what? At this point you may need to modify your goal or extend the amount of time that you allotted to achieve the goal. Do not feel that you failed your goal just because you have not yet reached the level of performance that you wanted to obtain. Instead view it as another opportunity to reassess your plan and get back to work. Do not become discouraged that you didn't reach your goal as planned. View it as a minor setback that will allow you another opportunity at success provided that you reassess, develop or modify your plan, and then work your plan. Setbacks are often a part of the process when dealing with goals. The key is to not give up, remain consistent, and to stay motivated.

Exercise 5: Using the following S.M.A.R.T. goal format write down one officer survival goal that you want to improve:

Goal				
Specific	Measurable	Attainable	Realistic	Time-Lined

Write your S.M.A.R.T. goal statement:_____

_____

_____

_____

_____

Confidence

    Confidence is the belief in ones abilities. When referring to officer survival it is critical that officers are confident in their ability to prevail in a violent encounter despite external factors that you do not control. If you lack the confidence to prevail then you have already lost regardless of all other factors. I have seen extremely talented martial artists who had the knowledge, skills, and abilities to easily dominate opponents yet failed to do so only because these individuals lacked confidence and did not believe in their abilities. Despite being strong, flexible, physically fit, fast, knowledgeable, and tactically sound these individuals lost the fight in their mind before the first punch was ever thrown. The loss of the fight was manifested in the mind only to become a reality in the fight. In sports typically the worst thing to happen is that you lose. In law enforcement, the outcome can have dramatic and lethal consequences.

    Confidence is increased through preparation and past success from training and/or real world experience. When you engage in quality practice sessions (preparation) over a period of time you increase your skill level leading to positive outcomes which increases your level of confidence. Success breeds confidence so it is vitally important that all training classes and workout sessions build success into each event for you to build upon. As you successfully use these skills during practice, competition, scenario based training, and real events your confidence level will improve.

If you were to write this in a simplified formula it would look like:

Preparation + **Success** = **Confidence**
(Quality Training and Practice) (Training/Real Success)

Knowing that you are physically fit, mentally prepared, and well trained in officer survival skills such as verbal de-escalation, defensive tactics, firearms, etc. increases your confidence. When you add this to successful training evolutions and real world application then you are well on the way to building confidence that is stable and long lasting. If your confidence is up and down like a rollercoaster it is not true confidence. In order for your confidence to be valid it must be long-term, stable, and based on success in training and on the job application. Officers who exhibit confidence tend to train consistently, focus on factors within their control, do not let setbacks derail their progress and have a firm commitment to prevail.

Confidence can be broken down into two types:

1. Global Confidence – is how you perceive your overall ability.

2. Task Specific Confidence – how you perform certain tasks such as repeatedly and accurately shooting a target from 25 yards with your firearm within a specific time constraint.

Sports Example: In the sport of mixed martial arts you have an elite world class fighter with an undefeated record who is extremely confident. Overall, his global confidence for winning fights is very high. And while he is confident in many of his skills, his task specific confidence for throwing kicks is low. Despite not excelling in kicking this fighter remains confident in his overall ability to win fights.

Law Enforcement Example: You have an officer who is physically fit, trains defensive tactics skills on a regular basis, and challenges herself by participating in scenario based training. This officer regularly performs well in training and has high global confidence. However, she lacks confidence in defending herself when on the ground when mounted by her adversary due to her small stature. Therefore, her task specific confidence from the mount position is low which overtime can negatively impact her global confidence. This officer's internal self-talk may be, "*I'm fine as long as I don't end up on the ground.*" During a confrontation she will not be focused on the threat as much as she will be thinking about not being taken down to the ground. In this situation, the officer would continue to work on improving ground fighting skills, specifically defense from the mount, to increase her task specific confidence which will positively impact her global confidence.

> In order for confidence to be valid it must be:
> - Long-term
> - Stable
> - Based on success in training and on the job application

Being confident in your abilities and knowing that you can successfully resolve use of force encounters is important for all law enforcement officers. But, just as confidence can be obtained it can be lost. Common ways that confidence can be lost or diminished include:

1. Not performing well
2. Poor practice sessions
3. Unrealistic expectations
4. Negative feedback from others

Officer Survival for Probation and Parole Officers

Let's examine each of the ways that confidence can derail you from peak performance.

Not Performing Well

When you are in a situation where you use your skills in a real encounter but you fail to perform at a level that is acceptable to you then your confidence can diminish. For example:

Assume that you are conducting a probation/parole violation arrest on a violent offender. This is a pre-planned arrest and the offender has been placed in a sterile room at the probation/parole office designed specifically for conducting arrests. You have two police officers as back up. You inform the offender that he is under arrest and direct him to stand up, turn around, and place his hands in the air. You verbally direct this offender into a position to initiate the handcuffing process. You approach the offender as you have been trained and as you put the first handcuff on he pulls away taking you off balance. He has one handcuff secured on his right wrist as the other handcuff is dangling. Now you are face to face with a non-compliant offender who decides that he does not want to go to jail today. You issue a loud, clear, and concise verbal command for the offender to turn around. Instead of complying the offender gets in a fighting stance and begins to lunge at you. One of the police officers uses his Taser on the offender as the second police officer regains control, applies the other handcuff, and takes him into custody.

This "routine" office arrest did not go as planned. You have practiced handcuffing regularly in training and have successfully handcuffed numerous offenders without incident. This time the offender was non-compliant and resisted. Now your confidence is rattled. You begin an internal conversation asking yourself the following questions:

- What if the police officers were not there to back me up?
- What if the police officers would have got injured?
- What if the offender grabbed me and took me hostage?
- What if the offender tried to grab my firearm or baton? Would I have been able to retain my weapons?
- Will I be able to handcuff the next non-compliant offender I have to arrest?
- Have I trained enough on proper handcuffing?
- Did I do something wrong?
- Did I forget a step?
- Have I become complacent and just assumed that he would comply?

Now think forward to your next planned office arrest. What do you think you will be focusing on? You will be thinking about how your last arrest did not go smoothly. If you lose confidence your focus will not be on proper techniques and tactics when arresting the next offender but how things went wrong with the last offender. In order to avoid this situation you need to train on handcuffing for the worst case scenario – a non-compliant offender who refuses to be arrested.

Poor Practice Sessions

A poor practice session can be the result of many factors. You might be tired, stressed, not feeling well, have a sick kid or parent at home, or maybe you are just having a bad day. At one point or another most officers have an "off day" during practice. If you normally are consistent with your performance and have one bad day then you should not let this negatively impact your confidence. Chalk it up to a bad day and move on. Now if you are consistently having poor practice sessions then your confidence level will drop. Let's assume that you are at the firing range to practice your shooting skills. The previous two times you practiced you had "bad days" and now you are concerned that you will not perform well during today's practice session. This thought process has already started you down a self-fulfilling prophecy. The focus of today's range session is malfunction drills under stress while engaging multiple threats. Unfortunately your performance today was poor. You failed to clear a class 3 malfunction in the allotted time period. And when you did clear the malfunction you missed two out of three targets. This is the third training session in a row with poor performance. In one month you are required to do your annual firearms qualification and do not think that you will perform well. Your confidence has tanked.

Unrealistic Expectations

Unrealistic expectations occur when you believe that you will perform at a level beyond your current ability. If you never passed a firearms qualification with a perfect score it probably is not a reasonable expectation that you will do so during your next qualification. If you have never performed a one shot draw from the holster with an accurate hit on the target in 1.0 second there is no reason to believe that you would be able to do so during your next time event of this drill. Now if you are constantly practicing towards these goals and making progress there is a chance of meeting such a challenge but it will only happen with dedicated, consistent, and focused practice. There are also things that we may never be able to accomplish. I am never going to be able to dunk a basketball for a regulation height basket. No matter how much I practice I will never dunk a basketball. I would never set myself up with such an unrealistic expectation and neither should you.

Negative Feedback from Others

Many people are impacted, both positively and negatively, by the people around us. When the comments are positive our confidence can rise. But when individuals provide you negative feedback it can have an adverse effect on your confidence. This is especially true if you value the person's opinion or look up to this person as a role model. Think back to the poor practice session just reviewed with the officer who has difficulty clearing weapon malfunctions. If the instructor were to make a comment such as, *"you are never going to get the malfunction drills down"* or another officer says to you, *"be sure your gun doesn't jam in a gunfight or your dead"* you will realize that such negative comments will take a toll on you even if said in jest. Now, on the way home from the range you are thinking to yourself, *"What if my gun does jam in a gunfight? Am I going to clear it in time?"* When trainers, other officers, friends, or supervisors plant seeds in your mind with negative comments it can impact your confidence to perform when it counts. It is common for officers who work in law enforcement to give each other a hard time with no harm intended or to be very competitive with each other. Most of the times such comments are not said in a mean spirited manner and there is no intent to cause any distress. Whatever the intent is with such comments it is always a good practice to not give them a second thought and to remain positive and focused on what you need to accomplish. Some officers will use such negative feedback or jesting as motivation to work hard in order to improve their deficient skills. These officers take a negative situation and reframe it to a positive by correcting the situation with training, ongoing practice, and a plan of action.

Regaining Lost Confidence

One of the most challenging things to do is regain your confidence when you are not performing well. Confidence is the belief in your abilities but it is extremely difficult to believe in your abilities when performing at a level that does not meet your expectations or established standards. And while there is no magic fix there are some strategies that you can use to help regain your confidence.

Re-evaluate your Training

It is advantageous to periodically review your training regimen and evaluate if you are training in a way that increases your skill set and creates success. A poorly planned training regimen or one that lacks focus can prohibit you from accomplishing your written goals. If you are not making progress or become stagnant then you are at a perfect spot to evaluate your training goals and make necessary improvements.

Questions to consider:

- Are your training goals realistic?
- Do you need to re-evaluate your training goals?
- Does your training foster success or does it set you up for failure?
- Is your current training increasing or decreasing your confidence?
- Do you need to remediate some or all of your training?
- Are you training alone, with a partner, or a group?
- Are you attending department trainings only or do you attend training outside of what your agency provides?
- Do you need to consider having a trainer look at your routine?

Failure to re-evaluate your training can lead you into a slump with no clear direction using stagnant goals. If you are not making progress you will eventually become frustrated and lose motivation to train your officer survival skills. Even when your confidence is high is it good to periodically re-evaluate your training to ensure that you are getting the most benefit from your training time.

Be Patient but Remain Persistent

Regaining your confidence is a journey that requires time and effort. Generally, there is no quick fix or shortcuts to success. The good news is that through patience and persistence you can achieve or regain a level of confidence that fosters successful outcomes. As long as you have a plan, goals, and a training program you can achieve confidence. And while it is important that your goals are time-lined it is also important that you give yourself enough time to achieve your goals. You need to build a track record of success to foster your confidence and this can take time. As long as you are making forward progress you are on the right track. Minor setbacks are not uncommon and should not discourage you. Remain dedicated and consistent to working on achieving your goals.

Remain Positive

When your level of performance falls to an unacceptable level it becomes very easy to focus on the negative. Your self-talk becomes:

"I can't…"

"I'll never…"

"I train hard but…"

"I'm not good at…"

"I'm going to fail at…"

"No matter what I do…"

Remember, attitude affects performance. If you are negative then expect a negative outcome. There is no substitute for a positive mental attitude especially when it comes to developing lifesaving officer survival skills. Anytime that you catch yourself using negative self-talk you need to immediately stop your thought process and replace it with positive self-talk. Staying positive is not enough and self-talk, including negative self-talk, is a skill than can impact performance. Your "inner critic" is exceptionally powerful especially when the critic has been negative over an extended period of time. This is why developing strategies to deal with negative self-talk and your inner critic is essential. I will discuss more on this topic shortly.

Take a Break

This might be a challenge for some people because they have this need to "do something" as opposed to doing nothing. Sometimes a short break from training will give your body and mind time to relax and get away from the stress of not performing well. As a law enforcement officer you can't afford to take too long of a break because many of your skills are perishable. But, there will be no harm in taking a week or two off to relax and recharge. When you get back to training you will be refreshed and reinvigorated. Now you can begin rebuilding your confidence with a fresh, positive perspective. Start off with a training program that ensures early success and work your way back to resolve problematic areas. Practicing fundamental skills is always a good way to start back up as these tend to be the rudimentary building blocks that more advanced techniques and tactics are built upon. Never move past the fundamentals until you have mastered these necessary basic skills.

Carry Forward Positive Past Successes

Think back to previous times in training or real world situations where you were successful with your officer survival skills. Knowing that you have been successful in a past event can be a confidence boost in knowing that you can continue to be successful in future events. Try to remember what your mindset, thoughts, feelings, and self-talk were during these previous successful events.

Concentration and Focus

Concentration can be defined as intense mental application or complete attention while *focus* is a point upon which attention is directed. Let's re-examine Howe's definition of Combat Mindset:

An aggressive combat mind-set is possessed by people who can <u>screen out distractions while under great stress to focus on the mission</u> and are willing to go into harm's way, against great odds if necessary.

As you can see from this definition, to have a combat mindset you must be able to:

1. Screen out distractions while under great stress
2. Focus on the mission

These elements are critical for officers who find themselves in a use of force situation. Not only must you block out distractions but you must maintain the ability to observe and respond to relevant information. Failure to maintain your concentration and focus on the threat(s) will almost ensure your defeat. Additionally, use of force situations often require split second decision making. If you fail to instantly assess the situation and develop an appropriate response you are rapidly decreasing your chances for a successful outcome. In such encounters your thought process must not be about why you can't deal with the situation that you find yourself in (i.e. negative self-talk). If you find yourself engaged in negative self-talk you are not only fighting the threat but you are fighting yourself from within. Instead you must remain focused on what action you will take to successfully resolve the situation and/or neutralize the threat(s). And, you must be able to do this within an extremely short time span while under stress. Under the best of circumstances this is a difficult task. This is why officer survival training is so incredibly important. To make matters even more difficult you must fight tunnel vision where all of your attention is focused on one threat at the exclusion of other potential threats.

Training provides you with the mental and physical skill set to focus on what you need to do as opposed to focusing on why you can't do what needs to be done. One of the most effective forms of training for use of force encounters is Stress Inoculation Training (SIT) which exposes an officer to stressful events in order to "inoculate" individuals to future stressors. Many officers avoid stress inoculation training and scenario based training because they know that they will purposely be placed in stressful situations. Officers avoid these classes for fear of failure, fear of looking foolish, failing to respond appropriately or because they do not want to acknowledge the reality that violence can be directed at them. Ignoring reality does not change reality. Such classes are critical aspects of officer survival training because they:

- Expose you to stress with the goal of inoculating you to the negative effects of stress
- Provide you opportunities to learn in a forgiving environment
- Provide an opportunity to develop and/or improve skills needed to successfully manage such encounters
- Increase your level of confidence because you build up a record of successful outcomes

Training is an opportunity for you to make mistakes, learn from the mistake, and incorporate lessons learned. It is never a good strategy to encounter a situation in the real world that you have not seen and experienced, in at least some variation, in training. If this is the case chances are you will not be adequately prepared to respond. You will lose concentration, focus, and confidence. Of course training rarely matches exactly all of the situations that you may encounter but it will provide you a mental database so that you can adapt and be flexible to situations you may encounter. The more realistic your training is the more prepared you will be when a situation happens for real.

Self-Talk

Winston Churchill once said, *"A pessimist sees the difficulty in every opportunity; an optimist sees the opportunity in every difficulty."* That statement sums up the difference between positive vs. negative thinking. This thinking is often manifested in self-talk which is either positive or negative.

Self-talk is the monologue that we have with ourselves that is expressed through internal conversation or by speaking verbally out loud. Self-talk can be positive or negative but either way it influences our feelings, emotions, and behavior.

Positive self-talk

Are the sayings that help foster a "can do" attitude, increases confidence, and assists with focus and concentration so that necessary and appropriate action is translated into performance especially in a crisis situation.

Negative self-talk

Is a monologue where fears are exposed leading to a lack of confidence, indecisiveness, loss of self-esteem, or the inability to take appropriate action, or worse, take no action at all.

Positive self-talk lets you know that you CAN succeed; negative self-talk tries to convince you that you CANNOT succeed. Negative self-talk decreases confidence, inhibits concentration, and increases anxiety which in turn leads to poor performance. During a crisis, law enforcement officers are not benefited by spending any amount of time with negative self-talk. Such action is self-defeating and can lead to officer injury or death. While it is important to understand that negative self-talk is unproductive and can result in a less than desirable outcome it is also a reality that negative self-talk is going to happen to all of us at one point or another. The key is to stop this process and move on to more productive and positive measures especially when your life is in jeopardy. This will be discussed shortly.

Peak Performance and Self-talk

Peak performance is not random and does not just happen without development of the following three skills:

Skill	Examples: Officer Survival Related
1. Physical Skills	Cardio-respiratory Endurance, Muscular Endurance, Strength, Flexibility, Speed
2. Technical Skills	Defensive Tactics, Firearms, Officer Survival Tactics, Taser, OC Spray, Baton, Searches, Warrant Execution, Arrests
3. Mental Skills	Mindset, Goal Setting, Confidence, Decisiveness, Concentration, Focus, Imagery, Positive Self-talk

Generally, your physical and technical skill set will be learned through quality initial training and then developed through consistent ongoing training to improve, reinforce, and refine skills. Officer survival skills must be efficient, effective, accurate, easy to learn, and easy to implement under stress. To improve your skills into well developed and refined movements you need to participate in a consistent training regimen that is goal oriented. But, performance is comprised of a multifaceted training program. It is correlated not only to physical and technical preparation but also to your mindset which includes your thoughts, expectations, self-talk, etc. Failing to develop physical, technical, and mental skills will leave you vulnerable during a crisis and will impair your ability to reach peak performance levels. Even if you are really strong with two of these skills but remain weak in one area you will be inadequately prepared to perform at your best. All three skills must be developed to a high degree in order to provide your best chance of performing at the requisite level. Unfortunately, many training programs glance over mental skills and provide only a very rudimentary level of skills that officers need. These training classes do not provide you the skills to address your inner critic and negative self-talk. In such cases you, as the officer, will need to take time on your own to develop mental skills or to seek out training that focuses on this necessary and vital skill.

Learning to control self-talk can help officers manage and respond to their internal monologue especially during a crisis when self-doubt can creep into your thought processes especially if you become overwhelmed with the situation that you find yourself. Officers must ensure self-talk is directed toward improving performance, not detracting or inhibiting performance. Just as you must regularly train your body to execute officer survival skills you also need to regularly train your mind with skills that will enhance peak performance on demand.

Examples of Negative Self-talk

- "I can't do this"
- "I'm going to die"
- "I'm going to fail"
- "I'm not in shape"
- "I'm a terrible shot"
- "I can't stay focused"

- "I haven't trained for this"
- "This is too difficult to handle"
- "I'm not good with confrontation"
- "I'm bleeding! I can't continue to fight"
- "I'm never going to see my family again"
- "It's too ____ (hot, cold, windy, *fill in the blank*) to..."
- "I'm too ____ (old, short, tall, heavy, *fill in the blank*) for this"

It would be bad enough to use such negative statements during training but can you imagine the impact if these were your thoughts during a crisis! You would be allowing yourself to fail and potentially have an outcome that changes your life for the worse.

Thought-Stopping to Neutralize Negative Self-Talk

Some people utilize negative self-talk so often that they become unaware of this self-defeating behavior and no longer are cognitively aware of their internal monologue. Negative self-talk becomes the proverbial self-fulfilling prophecy in that you tell yourself so often that you "can't" that you have set yourself up for failure before you even have begun. In order to stop these thoughts, that you may not even be cognizant of, you must first become aware that they are occurring and understanding that their impact is not providing any positive results for you.

Do not underestimate the power of your "inner critic" and how internal thought processes and self-talk negatively impact performance. For some people their inner critic has a very strong presence and has been active for a very long time. So much so that the person is no longer aware of their own thought processes. This inner critic brings you down and keeps you down often unconsciously without your knowledge. Such thoughts and negative self-talk will generally impact all areas of your life. When you find yourself engaging in negative self-talk there are some steps you can take to stop this practice and turn the situation around to a more productive and positive outcome especially relating to officer survival skills.

Thought-stopping is a technique where you replace negative self-talk with positive self-talk. The goal is to immediately stop the negativity and refocus on the task or necessary skill for the situation that you encounter.

Step 1:

The first step to this process is to become aware of your negative thoughts and negative self-talk. This will require you to become more in tune with your thoughts. You will not be able to stop your negative self-talk if you do not realize that you are having this internal monologue. Actively listen to what your "inner critic" is telling you. It is also important to understand when you are having such thoughts.

- Does it occur at the first sign that an offender is going to be non-compliant?
- Does it occur when you have a planned field arrest on a violent offender with a history of combative behavior?
- Does it begin the night before a training class, as you drive to training, as you are warming up, before you perform a drill, after the class is over or all of these situations?
- Does it happen during real events, training classes, or randomly throughout the day?
- Do you find yourself making excuses the night before training or on your way to training such as: your back hurts, you have a headache, your stomach is upset,

you didn't sleep well, you stayed up too late, you have work piling up, etc.?

Step 2:

Once you become aware of your negative self-talk the second step is to immediately stop the thought process by saying "STOP", "STOP IT", "NO", or another suitable cue to get you to refocus on the situation. You must be firm and forceful when giving yourself this instruction. Think of yourself as a drill instructor yelling a self-directed command to "**STOP**." If the use of words is not beneficial for you and you need a visual cue you can imagine an image such as a big "Stop" sign or a red traffic light instead.

Step 3:

This step involves replacing the negative thought/self-talk with either positive self-talk or an instructional command (instructional self-talk) to get you to refocus your attention on the needed skill based on the situation. Instructional self-talk is verbiage that will guide you through a specific task.

Next let's review some examples of this process.

Example 1:

Scenario: Officer failed to perform well during scenario-based training.

Negative Self-Talk: "I did terrible today, again!"

Thought-stopping: STOP

Positive Self-Talk: "I will work hard and do better next time."

Example 2:

Scenario: Officer is attending firearms training. From the 15 yard firing line he continually has low shot placement.

Negative Self-Talk: "I keep jerking that damn trigger!"

Thought-stopping: STOP

Instructional Self-Talk: "Front sight, p-r-e-s-s"

Example 3:

Scenario: You are reviewing terms and conditions of parole and a behavioral contract with a new offender assigned to your caseload. This offender has been on parole before and knows the process. The offender has never gotten along well with his past P.O.'s and is always adversarial. While going over the behavioral contract the offender says, "*I will do whatever the hell I want until my DOC number is killed. If you get in my way then I will handle you the way I handle all my problems which is why I'm here in the first place.*"

Negative Self-Talk: "I can't supervise this offender. He wants trouble"

Thought-stopping: STOP

Positive Self-Talk: "I can handle this guy and his confrontational attitude."

Example 4:

Scenario: Officer is conducting field work and is approaching the front door of a residence when he is shot in the leg causing profuse bleeding.

Negative Self-Talk: "I'm going to die"

Thought-stopping: STOP

Instructional Self-Talk: "Get to cover, apply direct pressure, call 9-1-1."

Negative self-talk is a valueless thought process with no positive attributes. And while we all engage in this thinking we must strive for tools and thought processes that assist with positive results. Negative self-talk will almost always guarantee poor performance or a negative outcome. Unfortunately, positive self-talk and instructional self-talk do not guarantee positive results. You still need the skills to back up your positive affirmations. This underscores the necessity for on-going training and improvement in your officer survival skills.

Exercise 6: List the negative statements you commonly say to yourself. Next, indicate where and in what situations you say these negative statements. This will help you become aware of the situations in which you're most likely to be negative. Then, list positive statements with which you can replace them.

Self-Talk Exercise			
Negative Statement	Where	Situation	Positive Self-Talk
EXAMPLES: I'm not going to pass my annual firearms qualification.	Driving to range, at range.	Firearms qualification	I have trained hard this last quarter. I will do my best to remain focused and relaxed.
Office day is too much for me to handle. I'm overwhelmed.	At home the evening before office day, while driving to work, at work.	Office day when offenders report.	I will handle this day one offender at a time.

Imagery

When talking about mental preparation officers routinely think about the use of mental rehearsal techniques such as imagery and visualization techniques as a training method to improve skills. Many law enforcement trainers use the terms imagery and visualization as if they are interchangeable terms. Attend training sessions and you will inevitably hear trainers in both law enforcement and sports tell their students to visualize. Actually, the terms imagery and visualization are two different mental rehearsal techniques that officers can use to aid in the development of mental toughness skills and improve their mindset. Let's review the definition of these terms:

Visualization is the process of creating a mental image of what you want to happen. The use of visualization techniques focuses primarily on *visual* input and tends to exclude your other four senses.

Imagery is a technique to enhance performance with the utilization of all your senses to include *sight*, *hearing*, *touch*, *smell* and *taste*. The goal is to create a detailed experience that feels very real where you create a desired outcome.

I prefer the use of imagery over visualization because imagery is inclusive of all your senses which in turn provides a more detailed and realistic experience. Additionally, thoughts produce the same mental instructions as actions. The use of mental imagery impacts many cognitive processes in the brain to include: motor control, attention, perception, planning, and memory. The brain is getting trained for actual performance during the use imagery. The benefits of using imagery include:

- Enhanced motivation
- Increased level of confidence and self-efficacy
- Improved motor performance
- Mentally preparing your mind for success

These are exactly the skills that law enforcement officers need when it comes to officer survival.

Think of imagery as a movie where you are not only the main character but you get to be the director, producer, writer, editor, casting director, wardrobe, and all the supporting staff. Your use of imagery is completely in your control where you not only get to script the story but you determine the ending which should always be a favorable outcome. You determine where the situation happens, when it happens, under what conditions, time of day, weather conditions, etc.

There are two points of view that you can take when using imagery:

1. You can have the perspective of seeing yourself as if watching a film on the television or a movie screen. You are watching yourself from an external viewpoint.

2. You can take the first person approach as if you are right there in the movie experiencing all the action as it is occurring. Everything happens is from your point of view directly from your eyes as you would see it occur in the real world.

When conducting imagery I prefer to use the latter perspective where I am an active participant in the movie as opposed to watching myself perform in the movie. I want to see everything as if I am right there in the scene. In other words you "experience" the situation firsthand as opposed to "seeing" it as in a move. I believe that this approach makes it a more realistic experience as opposed to watching it as if it is an out of body event.

When using imagery it is important to include all of your senses in order to make your mental preparation training session as realistic as possible. The more detailed and specific your scenario the better you will be prepared if a situation where to really occur in the performance of your duties.

Examples of using your five senses:

1. Sight (Visual) Images of the environment, threat(s), front sight of your firearm, injuries to the threat(s) or yourself, bystanders, emergency responders to

Officer Survival for Probation and Parole Officers

                                include police, fire and EMS, driving to your location, landmarks, etc.

                                Can be day time, night time, low-light environment, inside a home or apartment, at an offenders place of employment, a school for a juvenile offender, etc.

2. Hearing (Auditory)   Sound of gunfire, use of verbal commands, emergency sirens, screaming, calls from dispatch attempting to contact you on your department issued radio, parents of a juvenile who are arguing with each other, fellow probation/parole officers that are with you, police helicopter flying over the scene, etc.

3. Touch (Tactile, Kinesthetic)   Gripping your handcuffs, holding your baton and feeling the impact as you strike a target, shooting your firearm and feeling the recoil, conducting a magazine exchange, clearing a malfunction, employing OC spray, using a pressure point, using your radio, physically fighting a resistive offender that you are going to arrest, etc.

4. Smell (Olfactory)   OC spray, gunpowder, blood, body odor, dust, plants,

environmental smells, smoke, fire, chemical smell, etc.

5. Taste (Gustatory)   OC spray, sweat, water that you consume, etc.

Imagery can be used to enhance skills for difference situations. The three situations that I like to use imagery for include:

1. <u>Scenario Based Imagery</u> – This is where you go through a scenario from beginning to end using all five senses.

Examples can include:

- Leaving your probation/parole office to conduct a residential contact at an apartment complex.
- Conducting a field arrest with police officers as back up.
- Leaving your residence to go to the probation/parole office (after receiving anonymous death threats).

2. <u>Skill Based Imagery</u> – This is used to enhance a skill that you already know how to perform.

Examples can include:

- Drawing your OC spray and spraying a threat
- Drawing your firearm from the holster which is concealed
- Handcuffing an offender that you are going to arrest
- Clearing a class three malfunction with your firearm
- Conducting a tactical reload

Officer Survival for Probation and Parole Officers

- Using verbal skills to de-escalate an irate offender while in the office
- Escaping from a rear choke hold
- Weapon retention skills
- Using your baton
- Using your Taser

3. <u>Incident Correction Imagery</u> – This is where you take a real incident that did not go as planned and use this technique to change (correct) the incident to a positive outcome. Think back to the section on confidence when the officer attempted to apply handcuffs but the offender resisted. A good use of imagery is to replay the incident except this time you control the outcome and successfully handcuff the offender without incident.

Following are steps to assist you in the use of imagery. If you are new to this technique do not become discouraged if you find it difficult to use. Remain patient and give it a few tries to get an idea of the process and then it will become easier to practice this technique with little distraction.

1. Sit in a comfortable chair or recliner where you will not be interrupted by the phone, pets, or other people.
2. Relax your body by taking several deep and slow breaths. Inhale slowly through your nose, hold the breath for a few seconds, and then exhale slowly through your mouth. Repeat this about five times or until you feel relaxed and ready to begin.
3. Close your eyes and create a detailed, vivid, and convincing scenario. This scenario can be one you've previously experienced, one you think that you may encounter in the course of your duties, or a scenario

where you work on the development of a skill that you already have learned.
4. If you become distracted or find you are thinking about something else, acknowledge it, then let it go and refocus.
5. Focus on your breathing if you lose the scenario.
6. Maintain a positive attitude.
7. Imagine the sights, sounds, tastes, feelings, and smells of the experience.

Take note of as much detail of the scenario as possible. Examples:

- Who is involved in this scenario?
- Who is the threat?
- What is the threat saying or doing that places you in jeopardy?
- Where is this occurring?
- What time of day is it?
- What are the weather conditions?
- Is it daytime or night time?
- Are you inside or outside?
- What are you wearing?
- What safety equipment is on your person?
- Did you drive your personal vehicle or a department vehicle?
- What actions do you need to take to prevail using reasonable and necessary force, if necessary?

- Immediately after you neutralize the threat(s) do you need to call for medical attention for anyone?
- Do you have any injuries? (If yes, you will survive and must remain focused on what you need to do to prevail.)

If your imagery session is not going the way you want it to, simply open your eyes and start over with your breathing.

8. Always end an imagery session with a successful resolution to the situation. You have complete control of the scenario and the outcome. In all imagery sessions that involve use of force you must prevail. Remember, you are training your mind that will result in a tangible outcome for your body.

Next I will provide you with three examples utilizing imagery. Remember that you should be very specific and detailed to make your session as realistic as possible. For the sake of brevity, in these examples I may not be providing every single specific detail that I would be using in this process.

Scenario Based Imagery Example

Scenario: Arrest of offender in the probation/parole office

Background: Domestic Violence Offender

Charge: Aggravated Assault with a Deadly Weapon

Offender: Male, 26 years old, Caucasian, 6'1" tall, 215 pounds, athletic build

Prior Charges: 1. Assault on a Law Enforcement Officer
                             2. Resisting Arrest

3. Disorderly Conduct (2x)

4. Possession of Dangerous Drugs

The defendant is on a specialized domestic violence (DV) caseload. The defendant assaulted his now ex-girlfriend and cut her with a knife across her neck. The cut was minor considering the vital location on the neck but required five stitches to close. According to the presentence report the defendant stated:

> *"The cut on her neck was an accident and I never intended to cut her at all. She wouldn't have got cut if she didn't resist me. It was her fault, not mine. The stupid bitch is lucky that the cut wasn't worse than it is."*

As part of his conditions he is not to have any contact with the victim but he has recently violated this term on at least two separate occasions. The victim contacted the probation officer stating that she is scared for her life and that the offender came to her apartment two times this past week. The victim called the police both times and the offender left before the police arrived. The victim states she wants nothing to do with the offender and has not initiated any contact with him. She think he wants to kill her because all of the trouble he got into with his current charge.

Due to the offenders repeated non-compliance he will be arrested in the office for violating his terms and condition of probation/parole. The offender has <u>not</u> been informed that he is going to be arrested. Today is his normal day to report to the probation/parole office.

<u>Scenario Based Imagery Session:</u>

It is 1:45PM and I am in the probation/parole office waiting for an offender to arrive. A front office staff member walks into my office and informs me that the offender just arrived and signed in. She states that he appears to be acting normally and that he passed through security with no weapons. Although he successfully made it through the security screening process I do not assume that he does not have a weapon on him. He may have a weapon that does not alert the metal detector or hand wand that security uses. I turn to my office partner and tell her that I will be conducting an office arrest so that she is properly informed. I also say that this offender has a history of violence and resisting arrest. I remind myself to stay alert and focused.

I then pick up the phone and call the non-emergency phone number to the local police department to ask for assistance with this arrest. I inform the police dispatcher of the offenders domestic violence charge, his non-compliant probation status, his prior violence history along with resisting arrest and that he is a large muscular male. I request a minimum of two police officers to respond. The dispatcher states that it will be approximately 8 minutes before the officers arrive.

I then walk to my supervisors office and notify him of the planned arrest that we discussed earlier in the day. My supervisor informs me that he will standby during the arrest as an added precaution. All my probation/parole violation paperwork was completed yesterday so my focus is solely on the arrest that is about to happen once the police arrive.

I then walk out to the lobby to inform the defendant that I am running 15-20 minutes behind but I will be with him shortly. I do this for a few reasons: 1) to buy some extra time for the police officers to arrive, 2) to visually scan the offender to see what he is wearing, 3) to visually scan for potential weapons and 4) to get a general idea of his demeanor.

I walk back to my office where the arrest will take place and scan the office environment to ensure that I have removed all potential weapons of opportunities such as pens, pencils, staplers, paper weights, clip boards or any other items of concern.

Although I verified that I have all my safety equipment on before I left my residence this morning I conduct a quick equipment check: OC spray, firearm, two spare magazines, baton, handcuffs, handcuff key, flashlight. All safety equipment accounted for.

I am notified by a front office staff member that two police officers are at the back door of the probation/parole office. This is the location where we meet police officers when conducting arrests. I walk to the back door and escort the police officers to my office to show them where the arrest will take place. I brief the police officers on vital offender information to include a photograph, synopsis of the criminal history to include aggravated assault - domestic violence, use of weapons (knife), resisting arrest, assault on law enforcement, two counts of disorderly conduct and possession of dangerous drugs. I notify the officers that the offender is a large muscular male who is not intimidated by authority to include the police. I show the police officers where they will hide until I get the offender in my office. My office partner has on all of her safety equipment and is included in the briefing. My supervisor is also in attendance at the briefing. Should this offender resist there will be three probation/parole officers and two police officers to resolve the situation. I inform all officers involved that once I escort the offender into my office they are to immediately get into position to initiate the arrest. I inform the officers that I will immediately inform the offender that he is under arrest for violating probation/parole and then initiate the handcuffing process and search. I ask if anyone has any questions, concerns, or comments about the arrest. Everyone is good to go and they take their places.

I mentally remind myself to be in condition yellow and expect the unexpected; I take a few deep breaths before going to the lobby. I am ready to initiate the arrest of an offender who has a violent history.

As I walk to the lobby I am scanning the probation/parole

office. I open the lobby door and notice that the metal door handle is cold. I call the offender who looks at me, stands up and slowly walks toward the lobby door to my location. He appears relaxed and has a strong smell of cologne. He is calm and begins asking me how I am doing. I tell him that I am fine as I escort him to my office. As I am escorting him I conduct quick visual scan for weapons. As we approach my office I notice my supervisor keeping an eye on me from down the hall. Once in my office the offender automatically sits down in the chair as he has done numerous times before. Before the offender sat down both police officers were already in the best tactical position that they can be in for a normal size office environment. From a field interview stance I immediately tell the offender that he is under arrest for violating his probation/parole and that I need him to stand up, turn around and put his hands straight up in the air. The offender complies but begins to turn around to ask what he did wrong. I give him a loud, clear, concise verbal command to turn around and face the wall. He complies but then turns around again as he lowers his arms. As he locks eyes with me he then states, "*I'm not going to jail, I didn't do anything wrong.*" I notice that his jaw looks tense as he is staring at me. I know the offender is thinking about resisting and mentally processing his options. I raise both of my hands into a defensive position in case the offender decides to attack. Immediately one of the police officer pulls out his Taser X2 model points the red laser on the offender's chest and tells him to turn around. The offender complies with the police officers directive. The offender is again facing the wall away from all of the officers. I pull out my handcuffs and initiate the handcuffing process. I grab the offender's right hand with my left hand as I apply the handcuff with my right hand to the offender's right hand. I then immediately apply the other handcuff to the offender's left hand in case the offender decides to resist. I am in a solid and balanced stance in case he attempts to resist. Both handcuffs are on within one second of each other with no delay. The offender states, "*I won't resist, it's all good. There is no reason to Taser me.*" Once both handcuffs are securely applied I ask the offender the following questions:

> Question 1: Do you have anything on you that will poke, stick, or injure me in any way?
> Answer: "No."
>
> Question 2: Do you have any needles on you? (I realize this is redundant to the first question but I do not want to take any risks with being infected with a blood borne pathogen.)
> Answer: "No."
>
> Question 3: Do you have any weapons on you such as a knife, razor, gun, stick, or grenade?
> Answer: "No."

I remind myself to always wait for the offender to answer my questions so that I do not rush to search and then accidentally get poked by a hypodermic needle or other item. Once the offender answers these questions I initiate a thorough search to check for weapons or contraband. (Note: I will not go through the procedure of conducting a prisoner search in this example but when using imagery I would follow the process completely and accurately not to miss any steps.) When conducting a search I am looking for weapons, drugs, drug paraphernalia, hidden handcuff keys, and other contraband. After the search I will double lock the handcuffs to ensure that they do not tighten on the offender and to confirm that they are applied correctly.

Once the search is completed I may stop the Scenario Based Imagery session or I can continue on with the scenario until I book the offender into jail. For this scenario I used imagery to conduct and arrest and search of the offender in the probation/parole office with the assistance of two police officers. Your imagery session would provide more detail such as what your office partner is doing, what your supervisor is doing and the police officers' actions consisted of during the arrest. You can also do a scenario where the offender resists the arrest and use of force must be applied. Remember to be specific and detailed in your imagery session and use all of your senses.

Skill Based Imagery Example

Skill: Shooting my department issued firearm from the 25 yard line and obtaining consistently accurate shot placement.

Goal: To enhance my skill in smoothly drawing my firearm from the holster which is concealed and accurately hitting the target from a distance of 25 yards. During my next firearms qualification I want to accurately fire six shots center mass from 25 yards.

Skill Based Imagery Session:

It is 10:00AM on a cool November morning at the range. The temperature is about 65 degrees with a slight breeze. It is a bright sunny day out. I am at a range table loading my firearm and two spare magazines with training rounds. As I load the magazine I mentally remind myself to:

> *"Be smooth, focus on the front sight, and press the trigger. Do not rush as I have plenty of time to fire one round. Time will not be an issue."*

Once my magazines are loaded I put the two magazines in their carrier. I then put on my hearing protection and eye protection. I then walk to the firing line with all my equipment ready to go. I am now standing on the firing line 25 yards away from the standard law enforcement target. I load a magazine into the Glock 23 and rack a round into the chamber. I remove the magazine and top it off with one round. I replace the magazine into the firearm and then conduct a function check to ensure that a round is in the chamber. I secure the firearm in the holster. I am wearing a light jacket and will be firing from concealment. I have all my safety gear on and I am ready to shoot.

I start out from a field interview stance. I take two deep breaths as I focus on a small portion of the target that is located center mass. I move my right arm to move my concealment jacket out of the way with my thumb and once the jacket is cleared out of the way I grip my firearm. I unholster my firearm as I maintain visual contact with the target. Immediately after clearing the firearm from the holster I turn the barrel of the weapon toward the target. I punch the weapon out as my left hand meets up with my right hand forming a solid grip. I acquire focus on the front sight in order to obtain a sight picture. I ensure that there is equal space between the sides of the front sight as they are aligned with the rear sight. My sight picture is perfect. I move my right index finger to the trigger and take up the slack. I have made a conscious decision to fire one round at the threat (target). I press the trigger until a round is fired. I hear the muffled pop of the round firing, I see a hint of smoke in the bright daylight, and can smell the gunpowder. Immediately I obtain another sight picture being sure to focus on the front sight. Before holstering I mentally ask myself the following questions:

1. Is the threat neutralized? If not, do I need to re-engage?
2. Are there other threats that need to be addressed?
3. To break the possibility of tunnel vision I tell myself: Scan left, scan right.
4. Is it now safe for me to holster my firearm?

After answering these questions I holster my firearm. I

never rush this process and I never rush to holster my weapon. It is imperative that use perfect form and technique. I never sacrifice accuracy for speed. After holstering my firearm I walk toward the target to verify my shot placement. As I get close to the target I verify that the shot went exactly where I was aiming and intended the bullet to strike the target.

I would then repeat this skill based imagery session again where I would walk back to the firing line and do the process over again. I may mix it up and fire two or three rounds at the target instead of one round. Other times I may engage multiple targets.

Incident Correction Imagery Example

Incident: Field arrest at a half-way house of a non-compliant offender. This incident happened on a weekday at approximately 6:30PM during dusk. The offender was hiding behind the front door on the second story of a building. I was standing outside of the apartment as the front door was opened by a resident who lived in the apartment. When asked if the offender was home the resident who answered the door said no. As I walked past the door to enter the apartment the offender that I was looking for jumped from behind the front door and ran out of the apartment past four other community corrections officers and two fully uniformed police officers. As he was making his escape out of the apartment the offender forcefully pushed one of the community corrections officers out of the way.

Normally, I check the gap between the door were the door is hinged and screwed into the door frame. This time I did not look through the gap because the door appeared to be all the way open. On this field arrest I used poor tactics and made a faulty assumption that no one would hide behind the door because it appeared to be fully open. In this case the offender was extremely skinny and was able to hide. Fortunately, this offender was not a dedicated threat and had no intention of harming me or other officers. He just wanted to escape which he did despite the police department calling in a helicopter, police K-9, and setting up a perimeter of the neighborhood. A two hour police search of the neighborhood ensued with the offender getting away. Had the offender been a dedicated threat he would have caught me off guard and possibly been able to obtain my firearm which was concealed or to get me in a headlock possibly turning this arrest into a hostage situation with an officer as the hostage.

Goal: To replay the incident utilizing correct tactics, not making faulty assumptions, and arresting the offender without incident.

<u>Incident Replay Imagery Session:</u>

Note: Incident Replay will begin at the front door of the apartment which is a halfway house located on the second floor. Behind me are four community corrections officers and two police officers. The other community corrections officers are not armed with a firearm. They have a baton, OC spray, handcuffs, radio, and a protective vest with a probation placard. In addition, all officers have their badge hanging around their neck on a lanyard. I am the only armed community corrections officer on scene.

I knock on the door and wait for an answer. Using proper safety tactics I am standing on the side of the door in case an offender or other person was to shoot through the door. A young Caucasian male answers the door. He knows I am a law enforcement officer by the badge hanging from my neck and because I am wearing body armor with a placard that reads "Probation" on the front of the vest. I ask if John Doe is home to which the resident states, "No, I haven't seen him." As the resident is answering the question I complete a visual scan of the inside of the residence but don't notice anything out of the ordinary. I do notice that there are two bedroom doors in sight that are closed. I make a mental note to keep an eye on those doors. I notice that the front door looks fully open but I pull out my LED flashlight with my left hand, being sure to keep my right hand free, and shine the light though the crack of the door where the door is attached to the door frame. As I shine the light through the crack I notice a skinny black male hiding behind the door. I immediately give a loud verbal warning to all of the other officers, "*subject behind the door*" and I immediately step in attempting to keep the front door wide open with my left foot so that the offender cannot move. As I am applying pressure to the front door the police officers rush into the apartment with firearms drawn. The four community corrections officers rush in to obtain dominance of the room and to control the resident who answered the front door. As I have my body pressing on the front door one of the police officers grabs the offender by his right wrist and pulls him from his hiding spot behind the door. The police officer guides the offender to the ground as I maintain control of the offender's left hand. I notice that he is sweating and is slippery. The police officer is giving the offender a loud, clear, concise verbal command to get to the ground and do not move. The offender complies. I immediately get out my handcuffs and handcuff the offender who is in the prone position. As this is occurring the police officers immediately clear the rest of the apartment for other potential threats. One of the community corrections officers does a search behind the door to see if the offender dropped a weapon. No other subjects were located and no weapons were found. As this is occurring I ask the offender if he has any weapons on him to which he denies. Once the apartment is cleared and secured I raise the offender to his feet and conduct a thorough search for weapons and contraband. (Note: I will skip the search process but during your imagery session you want to conduct a complete and accurate search for weapons and contraband.) The offender is taken in custody and transported to jail by the police officers.

This Incident Replay Imagery Session is partially based on a real incident. It shows that one minor mistake can lead to a snowball effect of problems. This situation resulted in one female officer getting forcefully pushed by the offender as he executed his escape. The police called for a perimeter requiring numerous officers, a helicopter, a police K-9 and the inconvenience to a residential neighborhood just across the street from the halfway house. Fortunately this offender was not looking to harm any officers and just wanted to escape arrest which he did. He was eventually caught on a warrant and sentenced to a prison term resulting from a probation violation. Had this offender been a dedicated threat this could have gone in a much different direction.

Incident Correction Imagery is a great technique for officers to use as a way to correct and learn from mistakes so that you will not make the same mistake if you ever find yourself in a similar situation.

Officer Survival for Probation and Parole Officers

Exercise 7: This will be a multi-part exercise that will occur over an extended period of time.

Step 1:

Write down a scenario that you can use to practice the following imagery techniques.

    Scenario Based Imagery: _____

_____

_____

_____

_____

    Skill Based Imagery: _____

_____

_____

_____

_____

    Incident Correction Imagery: _____

_____

_____

_____

_____

Step 2:

Over a fifteen day period you will practice these imagery techniques based upon the scenarios or incidents that you have written down. You will spend five days in a row practicing scenario based imagery, five days in a row practicing skill based imagery, and five days in a row practicing incident correction imagery which will give you a total of fifteen days practice. Do NOT mix and match your imagery sessions. Stick to the same scenario for five days in order to give you sufficient time to practice your imagery technique and to get used to this process. I recommend doing this exercise during the work week and take the weekends off to relax. You are to only practice one time per day. I recommend setting a timer or alarm to provide you 20 minutes to practice. After the twenty minutes is up then you are done for the day. You may realize that you need more time to get through your scenario but for now just limit your time to 20 minutes. Once you get your technique down you will not need to use a timer at all and can go through your scenario at whatever pace works for you.

Step 3:

After each practice session keep a notepad close by to make some notes or observations immediately after you have completed your imagery session. You may notice that there are skills you need to work on or have some observations that have never occurred to you. Do not let this learning opportunity go to waste. Write down any thoughts and ideas that come to you as a result of using imagery.

Do not become discouraged if this exercise is difficult or challenging. Like any skill you need to practice to become proficient. There is a reason why all successful athletes use imagery as part of their training. And, their life is typically not in jeopardy as a result of missing a basket, goal or home run. As a law enforcement officer you may not be so fortunate. Your mind is your best weapon so give it the attention and training it deserves.

This chapter should reinforce the importance of having a combat mindset that will provide you with an impenetrable layer of mental body armor. During a life or death encounter you must be mentally strong to never give up, never give in and never entertain the thought of failure. You must not only win; YOU MUST PREVAIL.

Chapter 3: Survival Fundamentals

Train like your life depends on it because it does.

Don't just win; Prevail!

This chapter will review fundamental, yet critical, information that is beneficial for all officers to know, understand, and implement into their survival skill set. The goal is to expose officers to processes that will assist with:

1. Situational awareness
2. Decision making skills
3. Understanding psychological and physiological reactions to stress
4. Utilization of tactical breathing to minimize the negative symptoms of stress as a result of sympathetic nervous system activation

Without an understanding of this information you, as an officer, will be at a severe disadvantage when it comes to avoiding encounters and, if necessary, resolving incidents. It is not the time in the midst of a critical incident to find out how your mind and body will respond to acute stress levels or what you could have done to avoid the incident in the first place. A common safety mantra within community corrections is the concept of avoidance. The best defense is avoiding potential problems before they even begin. To accomplish the goal of avoidance officers must maintain a vigilant guard of situational awareness in order to spot potential threats before they form into an actual threat.

As an officer survival instructor it was always interesting to instruct officers who wanted to learn the "advanced" or "cool" techniques and tactics before they mastered the basics. Most community corrections officers will not clear buildings looking for a violent absconder, use their baton, or discharge their firearm in the line of duty. Yet, officers wanted to know advanced baton techniques to control an unruly offender or how to use their firearm to engage multiple targets from behind cover or while on the move. The reality is that one cannot truly understand the "advanced" skills without a thorough knowledge of the basics. Do not underestimate the basics as they are the building blocks to all other officer survival skills. When it comes to the basics the natural starting point is an understanding of situational awareness.

Situational Awareness

The first references to situational awareness come from the U.S. Air Force and relates to understanding the dynamics that a fighter pilot engages during an aerial dogfight. The fighter pilot needs to know not only where the enemy plane is but what its next move will be. This involves gathering information, analyzing it, making projections based on that analysis and then taking appropriate action. This was described by Col. John Boyd, USAF (Ret.), as the "observe-orient-decide-act loop" or OODA loop. It is also been referred to as the OODA cycle, Boyd's cycle, or Boyd's loop. To win a dogfight, the pilot must "get inside" the opponent's loop, while losing one's own situational awareness was called being "out of the loop". Col. Boyd was often referred to as "40 second Boyd" for his standing bet as a flight instructor pilot that beginning from a position of disadvantage, he could defeat any opposing pilot in air combat maneuvering in forty seconds. If he failed to do so he would give the pilot $40. It is believed that Boyd never lost a challenge. Boyd's OODA loop will be discussed in further detail later in this chapter.

In the most basic sense situational awareness means understanding what is going on around you. While such a statement, at first glance, appears to be simple there is much more to this concept. Understanding what is going on around you means that you have to observe, gather, analyze, and potentially respond to information from your environment. Gather too little information and you will not have the full scope of your environment. Gather too much information and you will quickly have information overload which may slow down your decision making process or worse will cause failure to see and respond to a threat. It is vitally important to have the ability to determine which information is relevant and which information is meaningless. Situational awareness requires that you cognitively process numerous pieces of information simultaneously. Based upon the collected information you must then decide what course of action, if any, is necessary.

Situational awareness is still a term that is extensively used by the military. According to the Army Field Manual 1-02, situational awareness is:

> *"Knowledge and understanding of the current situation which promotes timely, relevant and accurate assessment of friendly, competitive and other operations within the battlespace in order to facilitate decision making. An informational perspective and skill that fosters an ability to determine quickly the context and relevance of events that are unfolding."*[xxi]

The emphasis is on understanding actionable information and responding in a timely manner. While this definition is from a military manual it is still applicable to community corrections officers. As stated in the previous chapter, when violence is directed at you job titles become irrelevant. The military definition stresses factors that are applicable to officers such as:

- Knowledge and understanding of the current situation
- Promotes timely, relevant, and accurate assessment
- Facilitate decision making
- Ability to determine quickly the context and relevance of the events that are unfolding

Whether you are a member of the military, police officer, corrections officer, detention officer, private security, community corrections officer or a safety oriented civilian, understanding the process of situational awareness is critical. Failure to have, or the ability to maintain, situational awareness mitigates your ability to effectively solve problems. If the problem is violence and you fail to recognize the problem then you may very well be injured or killed. This is yet another reason why it is so important for officers to at least acknowledge the potential for danger even if this possibility is remote. Ignorance of danger or denial of a threat increases your chances of becoming victimized and is not an acceptable safety strategy.

The ability to be aware of your surroundings (situational awareness) in order to identify potential threats and dangerous situations is more a mindset than a hard skill. Another important facet that should not be overlooked is your ability to trust your instinct or your "gut" feeling. Your intuition is a form of self-preservation that should not be ignored or minimized. Often a person's subconscious will notice subtle signs of danger that your conscious mind is not able to process. We have all heard stories of victims who state that they felt something was wrong but chose to ignore such feelings. Always, always, always trust your instinct and never ignore them even if you are not consciously aware of what the specific problem is at the time. Trust your gut feelings (intuition) as there is a reason that you are receiving this early warning signal. In probation and parole there is no offender contact that is so important that you should knowingly place yourself in harm's way.

Color Codes of Awareness

The use of "Color Codes" as a method of identifying a state of awareness was popularized by the late Col. Jeff Cooper who was the founder of the American Pistol Institute which is now the Gunsight Academy. The color code system is essentially an indicator of your state of mind. It provides you with the ability to recognize when a situation is changing and provides you an opportunity to mentally acknowledge the changing environment and respond when necessary. It should be noted that there are different versions of color codes being used and the one that I will discuss is common among law enforcement.

Color Code State of Awareness used in law enforcement:

Condition White (Totally Relaxed):

Synopsis: You are relaxed, unaware, and unprepared to respond to violence directed at you.

You are completely unaware of your surroundings and what is happening in your immediate environment. You have no situational awareness. You are not ready for anything that may occur whether good or bad. If you were to be attacked in Condition White you would be completely caught by surprise and your survival may be determined by the skill level of your assailant. Remember, depending on the incompetence or your assailant is not a survival strategy! If caught by surprise in Condition White you will have the proverbial 'deer in the headlights' look. In such a situation you have an extremely limited amount of time to mentally compose yourself and make a rapid and accurate assessment of the situation that you now have found yourself in unexpectedly. Failure to accurately assess the situation and, when necessary, respond appropriately could lead to serious bodily injury or death.

Condition White is for when you are in the safety, security, and comfort of your home or when sleeping.

Community corrections officers should *never* be in Condition White while at work.

Condition Yellow (Relaxed Awareness):

Synopsis: You are alert, calm, and relaxed.

In Condition Yellow you have and maintain situational awareness. You know what is happening in a 360 degree span around you. Potential threats or individuals who want to do you harm will not take you by surprise because you are aware of who is in front, beside, and behind you, as well as, above you and below you depending on your location. You are mentally ready to respond in case you observe something even if there is no specific threat.

In Condition Yellow your mindset is:

> *Today may be the day that I am attacked. If so, I will be ready, willing, and able to react, respond appropriately, and in a timely manner within department policy and law. I refuse to be a victim.*

While in Condition Yellow your keen level of awareness eliminates the possibility of a threat from having the ability to sneak up on you to do you harm. You are relaxed but prepared. The key is that you are relaxed as you go about your duties. Condition Yellow is not a state of hypervigilance where you become paranoid of everyone you see and every noise that you hear. It is possible to remain in Condition Yellow for long periods of time with no ill effects or additional stress.

Community corrections officers should *remain* in Condition Yellow while at work. Condition Yellow is your early warning security system that allows you to maintain situational awareness of your environment. Condition Yellow makes you a less attractive target because you are alert and aware. You do not project weakness and you do not present as an easy target.

Condition Orange (State of Alarm):

Synopsis: Something is not right.

You have mentally keyed in on a specific and potential source of danger. You do NOT choose to ignore this source of danger and must acknowledge its presence and that it is real. Now is the time to develop a plan and identify potential options. In the Calibre Press Street Survival Seminar they discuss "***When/Then Thinking***" meaning: "When this happens; Then I will…" Now is the time to initiate When/Then Thinking.

Due to the recognition of a specific state of alert you are both mentally AND physically prepared to take action if necessary.

<u>Condition Red (State of Combat):</u>

Synopsis: The potential threat(s) is now a real threat to your personal safety.

In Condition Red you are "in the fight" and responding. You are taking <u>immediate</u> and <u>decisive</u> action to:

- Neutralize the threat(s)
- Disengage (Tactical Retreat)
- Get help

For some officers the thought of retreating or obtaining help sounds less than manly or heroic. Tactical retreat is leaving the presence of an aggressor or aggressors when possible without engaging in a physical confrontation. Tactical retreat is not always an option such as in cases where your ability to leave is not available. Remember that community corrections officers are not first responders and when possible it is best to retreat and get assistance from the police. Tactical retreat and getting help is not a sign of weakness and has nothing to do with lack of courage. It has everything to do with making the right decision to be safe.

Never let your ego dictate your response.

Condition Black (Panic):

Synopsis: Panic which causes you to freeze or prohibits you from taking pro-active steps to stop the threat(s).

Condition Black is when you become so overwhelmed by the event that you become paralyzed with fear. You can literally "freeze" in terror. Fear that results in the officer freezing, resulting in failure to take action, is never an acceptable response to violence. The result from such fear is that you become completely ineffective in protecting yourself and will likely be injured or killed unless you immediately regain control over your fear. It is critical that you, in a timely manner, gain focus and concentration on the threat or threats that put your life in jeopardy. Failure to do so will result in a negative outcome.

Entering Condition Black against a dedicated threat is a recipe for disaster.

Utilizing the Color Codes to increase your level of awareness is a significant step in having the ability to recognize danger so that you can avoid potentially dangerous situations or respond appropriately if necessary. It should be very obvious that Condition White and Condition Black are never acceptable awareness levels. This is another reason why regularly attending realistic training that is dynamic and inoculates you to stress is not optional but mandatory. If your department does not offer such training then seek it out on your own time and at your own expense. While understanding the color codes is not difficult or complicated it can take practice to increase your level of situational awareness. Next I will provide some exercises for officers to increase their level of situational awareness.

EXERCISE 1: Condition Yellow

    To develop situational awareness you need to practice. People tend to be creatures of habit and conduct themselves the same way day in and day out. This explains how you drive to work in the morning and don't remember a thing about the drive. You magically leave your house and somehow appear at work. It is easy to become so accustomed to the routine that you completely tune out what is occurring all around you. Never be in a situation where you get from point A to point B with no memory of the drive. In relation to officer survival this is not how you want to conduct yourself. It is critical to have complete situational awareness to be able to identify potential threats so that you can change your course of action to avoid a problem or respond to the problem when all other options are no longer available.

    You will practice this exercise on a Monday, Wednesday, and Friday of your work week. If you have a flexible schedule then do this exercise in a manner that will conform to your work schedule but do not conduct this exercise three days in a row in order to give yourself a break as you learn to incorporate this new skill. Be sure to separate a day between this exercise.

Objective: Maintain a state of Condition Yellow during your entire workday from the time you leave your residence until the time you return to your residence.

Directions: From the moment you leave your residence you will assume that you are being followed and will strive to maintain situational awareness throughout your workday. The person that is "following" you wants to do you harm so you must remain vigilant. You are to continually scan your environment to include: the drive to and from work, the walk to your office once you exit your vehicle when you park, while in your office, and for the remainder of your duties throughout the workday. Scan your environment whether you are conducting residential contacts, school contacts, employer contacts, going to detention or jail to contact an offender, or attending a unit meeting.

Items to note for this exercise:

1. How many times throughout the day did you drift into Condition White? Have a notebook handy and keep a running tally throughout the day of how many times you caught yourself or where caught by someone else in Condition White. Keeping a record will help determine your baseline.
2. Did you observe people, places, or things that you have not noticed in the past?
    a. If yes, what did you notice?
    b. Why did you not notice them before this exercise?
    c. What implication could this have on your safety if you failed to notice?
3. Throughout the day did you notice anything that was suspicious or out of place?
    a. If yes, specifically what did you notice?

b. If you were in Condition White and failed to notice something suspicious what implication could this have on your safety?
4. Was anyone able to sneak up on you or take you by surprise?
   a. If yes, who was it (offender, co-worker) and what were the circumstances?
   b. What can you do to prevent this from happening again?
5. Was this exercise mentally or physically taxing on you?
   a. If yes, in what ways?
6. By day three of the exercise was it becoming easier to remain in Condition Yellow?
7. What insight did you learn from this exercise?

It is important to take the time to answer these questions in order to completely process this exercise. Unless you are a highly skilled individual it is very unlikely that you would get through three whole days without slipping once in a while into Condition White. If you made it through three days and remained in Condition Yellow the whole time then congratulations is in order. You are well ahead of many of your fellow officers. This exercise is not about being "perfect" but more about improving your current level of situational awareness and determining what your starting point is so that you can work on improving your current level of situational awareness.

EXERCISE 2: Thirty Day Drill

If you feel that you need more time with exercise 1 then repeat it as necessary before continuing. Exercise 2 is designed to take your skill to the next level with Condition Yellow and situational awareness. First, do **NOT** tell anyone that you are doing this exercise or people will try to sabotage you by doing a "gotcha" which detracts from the essence of this exercise.

Objective: Maintain a state of Condition Yellow for 30 consecutive days to include weekends.

Directions: For the next 30 consecutive days, 24 hours a day, you will document in a log anytime that you drift into Condition White or get caught by surprise, when outside the comfort and safety of your residence, such as at work and any time that you are in a public location such as grocery shopping, eating out, going to a movie, hiking, getting gas, walking your dog, etc.

In the log you want to document the following specific information:

- Date and time that you got caught by surprise or slipped into Condition White
- Location, i.e., gas station, grocery shopping, at park with your kids, etc.
- Circumstances, i.e., co-worker snuck up on me, family member caught me off guard while maintaining the front yard, ran into an old friend at the grocery store but failed to notice him first, etc.
- Self-Critique – what steps can you take to avoid this situation from happening again?

After the thirty days is done look over your documentation to obtain the following information:

1. Add up the number of times during the thirty days where you caught off guard.
2. Are there any noticeable trends such as:
   - Day of the week
   - Time of the day
   - Location – work, in public

3. What information are the trends telling you?

The goal is to be able to go 30 days with no incidents. Operating in Condition Yellow, especially while on duty, is a critical skill that must be mastered by all officers. Once you get to the point where you have solid situational awareness and are comfortable operating in Condition Yellow the next concept to understand is the OODA Loop.

OODA Loop: Observe-Orient-Decide-Act

The OODA Loop, developed by Col. John Boyd, USAF (Ret.), is a simple yet profound model. Boyd wanted to understand why U.S. fighter pilots consistently won air-to-air combat engagements with their F-86 fighter aircraft in combat over Korea against pilots that flew Mig-15 aircraft which had better maneuverability. Conventional wisdom would indicate that planes with better maneuverability and similar speed would dominate most dog fights but this was not the case. Boyd intensely studied the characteristics of the planes but came to the realization that he was focusing on the wrong subject. Boyd's conclusion was that it was not necessarily the characteristics of the plane but the skill of the U.S. pilots that resulted in superior performance. More specifically, the skill of the U.S. pilots to acquire their adversary first. Boyd proposed that the U.S. pilots were more successful because they were better at making decisions due to their ability to process through the "loop" faster than their adversary. This was the genesis of the OODA Loop which stands for: Observe, Orient, Decide, and Act.

The predominant factor in the OODA Loop is to observe first and move through the loop faster than your adversary so that your adversary is responding to information that is no longer relevant because the situation has already changed. In the case of a fighter pilot that can literally translate to survival. Your adversary becomes of a victim of perpetual catch up unless he is able to reset your OODA loop so that you now are in a position where you have to restart at observe and then move through the loop. All human conflict is bound by this process whether the participants are aware of it or not.

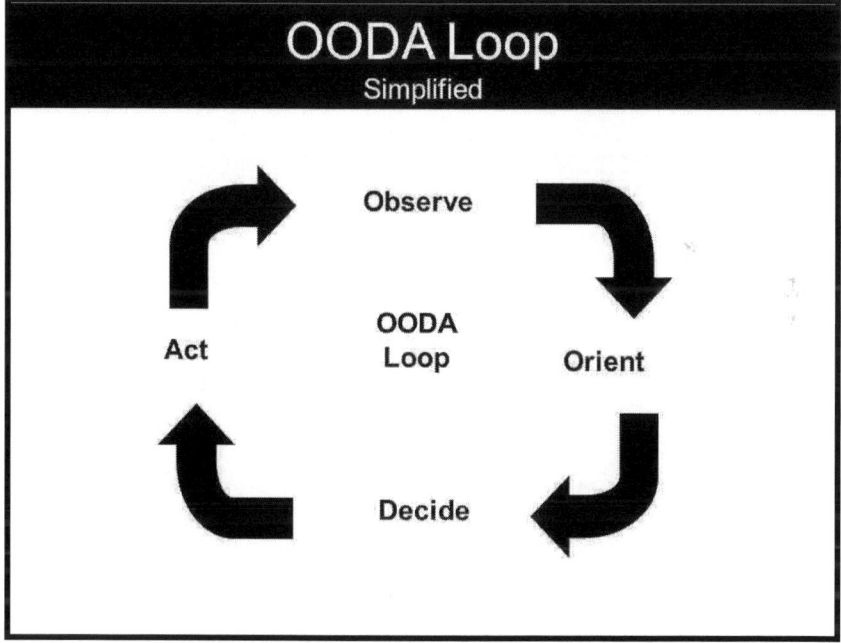

Figure 1: The OODA Loop sequence is: Observe, Orient, Decide, Act

Key points for each step of the OODA Loop:

Observe:

- One or more adversaries enter into the cycle.
- The more adversaries that you encounter the more OODA loops you are dealing with resulting in a significantly more complicated engagement.
- Whoever observes first has an advantage. You cannot defend yourself if you fail to observe a threat(s).The party who has failed to "Observe" is behind the loop and at a distinct disadvantage. Failure to rapidly observe in this situation can quickly lead to failure (i.e., death).
- Just because you "look" does not mean you "see." You must "see" what you are looking at and conduct accurate identification. Failure to make an accurate identification can lead to decisions being enacted based on incorrect information. As an officer this can result in bad decisions leading to unjustified actions resulting in a process that has significant consequences. For example, does the threat have a gun in his hand or is it a harmless cell phone, cigar, pen, rolled up magazine, or other innocuous item?

    - When you "look" you must "see" and comprehend what it is that you actually are seeing. This is a critically important skill especially when referring to target identification.
    - It is not uncommon to hear stories of people involved in auto accidents while changing lanes. The driver will often say, *"I 'looked' and thought the lane was clear. I didn't see another vehicle."*

    This is a perfect example of someone who "looks" but fails to actually "see" what is really occurring. Target identification is a critical skill that must be finely developed. As a firearms instructor I have facilitated judgmental shooting drills where there are multiple targets lined up in a row that have various targets. Some targets may have a bad guy with a weapon, a mom holding a child, a plainclothes police officer holding his gun with a badge displayed, or a plainclothes officer only holding out his badge with his arm extended. The officer who is participating in this drill is turned facing away from the targets and is directed to turn around and engage only threatening targets. Inevitably there will be officers who shoot the police officer who is only holding a badge. I have heard these officers say, "I thought it was a gun," or "I saw it was a badge but I pulled the trigger too fast." In a real situation this is never an acceptable response. It is critical to not only 'look' but to 'see' and understand what it is that you are looking at. Never underestimate the importance of this topic especially in a training environment. Training must prepare officers to function in a real world environment where stress and timing will always be an important factor. Target identification is a critical skill.

- If you lack situational awareness it is difficult to progress through the OODA Loop because you can become stuck at "observe."

Orient:

- Once you observe the threat(s) you must orient yourself to the threat and/or the situation itself.
- You will generally be under a time constraint to orient yourself. Incidents tend to be dynamic and the environment is typically in a constant state of change. Failure to "Orient" in a timely manner can lead to a

change in the encounter which forces you to restart the loop at "Observe."
- You will be under pressure and must make sense of the situation based on your observation. For example, you see a man who is threat to you with an object in his hand. You have to determine what the object is based on your observation and do this while under stress.

Decide:

- The ability to properly orient leads to a decision.
- The inability to process can lead to no decision being made where you become frozen (Condition Black.)

Act:

- Implementation of your decision.
- After implantation, you are now back at the beginning of the loop ready to re-observe.

The OODA Loop is about effective use of time. We all have the exact same amount of time so it becomes extremely important to make effective and productive use of very small time increments which can lead to your victory. Boyd's intention was getting inside the mind of your adversary to disrupt his decision making ability by providing outdated or irrelevant information so that the adversary cannot make a decision. In other words, to get inside your adversaries loop. When you move through the loop faster than your adversary then your adversary is always at a time deficit because he must go back to the beginning of the loop and start at observe.

One of the insightful aspects of understanding the OODA Loop is that Boyd did not focus on technology, plane characteristics, plane capabilities, or other such external factors. He came to the realization that it is the human (aka, pilot) that determines the outcome of a dog fight. This is a good reminder for officers to not rely as much on your equipment but to develop your skills with the equipment that you have been provided. U.S. pilots resoundingly proved this point during the Korean War. Boyd's OODA Loop has gained so much popularity due to its insightfulness that it is not only used in the military but law enforcement, business, sports, politics, economics, and other fields far removed from any battlefield.

> *Machines don't fight wars. Terrain doesn't fight wars. Humans fight wars. You must get into the mind of humans. That's where the battles are won.*
> *Col. John Boyd*

So, how does understanding of the OODA Loop benefit community corrections officers?

A few key factors are important to understand in relation to the OODA Loop and your role as a Community Corrections Officer:

1. Time is equal for everyone so use it to your advantage. Those who "observe" first are at an advantage. Those who fail to observe first will be behind the curve in the OODA loop. This is not an advantageous place to be when it comes to officer survival. (Figure 2)

2. It is you, the "officer," that matters and determines outcomes much more than the equipment that you are issued by your department. Just because your department may not issue the latest and greatest gear does not mean that you are doomed for failure. You are more valuable than the equipment around your waist so train to your capabilities. Your success is determined more by your software (brain) than by hardware (gear). Anytime that you allow your gear to determine the outcome of victory or defeat you have

set yourself up for failure by underestimating how your role in a confrontation perpetuates success much more than your gear.

The reality is that many departments have limited budgets and many projects compete for these limited funds. Administrators are stuck making difficult decisions and tough choices have to be made to determine where limited dollars will be allocated. Too often officer safety is not the priority until a critical incident occurs resulting in an injured or killed officer. I do not agree with this reactive posture by departments but for many this is how it will remain. As a result safety equipment quickly becomes outdated and before you know it you are working with safety tools that are not the latest and greatest. If this is the case for your department then focus on developing your skills even if it is at your own expense and on your own time. Just as your department has difficult choices to make you also have difficult choices to make regarding training.

3. The ability to move through the OODA Loop more quickly than your adversary provides you a great advantage at a successful outcome even if your adversary appears to have perceived advantages over you such as size or strength. We see this in sporting events such a mixed martial arts (MMA) when one fighter is physically stronger, faster, or taller but still loses the fight due to poor decision making. Another good reason to train hard and never give up!

It is important to remember that everyone goes through an OODA Loop process even if they are not cognitively aware of the process or its name. In other words, when you are engaged in a confrontation with an adversary you are processing your OODA Loop but so is your adversary. If you have multiple threats the situation becomes more challenging because you still have your OODA Loop to contend with but now you have multiple threats each with their own OODA Loop. The good news is that the OODA Loop of your adversary can be short circuited causing a restart at observe.

If an adversary makes a decision to do you harm and initiates an attack you are already behind the curve in relation to the OODA Loop (Figure 3). Now you are in a situation of trying to catch up and either move through the OODA loop more quickly than your adversary OR you need to initiate an action that resets your adversaries OODA loop back to observe. The key to success is the ability to create situations where one can make appropriate decisions more quickly than one's adversary. Time is the dominant parameter. The officer who goes through the OODA cycle in the shortest time prevails because his opponent is caught responding to situations that have already changed. Having multiple adversaries (Figure 4) makes this situation even more challenging because the officer has to prioritize which threat takes priority without losing situational awareness of the other threats. Also, when dealing with multiple threats you have to multi-task a lot of vital information such as which threat(s) take priority, what action is needed to keep you safe, what information from the environment is relevant and what information should be discarded. This is a lot for anyone to handle especially under stress and time constraints.

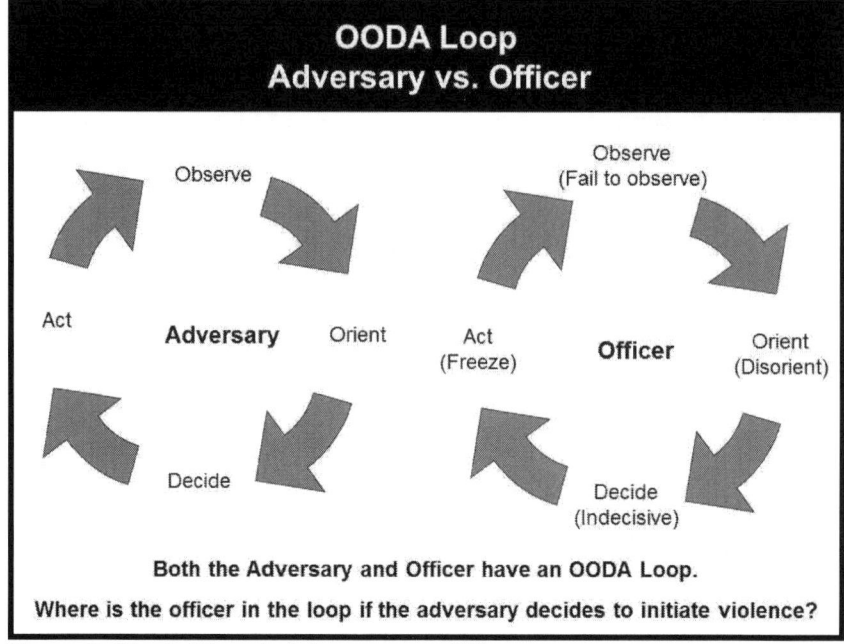

Figure 2: Single Threat: Adversary vs. Officer

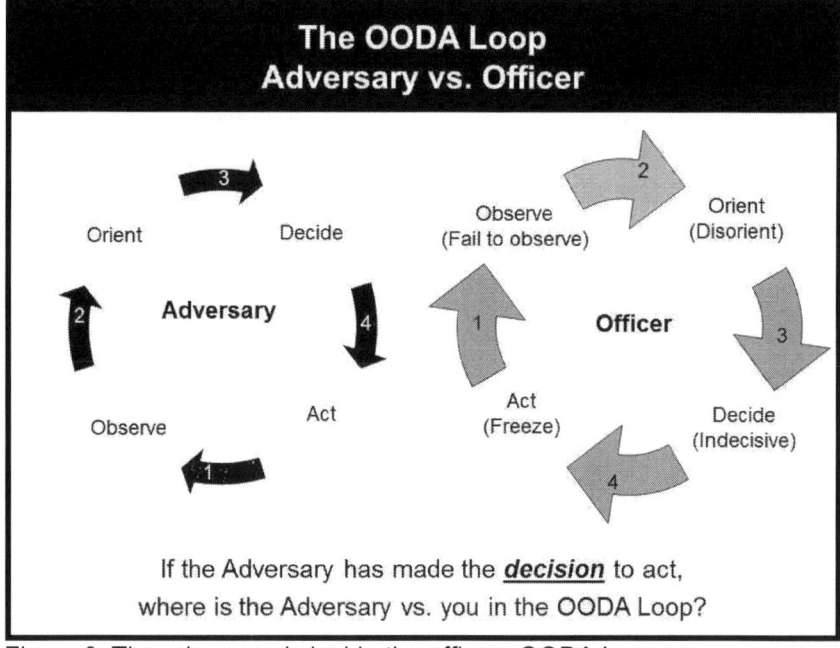

Figure 3: The adversary is inside the officers OODA Loop.

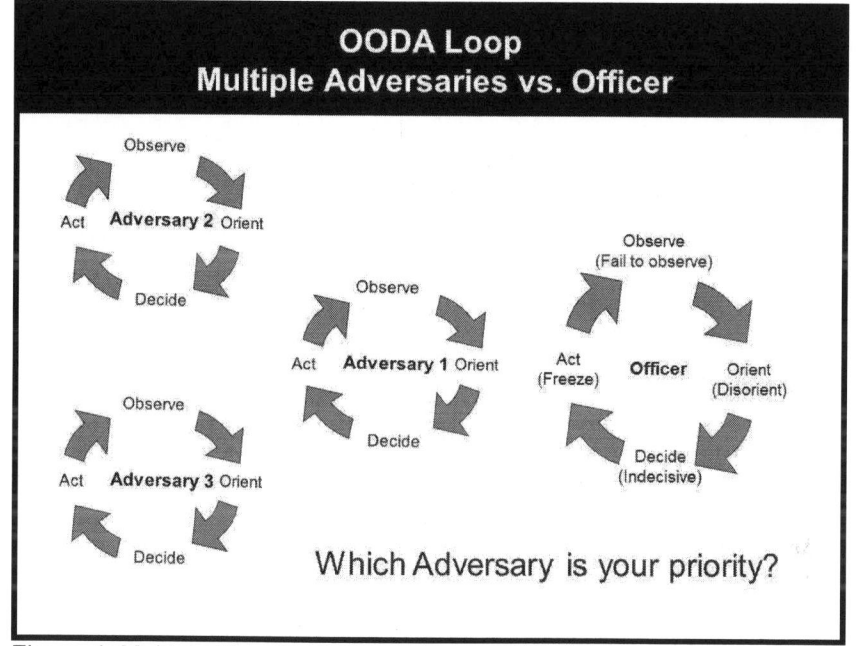

Officer Survival for Probation and Parole Officers

Figure 4: Multiple Threats: Adversaries vs. Officer

> *"You can only beat the opponent, who makes a mistake"*
>
> *Tony Blauer*
>
> The difference between sports and professional law enforcement officers is significant especially relating to outcomes. In sports you generally either win or lose. In law enforcement losing can result in death or permanent disability. As an officer it is important that you train realistically and not approach your training as a sporting event.
>
> As stated earlier in reference to the OODA Loop: *All human conflict is bound by this process whether the participants are aware of it or not.* It is important that you have the ability to capitalize on any mistake that is made by your opponent (sport) or adversary (real life). Oftentimes you will only be provided one opportunity to take advantage of the mistake. Taking advantage of the mistake is your opportunity to "get inside his loop" and reset him back to "observe."

Your ability to cycle through the OODA Loop more quickly than an attacker is a vital skill to possess. If you fail to have situational awareness you are significantly diminishing your ability to observe a threat and more likely than not you have failed to remain in Condition Yellow. It is impossible to respond to a threat that you do not even know exists. It is also important to have the ability to reset your adversaries OODA Loop back to "observe" especially when you are taken by surprise and find yourself behind the curve of the OODA Loop.

It is critical that officers continually improve their situational awareness skills. This can be achieved in part by understanding the Color Codes and the OODA Loop. Another necessary component is attending scenario based training where you progressively build your skill set with more challenging scenarios.

Color Codes and OODA Loop

Having reviewed the color codes and the OODA Loop it should be obvious that there is overlapping of ideas between these two important concepts. The color codes are about the state of your mind and your ability or willingness to recognize what you need to do given a set of circumstances. The color codes stress the importance of situational awareness so that you can pick up environmental cues indicating that a problem exists. As a situation escalates you can mentally, and if necessary physically, escalate your actions, planning and response. The OODA Loop provides you a time sensitive decision-making model that occurs regardless of your cognition. Both the Color Codes and the OODA Loop stress the importance of situational awareness.

It is vitally important that you understand the importance of Condition Yellow and the ability to 'observe' cues of potential threats in your environment. Lack of situational awareness is never a luxury that benefits an officer. The sooner you observe the better chance you have for a successful resolution which may be as simple as avoidance and disengagement. You simply head in a different direction from where the danger is emanating. On the flip side it is equally important that when in Condition Red that you are "in the fight" and committed to a successful resolution despite whatever odds may be against you. You must commit to: NEVER GIVE UP.

When faced with a potentially dangerous situation it is common to experience both psychological and physiological reactions to stress. Most community corrections officers do not experience dangerous situations as a routine part of their job. So, when a 'situation or crisis' occurs it is very normal to become nervous. And, there is nothing wrong with being nervous or experiencing fear. In fact, this response often aids in better performance as long as you do not let your fear prohibit you from taking necessary action. Failure to understand how your body and mind will respond to extreme stress and anxiety may lead to inaction (Condition Black) or loss of concentration and focus. Being aware of these stress responses may help you take steps to mitigate these effects and, at a minimum, will provide you with an understanding of your bodies reactions to stress.

Psychological and Physiological Reactions to Stress

A lot of research has been and continues to be conducted to understand the impact of stress on human performance. Many studies indicate a strong correlation between stress and performance. As the level of stress increases the body shows a corresponding increase in heart rate, blood pressure, and cortisol levels. The results can, but not always, lead to a decreased level of performance and impaired decision making abilities. This is especially true if the level of stress you experience gets out of control. A certain amount of stress is beneficial to performance while too much stress diminishes performance.

Anxiety is an emotional response to a situation that is perceived as dangerous. If the situation is not perceived as dangerous or threatening then there should be no change in the officer's anxiety level. What you perceive as dangerous another officer may perceive as not dangerous. Therefore your perception to the situation is a key factor in how you respond. In addition, your level of training, specifically stress inoculation training, will help to mitigate any negative or non-productive reactions to stress. It is important to experience the effects of stress in training and not have the experience for the first time in a real world situation where you may not understand how stress will impact your mind and body.

Officer Survival for Probation and Parole Officers

> The components of anxiety, stress, fear, and anger do not exist independently of you in the world.
>
> *Wayne Dyer*

Nervous System

The nervous system has two main divisions consisting of the central nervous system (CNS) and the peripheral nervous system (PNS) (Figure 5).

Central Nervous System

The CNS consists of the brain and spinal cord. It acts as the control center of the human nervous system, processing information and issuing commands. The brain is composed of three major parts: the cerebrum, cerebellum, and the medulla oblongata (brainstem).

Cerebrum: is the main portion of the brain and is associated with higher brain function such as thought and action. It is divided into two large sections called hemispheres. The outermost layer of the cerebrum is the cerebral cortex which is responsible for memory, attention, perceptual awareness, thought, language, and consciousness. Deep within the cerebrum is the limbic system, often referred to as the "emotional brain." The limbic system is responsible to regulate autonomic and endocrine function, particularly in response to emotional stimuli such as anger, fear, sorrow, and pleasure. They set the level of arousal and are involved in motivation and reinforcing behaviors. This system contains the thalamus, hypothalamus, amygdala, and hippocampus.

Cerebellum: is associated with regulation and coordination of movement, posture, balance, and learning motor skills.

Medulla oblongata: deals with autonomic, involuntary functions, such as breathing, heart rate and blood pressure, as well as, controlling reflex activities such as coughing, gagging, swallowing and vomiting.

Peripheral Nervous System

The PNS connects the CNS to other parts of the body and is composed of sensory nerves and motor nerves. These nerves relay information from our brain through the spinal cord to the body and back to the brain. The PNS is comprised of the somatic nervous system (SNS) and the autonomic nervous system (ANS).

The somatic nervous system is part of the PNS and conducts impulses from the central nervous system to skeletal muscle which produces movement and is under voluntary control.

The autonomic nervous system is the command network of the PNS used to maintain the body's homeostasis. It automatically regulates heart rate, respiration rate, pupil size, digestion, perspiration, and the urinary and reproductive tracts. The ANS is divided into the sympathetic nervous system (SNS) and parasympathetic nervous system (PSNS). The SNS is responsible for the "fight or flight" response, corresponds with arousal and energy generation, and inhibits digestion. The PNS is involved in relaxation and decreased arousal. Each of these subsystems, the SNS and PSNS operates in reverse of the other. Both systems innervate the same organs but act in opposition to maintain homeostasis. For example, if you were to become frightened by a the sound of a gunshot the sympathetic nervous system

Officer Survival for Probation and Parole Officers

causes your heart rate and blood pressure to increase; the parasympathetic system reverses this effect and lowers your heart rate and blood pressure.

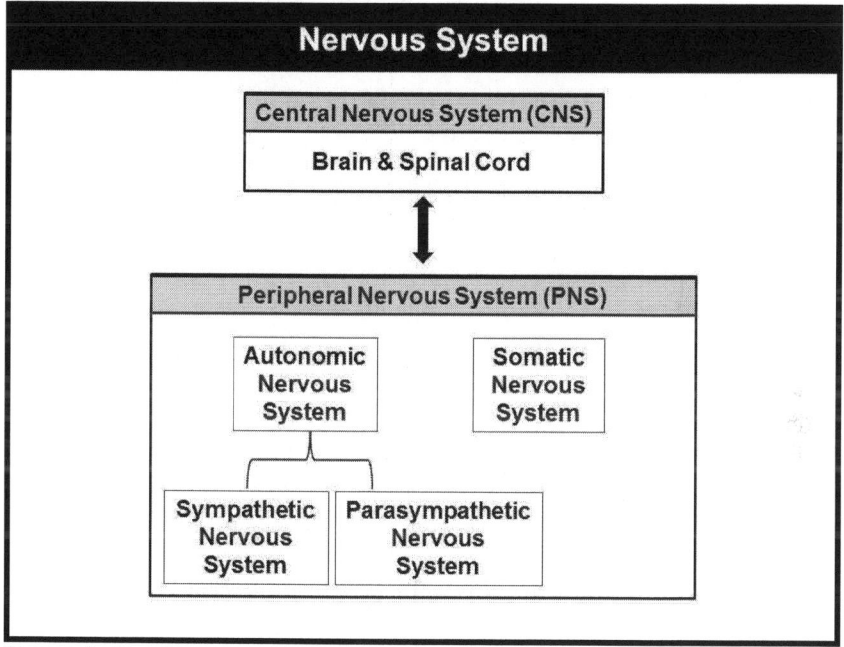

Figure 5: The Nervous System

    The fight or flight reflex is a Sympathetic Nervous System (SNS) reaction. All humans are hardwired with this survival response to perceived danger or life threatening situations and this process has helped to keep us alive for thousands of years. This process prepares your body to respond to the danger. When our fight or flight response is activated chemicals such as epinephrine (adrenaline), norepinephrine (noradrenaline), and cortisol are released into our bloodstream causing our body to undergo a series of changes in order to respond to the threat in our environment. Our awareness intensifies, vision is more acute, perception of pain is diminished, and our impulses quicken. Our body becomes prepared both physically and psychologically for fight or flight. Our life may depend on this automatic process.

When the SNS is activated the body responds with the following effects:

Effect and Benefit

<u>Pupil Dilation:</u> Provides better vision.

<u>Increased Sweating:</u> Metabolic rate increases causing the body to generate more heat. Perspiration helps to keep the body cool and prevents overheating.

<u>Increased Heart Rate (Pounding in your chest):</u> Provides increased blood flow to your muscles and diverts blood flow to less important areas such as skin. Decreased blood flow to the skin explains why superficial cuts bleed less during a fight-or-flight response.

<u>Increased Blood Pressure:</u> Provides extra blood, oxygen, and glucose to the muscles to supply energy.

<u>Increased Blood Glucose Levels:</u> Provides energy to muscles which can aid in strength.

<u>Increased Respirations:</u> Provides increased levels of oxygen to muscles.

<u>Dilation of the Bronchial Tubes in the Lungs:</u> Breathing changes from slow and relaxed to fast and shallow.

<u>Increased Muscle Contraction:</u> Provides extra speed and strength.

<u>Inhibits Digestion and production of Saliva (Dry mouth):</u> Diverts more blood and oxygen to muscles.

<u>Improved Blood Clotting:</u> Reduces the risk of blood loss if injured.

You may also experience the following symptoms as a result of the chemical dump your body receives from the fight-or-flight hormones: dizziness, nausea, trembling in your hands, knot in your stomach, tingling sensation in your arms, legs or face, and urge to urinate and/or defecate. In a crisis situation you will more than likely be very nervous and having these symptoms does not mean that you are not up to the task or that you are a coward. This is how your body responds to such events and it is important to understand the potential reaction that your body will have prior to an event so that you know it is completely normal.

While most people would not like to discuss this issue you should realize that there are cases where law enforcement officers and military personnel have urinated and/or defecated in their clothes during a crisis. Typically, we don't brag about these details to our friends over a frosty adult beverage after a hard day of work. We would rather forget those details of an incident. Yes, this would be an embarrassing situation but it is a potential response from your body that most officers would rather not divulge or discuss. If you are in such fear during an incident that you urinate or defecate you must remain focused on your survival and, to the best of your ability, resolve the situation so that you prevail. I would rather urinate in my pants and live to tell the story then let the embarrassment of the situation prevent me from surviving. I would rather testify in court against a violent offender by telling a jury that I defecated in my pants because the situation was life threatening rather than having my family sit at my funeral. If you ever encounter a fellow officer who has had this experience do not give them a hard time about it. Chances are the officer is not proud of their "accident" and would rather just forget that it happened. Be professional and respectful and don't bring it up or give the officer a difficult time even if you don't mean any harm. It just isn't a funny situation for any officer to experience. Sometimes it is important to look at the big picture and keep things in perspective. Perspective is key! Embarrassment is short term. Keep things in perspective and survive the encounter. Survival is what matters.

There are many factors that influence how your body will respond to an activation of the sympathetic nervous system which leads to a fight-or-flight response.

Factors include:

- How you perceive the event
- Prior experience to the stressor, if any
- Your level of training (another reason for participating in realistic & dynamic scenario based training)
- Your level of confidence
- Your exercise patterns (working out helps you to handle stress hormones)
- Overall level of health
- Diet
- Personality

As we have seen, under stress (arousal) the body undergoes several changes. As a law enforcement officer it is important to understand that to a degree these changes are manageable with *training* and *practice*. Your level of training, life experience, and confidence in your abilities will be a factor in determining how you respond to such stress.

Survival stress responses for law enforcement officer can include:

- Fight – Using force that is *reasonable* and *necessary*.

- Flight – Leaving the situation. When the brain is overwhelmed by a threatening situation there is an innate urge to flee (i.e. run) in order to protect yourself. It is important to understand that 'flight' is not always possible depending on the circumstances. If

the option of flight is not available you may have no other choice but to fight.
- <u>Freeze</u> – The situation is so overwhelming either from fear or sensory overload that you freeze and are incapable of any action. This is Condition Black.

The sympathetic nervous system is designed to prepare your body to fight or flee. But, sometimes your level of stress (arousal) is so high that you become overwhelmed at the situation. Too much arousal turns into fear (panic) which can result in negative response or no response at all. In other words fear is preventing you from responding appropriately to stop the threat (fight) or leave the area (flee). It is important to understand that fear is good and should not be completely eliminated. Fear lets us know that something is not right and that you may be in danger. As a result, the fight-or-flight system kicks in as a method that will prepare you to respond to the danger or threat. Fear becomes problematic when it controls you to the point that you cannot respond as in condition black.

Fear is good; uncontrolled fear is not good.

Fear that leads to a positive response is good;

fear that leads to Condition Black is not good.

Perceptual Distortions

When fight-or-flight stress hormones are released into your body you may experience perceptual changes during the event. Again it is important to be aware of these possible effects before you are engaged in a life or death situation.

Effect and Meaning

Tunnel Vision: Loss of peripheral vision. Narrowing field of vision.

Loss of Depth Perception: Inability to judge depth or distance.

Loss of Near Vision: Difficulty seeing objects that are close.

Visual Clarity: Ability to notice specific details that you would not ordinarily notice such as seeing a bullet in the air.

Auditory Exclusion: Temporary loss of hearing. You may not be able to hear your weapon fire or verbal commands from a partner.

Intensified Sound: Can occur in a low light environment where vision is diminished and hearing becomes more important.

Sensory Exclusion: You do not feel pain from injuries such as knife or gunshot wounds. Your sense of pain shuts down during the stress of the event.

Autopilot: Acting without conscious thought often as a result of ongoing quality training that has ingrained proper technique (aka, muscle memory)

Slow Motion Time: Perceiving an event to happen in slow motion.

Temporary Paralysis: The inability to move or take appropriate actions. Can be associated with Condition Black (Freezing).

Dissociation: A sense of detachment where you feel as if you are not part of the situation but observing what is occurring from outside of your body.

Intrusive Thoughts: Thoughts that are completely irrelevant to the situation that you are involved.

Memory Loss: Missing part of your memory for events that occurred during the incident.

Memory Distortions: Having a memory of something that did not occur during an incident or failing to remember something that did occur.

According to a Perceptual Distortion Survey conducted by Artwohl and Christensen of 72 law enforcement officers, following is the breakdown by percentage of officers who experienced perceptual distortions[xxii]:

Percent	Perceptual Distortion
88	Diminished Sound
82	Tunnel Vision
78	Automatic Pilot
65	Heightened Visual Clarity
63	Slow Motion Time
61	Memory Loss for Parts of the Event
60	Memory Loss for Some of Your Actions
50	Dissociation
36	Intrusive Distracting Thoughts
19	Memory Distortion
17	Intensified Sounds
17	Fast Motion Time
11	Temporary Paralysis

Heart Rate and Skill Performance

Bruce Siddle the author of the book *Sharpening the Warrior's Edge* hypothesized a relationship between heart rate and performance to include motor skills. For law enforcement officers the motor skills that are being referred to include: fine, complex and gross motor skills.

Following is an explanation of these motor skills:

Motor Skill	Definition	Examples
Fine Motor Skills Deteriorates at 115 BPM	Skills performed by small muscle groups such as with the hands and fingers. Typically requires precise hand-eye coordination.	- Putting your car key in the ignition - Double locking handcuffs - Shooting a firearm accurately - Sight alignment - Tactical magazine exchange
Complex Motor Skills Optimal at 115-145BPM	Skills that require hand-eye coordination, timing, movement, and tracking. Techniques that consist of multiple movements.	- Moving and shooting with accurate hits on target - Deployment of pepper spray - Complex defensive tactics techniques
Gross Motor Skills >175BPM	Skills that utilize large muscle groups.	- Walking - Jumping - Running (great for fight-or-flight) - Squatting - Pushing/Pulling

Siddle states,

> "...at 115 beats per minute (BPM), fine motor skills (precision and accuracy skills) deteriorate. When the heart rate exceeds 145 BPM, complex motor skills deteriorate and the visual system begins to narrow. But when the heart rate exceeds 175 BPM, a warrior

can expect to experience auditory exclusion and the loss of peripheral vision and depth perception. This initiates a catastrophic failure of the cognitive processing capabilities, leading to fatal increases in reaction time or hypervigilance (freezing in place or irrational acts)."[xxiii]

The study of stress on performance led to the Inverted "U" Hypothesis which states that the quality of performance improves as arousal levels increase up to a certain point, beyond which it deteriorates. Too little arousal and you underperform; too much arousal and performance deteriorates possibly into Condition Black. The Inverted "U" Hypothesis is graphically represented as an upside down "U" where the *x* axis is arousal and the *y* axis is performance. These reactions lead to a loss of fine and complex motor skills which is why much of your training must be geared toward gross motor skills that can be used in stressful situations.

There is still a lot of research being conducted to determine peak performance zones or optimal zone of performance for athletes, law enforcement officers, and military warriors to perform at their best level. I'm not sure that science will ever be able to pin down a specific peak performance range due to individual variances. So, when you see a specific range it is important to realize that there is some latitude with the provided numbers. It would be incorrect to state that at this specific heart rate this is what will happen with your performance. It is more likely that each person has their own individual optimal zone of performance.

It should be noted that when we discuss heart rate, performance, motor skill deterioration, and negative effects from sympathetic nervous system activation there is a significant difference between increases in heart rate from hormones verses exercise induced increases in heart rate. For example, you could increase your heart rate to greater than 175 BPM through exercise yet not experience auditory exclusion or tunnel vision. But, you can feel such effects from a hormonally caused increase in heart rate. Although exercise and physical fitness are very beneficial for a healthy lifestyle it is important to understand that exercise alone will not prevent you from experiencing the negative effects from hormones that are released into your bloodstream during sympathetic nervous system activation. The best method for being prepared for SNS activation is through stress inoculation training that is dynamic, realistic, and attended on a consistent basis. Again, if your department is not providing you such training opportunities then you are not being adequately prepared with the necessary skills to survive a potentially lethal encounter.

Breathing: Tactical, Combat, Autogenic

When your sympathetic nervous system is activated due to an incident and your body is dealing with stress it is important to breathe properly to mitigate any potential negative effects of stress hormones. One of the physiological effects of fight-or-flight activation is an increased rate of breathing. Short rapid breaths can lead to hyperventilation which causes the carbon dioxide level in the blood to decrease thereby reducing blood flow to the brain. When this occurs you may experience symptoms such as: weakness, fainting, dizziness, lightheadedness, confusion, agitation, dissociation, hallucinations, tingling sensation in the fingers and mouth, and feeling as if you cannot breathe. None of these symptoms are beneficial for your survival in a crisis. It is critical to maintain control over your breathing which will assist in lowering your heart rate, improve motor skills, and improve cognition so that you can successfully neutralize the threat.

Proper breathing becomes a vital and relevant skill that all officers need to use during a crisis. The breathing skill goes by a number of names such as: tactical breathing, combat breathing, and autogenic breathing. For consistency I will refer to this skill as tactical breathing. It is a simple yet highly effective technique to lower your heart rate and diminish some of the negative effects of stress. Remember that breathing is controlled by the autonomic nervous system and occurs without conscious thought. When the sympathetic nervous system is activated your rate of respirations increases and you breathe in a fast and shallow manner. The goal is to consciously regain control over your breathing, an autonomic function, and thereby control your sympathetic nervous system response. The more you practice this breathing technique the faster the effects work thereby reducing the negative impact of SNS activation. This is where tactical breathing comes into play.

Tactical breathing is a four step, four count process as follows:

1. Breathe in through your nose for a slow four count expanding your abdominal region (like expanding a balloon in your belly)
2. Hold your breath for a four count
3. Expel the breath through your lips for a four count (let the air out of the balloon)
4. Wait for a four count before you repeat the process

When performing tactical breathing my internal dialogue is:

In, two, three, four

Hold, two, three, four

Out, two, three, four

Wait, two, three, four

I attempt to repeat this cycle four to five times depending

on the situation. The efficacy of this breathing technique, as with the individual optimal zone of performance, varies from person to person so it is important to practice tactical breathing to determine what works best for you. You may need to adjust how many cycles to perform or how long you should hold each breath. Be sure to breathe in through the nose, fill the balloon in your belly, blow out through the mouth to deflate the balloon, and then wait until you repeat the process. It is simple yet highly effective.

Tactical breathing can be implemented for community corrections officers before, during, or after an incident. Let's examine some situations where you, as the officer, will benefit from the positive results of tactical breathing.

Example 1: Before a potential incident

> In this example you and a partner are going to conduct a residential contact on a parolee who has been incarcerated numerous times as a juvenile and adult. He has a violent history, has ties to a white supremacy group, and is in superb physical condition. At the age of 29 he has spent a total of 11 years incarcerated in juvenile and adult facilities. He has been on parole for eight months and while he is compliant he has a tendency to push the limits and has absolutely no respect for authority or law enforcement. All of his drug tests are negative, he is holding a job as a motorcycle mechanic, and he is renting a room from a friend who has no prior criminal history. The last two contacts with this parolee where at the parole office. During his last office contact he made a comment stating that you, as the parole officer, better not disrespect him out in the community because he will not tolerate such actions from no cop (meaning parole officer). You have no idea where this is coming from as there have not been any problems that you are aware of since you have been his parole officer. The parolees' exact words were:

"If you disrespect me then it is going to be on. You know damn well that it has to be that way. That is just the way it is in my world and it ain't nothing personal. I don't want to go back but I will if you treat me like the fool. I've done a lot of time so doing more is no problem to me. You know I don't care so you best be cool with me."

The inference was that there would be a physical altercation if the parole officer shows any form of disrespect to the parolee. When this conversation occurred the parole officer immediately staffed the case with the parole supervisor who had a discussion with the parolee regarding his comment and the implications he was referring to regarding a fight. The parolee was polite during this meeting and said he doesn't want any problems and that he is only looking to be respected. The parole supervisor directed the parole officer to always have a partner when contacting this offender in the community.

Today is the first residential contact at the parolees' home since the incident at the parole office. As the parole officer is driving to the residence with his partner they discuss "what if" scenarios in case things go bad during the contact. The parole officer notices that he is getting nervous. He begins to sweat, his heart rate and breathing dramatically increases and his fingers are tingling. He knows he needs to regain his composure before getting to the residence of the parolee. As he is driving he begins a series of tactical breathing exercises. His partner is on his cell phone making a call and is not aware that anything is going on. After about 6-8 cycles his heart rate and respirations are much lower, he is no longer sweating and his fingers are not tingling. He is ready to go and complete the contact with the parolee. His partner is off the phone and they make the contact without incident.

This is a good example of using tactical breathing before a contact to regain control of your heart rate and respirations and to prepare yourself for the contact. As demonstrated in this example tactical breathing can safely be done while driving and many police officers utilize this technique when involved in high speed chases as a method of remaining calm.

Other situations in which the use of tactical breathing is beneficial is prior to conducting an arrest either in the field or your office and before conducting a probation/parole search of a residence.

Example 2: During an incident

In this example you are a juvenile probation officer assigned to a high school. While you are in your office the school principle, school counselor, and a security officer bring in a 16 year old boy named Brock who was acting out in class and not following the teacher's directions to remain in his seat. Brock was cursing at the teacher and he kicked his desk.

Brock is assigned to your caseload and is on probation for the third time. He was sentenced to probation this time for assault, underage drinking, and theft of means of transportation. Brock punched his mother in the face three times and took her car keys so that he could go out with his friends. The police found him at a local park with three other friends where they were all drinking beer and vodka. During the attack on his mother he broke her jaw and knocked out a tooth. Brock was recently released from juvenile detention after six months and is once again living with his parents. Brock was recently diagnosed with oppositional defiant disorder by a psychiatrist.

The principal wants you to inform Brock how his

actions are not acceptable and what the consequences mean to his probation status. Brock is so worked up that you cannot get a word in to see what is going on. The school counselor gets Brock to sit down and starts to calmly talk with him about his actions. Brock's face is getting red and no one seems to be in control of the situation. You feel that Brock is going to explode in a frenzy of anger and you know that he is capable of inflicting serious bodily injury. You start breathing heavy and your heart rate has skyrocketed. You feel lightheaded and faint. You immediately initiate tactical breathing as the counselor is attempting to de-escalate Brock from getting completely out of control. You complete five cycles and feel ready to respond to the situation. Brock abruptly jumps out of the chair and says, "Fuck all of you" as he proceeds to punch the security officer in the face and then runs out of the office. The principle immediately calls 9-1-1 for a police response. The police find and arrest Brock at his parents' home about two hours later. He is back at juvenile detention pending new assault charges.

Example 3: After an incident

In this example you are conducting office day at the adult probation office. The probationer that you are about to see is Mike who is a 44 year old biker sentenced to three years probation for possession of methamphetamine, possession of drug paraphernalia, and possession of marijuana. Mike works full time as a construction worker and has no prior criminal history. He did have a domestic violence arrest that is 10 years old but the charges were dropped.

Just yesterday you received a positive drug test for methamphetamine. This is the first positive drug test that you received on Mike since he was sentenced to probation 10 months ago. You contact his substance abuse treatment provider who states that Mike is attending and actively participating in all his treatment classes. During this office contact you are going to question Mike about the positive drug test.

Mike is a gruff guy who is always polite but not one for small talk or needless conversation. You call Mike back to a sterile interview room. You tell Mike that you talked to his substance abuse counselor who said that he is doing well in group classes, actively participating, and that he has never missed a class. You then tell Mike that you received a positive drug test for methamphetamine and ask him what is going on. Mike states that some old friends came over and they were just hanging out at the motorcycle club. He said it was no big deal and that he drank one beer and smoked a little meth with friends. Mike said he didn't want to drink or smoke the meth but these weren't the kind of people who you refuse to drink or smoke with. He said he knew it was wrong but what was he to do! I know it can get me in trouble with you as my PO but these guys don't care about my probation and they wanted to party. You begin to use your motivational interviewing skills by saying it looks like you were caught having to make a decision that would either keep your friends happy or one that will potentially get you into trouble with your probation. How is your drinking beer and smoking meth going to get you off probation? Mike says he doesn't need a lecture from a probation officer. You then say you are trying to get him to understand how his choices have consequences. At that point Mike jumps out of his chair, point his finger at you and says, "Stop lecturing me or I'm going to get really pissed off at you." At that point you stand up and get ready to tell Mike to calm down when he does a hard two hand push and violently shoves you into a wall telling you to shut the hell up. He immediately leaves the office without further incident. This whole incident occurred in less than one minute and you never anticipated that it would escalate so fast and to the point of violence.

Other officers immediately come to your aid. One of the officers notices that Mike pushed you so hard that your head slammed into the wall leaving a small dent in the wall. You are surprised that your head does not hurt and you feel no pain. Your heart rate and breathing are very rapid that you can't even talk. You recognize the signs of SNS activation and you immediately begin tactical breathing until you are calm enough to tell your supervisor what just occurred. About forty minutes later you notice that your head hurts and that you have a bump to the back of your head.

As you can see from the previous examples the use of tactical breathing is an important skill that can be used before, during, or after an incident. Like any skill, tactical breathing must be practiced in order to be maximally effective during a crisis. Another area where tactical breathing is vitally important and can be practiced and developed is in the training environment.

As an officer survival instructor I have seen numerous cases where officers in training situations let their level of anxiety get so out of control that they: 1) completely fail to perform literally forgetting what they were supposed to do, 2) freeze, or 3) refuse to participate in the drill. I have seen this occur in the following situations:

- Conducting scenario based drills with the RedMan suit
- Written proficiency tests for defensive tactics and firearms
- Physical proficiency skills testing for defensive tactics
- Firearm disarming skills
- OC (pepper spray) application

- Firearms malfunction drills that are timed (clearing a class 3 malfunction)
- Low light firearms qualifications
- Firearms qualification
- Force-on-force training with non-lethal training ammunition

It is amazing what a little motivational speech in conjunction with tactical breathing would do for these officers. It is impressive and inspirational to see an officer progress from fear and anxiety to performing at the requisite level despite the fear and anxiety. As an officer survival instructor we do not want to eliminate fear as fear can make us cautious and deliberate in our actions. But, we also do not want fear to prohibit officers from taking appropriate action that can save their life.

An important lesson to learn and appreciate from reading this chapter is that:

> **During a crisis you must be able to effectively perform under stress, in a timely manner, and often under less than ideal circumstances in order to have a chance of success. Unfortunately, there are no guarantees of the outcome but failure to take action when action is required is the starting point for an outcome that can be deadly or have lifelong consequences.**

As a community corrections officer your ultimate goal is to avoid critical incidents and life threatening situations. But, the reality is that while we strive for avoidance we are sometimes placed into situations where avoidance is not possible and action is required. In order for you to increase your ability to successfully respond to a critical incident you must be able to have the following fundamental skills: situation awareness of your environment, the ability to make fast and accurate decisions, an understanding of the psychological and physiological reactions to stress that you may experience, and the ability to mitigate or reduce negative effects of stress. The Color Codes of Awareness, OODA Loop, an understanding of the stress process, and the ability to perform tactical breathing will provide you with valuable tools. What starts off as a "routine" day can quickly escalate into a life threatening fight even when you do everything correctly and try to avoid an incident. In such cases you will be nervous, your body will initiate a sympathetic nervous system response, you may experience perceptual distortions, fine and complex motor skills will diminish, your heart rate, respirations, and blood pressure will increase, etc. Your body responds in a way to help prepare you to fight or flee. Your training will help determine the efficacy of your actions.

Train like your life depends on it because it does.

Chapter 4: Use of Force

Are you prepared to use force?

Many probation and parole officers retire from their career in community corrections without ever having to utilize force. More often than not their verbal skills have prevented potential incidents from escalating to the point where force was needed to control an offender or other subject. Many community corrections officers are extremely competent with verbal skills to include verbal de-escalation as this is a skill that gets developed and refined on a daily basis. As indicated in an earlier chapter there is no national database or central depository that collects use of force information for probation or parole departments so we really do not know the true scope of use of force incidents. Despite not knowing the data on the subject I can guarantee you that use of force incidents do occur and that you, as an officer, may unexpectedly and without warning, find yourself involved in a use of force incident. It would be wise to eliminate from your mind the thought that use of force incidents happen to others but could not happen to you. This type of thinking is equivalent of putting your head in the sand and hoping for the best. This is not realistic.

It wasn't long ago that many departments did not have policies or procedure addressing use of force for community corrections officers. Those departments that did have policies where often inadequate and incomplete focusing on verbal de-escalation skills and possibly the use of a chemical agent such as pepper spray. Additionally, many departments did not have formalized training or curriculum for defensive tactics, chemical sprays, firearms, and safety policies to include a use of force policy. Fortunately, departments are moving in the right direction and are beginning to take staff safety issues seriously by implementing safety policies and procedures along with requisite training. When it comes to officer safety, departments must take a proactive approach instead of being reactive after the fact. Far too often departments only address safety issues and make changes after an incident occurs which typically results in an injury or death to an officer. This is not acceptable considering the foreseeability of officer safety incidents especially with the offender population that officers supervise on a daily basis many who have a documented criminal history consisting of violence, substance abuse, and other antisocial behaviors. Can you imagine a modern police department today that does not have training relating to officer survival to include training on defensive tactics, firearms, less lethal weapons, and policies to support these tools? It would be beyond comprehension to see a police department that does not address such officer safety topics. There should be no difference in the profession of community corrections and officers should not have to feel like they are pulling teeth to get their concerns addressed. Leaders of probation or parole departments who fail to seriously address and implement officer safety procedures, policies, and provide needed equipment and training are setting their department up for significant liability. Yet, such departments do exist and they will pay dearly as a result of lawsuits that will surely follow from use of force incidents resulting in an injury to an officer.

    Times are changing and departments are responding to safety issues but change is slow, difficult, and costly. As community corrections departments move in the direction of taking officer safety seriously there will inevitably be an abundant amount of time spent in meetings, focus groups, and committees to discuss the process of training staff, issuing safety equipment, and instituting new policies and procedures. In these meetings the divide between the "counselor" and "cop" will become very apparent. There will be vocal attendees, some who are decision makers, who have no experience in officer safety or officer survival. Some will stick with what they know best and what they have done in the past - nothing. Their mindset is, *"we haven't needed safety training or equipment in the past and we don't need it now. Yes, we have had minor problems but they don't justify the monetary cost along with the time and effort to train all of our staff."* Some administrators who are responsible for juvenile offenders will say things such as, *"They are kids! Do we really need to carry a gun to control a kid? Are we going to start shooting and killing kids now?"* It is as if these administrators actually believe that youthful offenders could not possibly be dangerous. But we know this is not the case. Just ask the family of Juvenile Probation Officer Mary Fine who was brutally beaten, sexually assaulted, and strangled to death by a 16 year old juvenile. It can be an uphill climb to move in the right direction. Some who attend these important meetings will focus more on what they do not want community corrections officers to become (i.e. police officers) as opposed to focusing on what steps the department needs to accomplish in the way of officer safety policies, procedures, equipment, and training. Some administrators and officers will become caught in this mental loop thinking that if a probation or parole officer carries a firearm, baton, OC spray, handcuffs, etc. that they will automatically start behaving differently or worse acting like a police officer. It is important that attendees and decision makers have a balanced approach between helping offenders change their behavior to law abiding individuals with the ability to hold offenders accountable for noncompliant behavior. They must believe that offenders, both adult and juvenile, can be a threat to officers to include a lethal threat. Let me put your mind at ease that carrying the same equipment as police officers will not, in the majority of cases, impact the way that a professional probation or parole officer acts or performs their job. Yes, there will always be exceptions and some officers will act inappropriately but in my experience this is the exception and not the rule. Also, it is typically not too difficult to address inappropriate behaviors with these officers and get them on board. If administration has such little faith in their officers abilities to conduct themselves both professionally and appropriately then they have a leadership problem in addition to an inadequate officer safety program.

Having trained with different municipal, state, and federal law enforcement agencies I definitely believe there exists a different mindset between police officers and community corrections officer especially at the administrative levels. Police focus on enforcing laws and catching the bad guys whereas community corrections officers tend to focus on behavioral change. In reality, police officers and community corrections officers work with the same offenders just at different points in time and with different goals in mind. Yet, the offender is still the same person and will always have the potential to be a safety risk to officers and the community even if they are currently compliant with their probation/parole grant and appear to be law abiding. Given the right set of circumstances anyone can become a threat to another person and this includes law abiding people with no criminal history.

This chapter will review topics relating to use of force that are important for officers and administrators to understand. Major topics in this chapter will include:

1. Officer safety equipment

2. Use of force continuum

3. U.S. Supreme Court decision: Graham v. Connor

Safe Distance for Offender Contact: Does it exist?

Realistically, community corrections officers typically interact with offenders at very close distances. It is often repeated in training classes to stay a safe distance from offenders. It is not uncommon to hear an officer survival instructor tell new officers to stay a minimum of one to two arm's length distance from an offender. At this range you are still in a very dangerous situation. An offender who is a dedicated threat who wants to cause you harm can easily cover a 1-2 arm's length distance in ¼ to ½ of a second. This is an extremely short time span and being that action is faster than reaction you will _ALWAYS_ be late in your response even if you are highly trained. By no means does this mean that you will lose the altercation but it does mean that you are playing catch up, need to reset the threats OODA Loop, and that you must respond appropriately.

Typically community corrections officers work in an environment that commonly places them in very close proximity to the offenders they supervise such as an interview room or their residence. Think back to all the times that you needed an offender to sign paperwork. The offender is very close to you and oftentimes is borrowing your pen, which can be used to stab you, to sign the document. Officers are never provided the luxury of supervising offenders at a safe distance. You are always way too close to offenders and always in a dangerous situation if the offender decides to do us harm. This is a reality for community corrections officers.

Safe Distance

Trainers often advise officers to stay a safe distance from an offender. Questions to consider:

1. At what distance would you feel optimally safe when supervising an offender?

2. In response to question 1, is your answer a realistic possibility and do you normally conduct business at such a distance?

3. If you are supervising an offender who instantaneously becomes a dedicated threat, at what distance do you want to be from this offender?

4. In your experience how common or possible would it be for you to obtain the distance that you answered in question 3?

Officer Safety Equipment

Due to variance in policy, philosophy, and training it is impossible to specifically know what safety equipment departments issue to their officers. It is understood that some departments may not issue any safety equipment to officers while others may issue some or all of the listed equipment. Following is an overview of common safety equipment that may be issued to community corrections officers along with basic information.

Handcuffs

Handcuffs are considered a *"temporary restraining device"* and are not designed to restrain a person for long periods of time. Subjects can be handcuffed from the following positions: standing, kneeling, and prone. High-risk subjects should be handcuffed while in the prone position. Like any piece of equipment there are weaknesses of the handcuff that all officers need to be aware of when using this device.

Weaknesses include:

1. Loose or incorrect application.
2. The rivet of the double strand/ratchet can be separated.
3. The handcuff chain can be broken (difficult but possible). Not all handcuffs have a chain that links the handcuffs together.
4. The swivel can be broken.
5. The double-lock mechanism can be released through movement. Again, difficult but possible.
6. Handcuffs can be picked or shimmed with improvised keys such as from a paperclip, a piece of metal, or other items that have the ability to manipulate the lock or locking mechanism.

Application:

- When handcuffing an offender/subject it is imperative that your firearm or other safety equipment must be holstered and secured prior to approaching the offender/subject.
- Load the handcuffs prior to cuffing an offender/subject.
- Handcuffs should be applied with the keyholes facing up toward the elbows to minimize the offender's ability to pick the lock.
- Approach the offender/subject to be handcuffed in a safe manner typically from behind at a 45 degree angle where their head is facing away from you so the subject cannot see your approach.
- Ensure that you apply the handcuffs rapidly to obtain control. The longer it takes to apply the handcuffs the more danger that you are in.
- Hands should be cuffed behind the back unless there is a situation that prevents this from occurring. Cuffing behind the back is significantly safer for the officer than handcuffing in front.
- Apply the handcuffs with the subjects' palms facing outward.
- Always double-lock the handcuffs to prevent them from tightening and possibly causing injury. Check that the handcuffs are not applied too tightly so that circulation is not restricted and to prevent nerve damage.
- Always complete a thorough search for weapons and contraband. Before initiating the search always ask the following questions and wait for a response:

    1. Do you have any weapons on you to include a gun, knife, sharp instrument, or explosives?
    2. Do you have anything on you that will stick, poke, or injure me?
    3. Do you have any drugs or needles on you?

Once you ask a question it is imperative to wait for a response and not rush into the search. Make sure that the person answers with either a "yes" or "no" answer to each question so that you receive a clear message that he either does or does not have a weapon or contraband that will hurt you. Always use a proper search technique that you were taught.

- Do not handcuff an offender/subject to yourself or a fixed object.
- Do not grab the chain between the cuffs. Some handcuffs have a hinge instead of a chain.
- Once you apply handcuffs you are responsible for the safety and well-being of the person that you handcuffed.
- Handcuffs should remain in a closed position to prevent the offender/subject from using them as a weapon against you. When the single strand or ratchet is in the open position it can be utilized as a very dangerous and effective weapon. The ratchet has teeth that can inflict further injury. In an open position the ratchet can cause serious eye damage, injury to the mouth, puncture the throat or neck, etc.

The very nature of handcuffing requires that you get extremely close to the offender/subject that you are securing. This is an inherently dangerous procedure that deserves your complete attention. When handcuffing be prepared for resistance and the possibility that you will need to disengage from the offender/subject or initiate a takedown to gain control. No matter how many offenders/subjects that you successfully handcuffed in the past never presume compliance on the subject you are currently handcuffing. Once a person feels the metal of the handcuff on their wrist and hears the infamous clicking sound that person knows their freedom is gone even if temporarily. This is the critical time when an offender or subject may decide to resist and fight. This is the time that their thought process may be, *"I'm not going to jail today."*

Never underestimate what a person will do to maintain their freedom. This is why it is so important to get the handcuffs applied securely in a fast manner. Once the first handcuff is secured on the wrist you must apply the second handcuff very rapidly. Be ready to respond appropriately if the offender/subject becomes non-compliant or brutally aggressive. Assume nothing and be ready for anything. Always follow the training that you receive in defensive tactics and officer survival training.

Handcuff Key

Handcuffs generally come with two small handcuff keys. Some departments will also issue a larger more user friendly handcuff key which provides easier manipulation of the locking mechanism. It is good practice to always have at least two handcuff keys with you at all times. Remember, many secure facilities prohibit officers from carrying handcuff keys into the facility. If this is the case be sure you retrieve your keys with you when you leave the secure facility.

In addition to the two handcuff keys you carry I also recommend that you "hide" a handcuff key on your person in case you are taken hostage and handcuffed with your own equipment. Hide the key in a location where it can easily be retrieved. Some places to consider would be in a rear pocket, in a small hidden pocket that you sew into the waistband on the back of your work pants, in a sock, in a shoe, etc. Find a place or two where you can comfortably and effectively hide a spare handcuff key so that if you are taken hostage and the possibility of escape is presented you have a key to remove the handcuffs. Carrying a hidden handcuff key may sound excessive to some but your perspective will instantly change if you are ever taken hostage and secured with your own handcuffs. Prepare for the worst case scenario.

Flex-Cuffs

Flex-cuffs are generally made of high strength plastic and can be one single loop that secures both hands in one loop or two individual loops in which each hand is secured in a separate loop. Some companies advertise flex-cuffs with a tensile strength of 400+ pounds. Again, these are a temporary restraining device and they can be broken using specific techniques. Never assume that you are safe when using handcuffs or flex-cuffs.

Leg Shackles

Leg shackles provide an additional layer of restraint and are designed to restrict an offender/subject from effecting escape by minimizing their ability to effectively run.

Application:

- Handcuffs should be applied first unless you are working with multiple officers and have the ability to simultaneously apply both handcuffs and leg shackles.
- Leg shackles should be applied when the offender is in a kneeling or prone position.
- Ensure that you apply the leg shackles rapidly to obtain control of the legs which can be powerful weapons capable of causing significant injury. As with handcuffs the longer it takes to apply the leg shackles the more danger that you are in.
- Leg shackles should be applied with the key holes facing down toward the ground to minimize the offender's ability to pick the lock.
- Always double-lock the leg shackles to prevent them from tightening and possibly causing injury. Check that the leg shackles are not applied too tightly so that circulation is not restricted and to prevent nerve damage.

- Because the chain on leg shackles tend to be long it is important that you do not get into a situation where an offender can wrap the chain around any part of your body especially around your neck.
- Assist the offender/subject in standing once the leg shackles are correctly applied and double locked.

The weaknesses that were noted for handcuff apply to leg shackles.

Belly Chain/Belt

A belly chain/belt is used in conjunction with handcuffs as a method to restrain an offender in the front of the body. This method is typically utilized when transporting a prisoner who will be detained for a long period of time. The belly chain/belt is more comfortable than being handcuffed behind the back while strong enough to secure the prisoner.

Application:

- Can be used with compliant or non-compliant prisoners.
- Wrap the belly chain/belt around the prisoner's waist so the handcuffs are positioned at the navel.
- Lock the handcuffs around the prisoner's wrists at the front of the body near the navel.
- Always double-lock the handcuffs to prevent them from tightening and possibly causing injury. Check that the handcuffs are not applied too tightly so that circulation is not restricted and to prevent nerve damage.
- When using a chain, lock the belly chain with a padlock using the rings on the belly chain. The padlock should be at the back of the prisoner to prevent tampering or lock picking. Always verify that the lock is secured.
- Pull on the belly chain to verify it is locked properly and secure.

Flashlight

A commonly issued flashlight is the Maglite® brand flashlight which is a good quality durable light that is constructed of anodized machined aluminum. It is available in LED for a brighter light with an adjustable beam that can go from a spot-to-flood beam. LED bulbs are durable and have an extremely long life lasting thousands of hours. This flashlight has the ability to have constant on or momentary on. It is a good general purpose flashlight but I would not recommend it as a tactical light for use with a firearm in a low-light situation. Although, if it is all you had it will work in a tactical environment.

For officers who are armed with a firearm I recommend carrying a high quality LED tactical flashlight that is small yet powerful. An LED (the acronym for Light-Emitting Diode) is a semiconductor chip that converts electrical energy directly into light. An LED is called a solid-state light source because it has no gas or liquid components, as do other light sources. These flashlights tend to put out a very solid beam of white light that do not have rings, shadows, or hot spots. Brightness is often measured in lumens. The higher the lumens the more output and brighter the light. Many departments do not issue tactical flashlights so officers who want one must purchase it at their own expense. They tend to be expensive but the money is well worth it especially if you need to use it during a low-light encounter. While I do not endorse any particular company I have used flashlights from SureFire, Streamlight, and BlackHawk and have been very satisfied with each brand. Over the last few years the availability of such lights has exploded on the market and there are now more choices than ever for such a light. These tactical flashlights come with many different options including the ability to adjust brightness levels and strobe functions. The strobe function is a great option to momentarily disorient a subject.

When it comes to flashlights I strongly believe in the

concept of redundancy meaning that I carry an extra flashlight in case the flashlight fails, batteries die, or it gets knocked out of my hand. I highly recommend that officers carry no less than two flashlights. You may hear people say the following phrase, *"Two is one; one is none"* which speaks directly to the concept of redundancy. Failures happen and batteries die – often at the worst possible time. Always have a back-up and embrace the concepts of redundancy! Remember, your unwelcome partner, Mr. Murphy, is ready to cause problems for you so anticipate problems and be ready with solutions to his devious methods. Redundancy helps to keep Murphy away!

There are also weapon mounted lights that attach to rails on firearms such as the Glock firearm which is commonly issued among law enforcement. Even if you have a weapon mounted light I still recommend that you carry two other tactical flashlights on your person. You do not want to use your weapon mounted light as a general flashlight without justification because you will also be pointing your weapon anywhere that you are shining the light. Always use safe firearm handling practices.

When carrying a flashlight it is also important to carry extra batteries. Many of the tactical flashlights utilize CR123A or 123A lithium batteries. These are high performance batteries that work well in flashlights that require a lot of energy. They are also effective in both cold and hot climates (-76°F to 176°F) and boast a ten year shelf life. The downside is that these batteries are expensive. Many high quality LED flashlights now use double AA batteries but these lights often have less lumen output than the 123 lithium batteries.

Chemical Sprays

There are three types of chemical sprays that have been commonly used in law enforcement over the years:

CN - Chloroacetophenone

- Lachrymatory agent
- Commonly referred to as tear gas

Target: Mouth and Nose

Effect: Profuse tearing, involuntary eye closure, and a burning sensation to moist skin. Poor efficacy on animals due to a lack of tear ducts.

CS - Orthochlorobenzalmalononitrile

- Classified as an irritant

Target: Mouth and Nose

Effect: Ten times stronger than CN. Produces extreme burning to eyes, copious tears, coughing, and tightness of the chest.

OC - Oleoresin Capsicum

- Classified as an inflammatory agent
- Referred to as pepper spray

Target: Face, Nose, Mouth, Eyes

Effect: Derivative of cayenne pepper. Produces involuntary closing of eyes known as a blepharospasm, impairs breathing as a result of uncontrollable coughing and gagging, intense burning to the skin, and temporary loss of muscular strength and coordination.

Most effective when inhaled and has a rapid onset of symptoms. Effective for up to 45 minutes.

Effective on animals, psychotic individuals and those under the influence of drugs and alcohol but nothing is 100% effective.

> Any chemical agent that contains an alcohol base should not be deployed around open flame or in conjunction with any device that may initiate a flame such as conducted energy device. Many departments no longer use alcohol based chemical agents to prevent a fire.

Today, most police officers, corrections officers, probation officers, parole officers, detention officers, and court security officers are issued OC spray due to its effectiveness and because there are no harmful side effects to those who are sprayed.

OC spray is classified as an inflammatory agent and causes involuntary closing of the eyes, coughing, gagging, intense burning to the skin, and temporary loss of muscular strength and coordination. OC spray is most effective when inhaled and the effects can last up to 45 minutes. New officers often ask how effective OC spray is when utilized in an emergency. My response is that it is effective if it stops the threat. If the spray fails to stop the threat then it is ineffective regardless of all other factors such as the percentage of OC or the heat rating. Many companies that produce OC spray will list the percentage of Capsicum in the bottle. It is easy to assume that the higher the concentration of OC the more effective the spray will be but this is not the case. Oleoresin Capsicum is a derivative of cayenne pepper. Pepper spray effectiveness is often measured by determining its Scoville Heat Unit (SHU's) rating which is a widely recognized method for measuring the "hotness" of a chili pepper and is based on the amount of capsicum the spray contains. The more capsaicin content the OC spray has, the hotter and more effective the spray will be resulting in a higher SHU rating. It is possible to have a can of OC spray that has a high percentage of Capsicum but a low Scoville Heat Unit rating. Yet, a more effective brand of OC may have a lower percentage of Capsicum but has a higher Scoville Heat Unit rating making the spray more potent. It is very common for law enforcement to use OC spray that has a SHU of 2,000,000 which is very effective.

OC spray typically comes with three options for a dispersal pattern to include stream, cone shaped mist, or fog. Stream is commonly issued to community corrections officers because it has the longest range and will spray between 10-12 feet depending on the brand. Also, it is not impacted as much by wind, provides the officer the ability to hit a specific target, and reduces the possibility of hitting other officers or bystanders. Anytime you deploy OC spray there is a very good chance that other unintended persons will be impacted by the spray which will permeate the environment. Some OC canisters contain a dye to rapidly identify the person who has been sprayed.

There are many sizes of OC spray that can be issued with 1.5oz being the most common for probation and parole officers to carry. A 1.5 oz. unit of OC spray with a stream nozzle will provide approximately 15 bursts of a 1 second duration with a maximum effective range of 10-12 feet. It is recommended that OC spray be carried on your person attached to your belt. OC spray should **not** be carried in a purse, pocket, backpack, or any other type of external carrying case. The reason is simple; if you need the OC spray you are not going to have time to grab it because it is not immediately assessable. In a crisis seconds count and you will not have time to go through your items to look for your pepper spray. Depending on your preference you can place the spray on your primary or reactionary side. I prefer to place it on my primary side which is the same side that I carry my firearm. This prevents me from holding a non-lethal weapon (OC spray) in my reactionary hand and a firearm in my primary hand. This should never occur but I have heard of situations where officers have OC spray in one hand and a firearm in the other which is a recipe for disaster. Carrying the OC spray and firearm on the same side eliminates this from happening. It also allows me to use my reactionary hand to control an offender if necessary. For officers that are not issued any other safety equipment other than OC spray I still recommend carrying the spray on your primary side so that you can use your reactionary hand as needed and not lead with the OC spray. This is a personal preference and you may choose to carry your OC spray in a different manner.

When the possibility exists that you may need to deploy OC spray it is important to use loud, clear, and concise verbal commands to get the offender/subject to comply. The goal is to obtain compliance without the need to spray. Depending on the situation you should be in a position of advantage but oftentimes the environment dictates where you will be located. If the offender/subject fails to respond to your verbal commands and you decide to deploy the spray to gain control then spray a one second burst, move your location, and re-assess to see if you need to: 1. spray again, 2. move in to secure the offender/subject with handcuffs, or 3. disengage to obtain assistance from the police. If you move in to secure the offender/subject with handcuffs then be sure to place the handcuffs on very quickly so that you gain control of the situation.

OC Spray Deployment

When using OC Spray:

- Utilize loud, clear, and concise verbal commands
- When working with a partner or police, communicate to let them know that you will be deploying OC spray so that they can avoid or minimize exposure
- When using a stream nozzle avoid spraying directly into the eyes if at a close range to avoid potential eye injury
- If offender is wearing glasses spray above the glasses
- Use in 1 second burst, move, and re-assess
- Apply handcuffs rapidly, double-lock handcuffs
- Once handcuffs are applied do NOT remove the handcuffs
- Move offender/subject to fresh air and rinse with water
- Conduct a thorough search of the offender/subject for weapons or other contraband
- You are responsible for any individual that you handcuff so do not leave this person unattended even for a short time
- Effects typically last up to 45 minutes
- Document completely and accurately
- Call for medical assistance if indicated

Once OC spray is deployed follow your department's policy regarding exposure. Move the offender to fresh air and rinse face with water but do NOT remove handcuffs. The effects can last up to 45 minutes. If the offender begins to experience respiratory or other medical problems then immediately have emergency medical services (EMS) respond. Alert EMS if the offender is wearing contacts. It is critical to remember that once you take an offender into custody you are responsible for that offender's well-being. Do not leave the offender alone for even a brief period of time especially if they are handcuffed and recently exposed to OC spray with impaired vision. Notify detention or prison staff that the offender was OC sprayed. Document completely and accurately in your use of force report.

A common question that always arises during defensive tactics training is, *"You don't shoot officers with a firearm in firearms training so why do I have to be exposed to OC?"* Comparing getting shot with a firearm and being exposed to OC spray is far from an equivalent comparison. Simply put, shooting an officer is lethal force which will result in serious bodily injury or death. We do not test lethal force on officers for obvious reasons.

Exposure to OC spray is important for a number of reasons:

- OC exposure is non-lethal and will not cause harm to the officer in training.

- When OC is deployed in a real incident there is a very good chance that you, as the officer, will also be effected by the spray. It is important for officers to experience OC spray prior to a real incident so that the officer knows what it feels like and that he/she can fight through the effects of the spray.

- Eliminates or reduces panic and fear by knowing that you have experienced OC spray without any negative impact.

- Increases officer confidence that the spray is effective and painful if they need to spray an offender/subject.

- If you are involved in a use of force incident involving OC spray that goes to court you can testify that you have been exposed to OC spray as part of your training and that you understand firsthand the effects of being sprayed.

OC Exposure in Training

Prior to any officer being exposed to OC spray in training instructors must verify that all participants have submitted medical waivers indicating that the officer is aware he/she will be exposed to OC spray and that he/she does not have any known medical condition(s) that would prevent the officer from being exposed to OC spray.

Two common methods that can be used to conduct exposure of OC spray include:

1. Direct Spray

    The officer will be directly sprayed in the face with a one second burst of OC spray. If using a stream nozzle the instructor should avoid spraying the officer directly in the eye to avoid any potential injury. This method will allow the student officer to feel the full effect of the OC spray. If there is concern about spraying directly into the eye the student officer can be provided vented goggles to prevent an eye injury.

2. Swab

The swab method utilizes a cotton ball or Q-tip that is soaked in OC spray and then swabbed underneath the eyes and nose of the officer. This method does not have the same effect as a direct spray.

The direct spray method is the most realistic and exposes the officer to the full effect of the OC spray. When conducting OC spray exposure I recommend using the direct spray method as the swab method fails to provide student officer with the full impact of the spray. In a real world incident where OC spray is deployed the officer may very well receive a full dose of spray which will be a very different experience than what was received from the swab method. Unless there are circumstances that would prevent a student officer from experiencing the direct spray I do not recommend the swab method for OC exposure. As the lead defensive tactics instructor where student officers were exposed to OC with the swab method and the direct spray method I can say conclusively that the direct spray method is significantly more impactful to the officer and much more realistic.

After officers have been exposed to OC it is important to allow a full 45 minutes for decontamination. Officers who have been exposed should fully rinse off with water. Of all the students that I have been involved with during OC exposure I do not recall any incidents of an officer having any negative effects from this training process or the OC.

Expandable Baton

In community corrections an impact weapon will generally refer to the use of an expandable baton. Batons come in varying lengths ranging 16"-26" in the open mode. The baton will consist of two telescopic shafts that lock into place once expanded. They are generally made out of high quality aerospace steel or lightweight aluminum alloy.

Parts of the baton include the following:

- Handle: Depending on the model the handle will be 6" - 9" in length
Foamed vinyl grips that provide a firm hold

- Shaft: Depending on the model the shaft will be 10" - 17" in length
When expanded the shaft will taper lock into place and remain open
When closed the shaft will collapse into the handle

- Cap: Located at the end of the handle

- Tip: Located at the end of the shaft

Benefits of an expandable baton include:

- Easy to conceal
- Low profile when in the closed mode
- Provides psychological deterrence especially when in the open mode
- No sharp edges that can cut/snag clothing or cut an assailant

A baton would be utilized by an officer when an offender/subjects actions are likely to cause you physical harm. When utilizing the expandable baton it is important to follow the training that is approved and provided by your department. There are multiple baton training programs that utilize different methods of using the baton. For example, some programs will have you strike the subject at a 90 degree angle to a limb while others will have you strike the limb at a 45 degree angle. Do not deviate from the training that is provided by and approved by your department or you may end up facing liability if you use the baton differently than authorized or trained.

In a situation where an officer is using a baton it is extremely important to use loud, clear, and concise verbal commands. Remember, probation and parole officers generally do not wear a uniform and oftentimes are out in public while working. If you utilize a baton in a public location it is very likely that other individuals will be around who may not know that you are an officer until there hear you providing verbal commands (they may assume that you are a police officer). Also, we now live in a society where just about everyone has a cell phone with the capability of taking high quality photographs and video. Within minutes of being involved in a use of force incident a video of your actions can be placed on the internet on a website such as YouTube for the world to see. If caught on video it would be to your benefit to be heard giving loud, clear, and concise verbal commands to the offender/subject.

Impact Weapon Targets: Primary striking points and striking points to avoid

Primary Striking Points
Common Peroneal Nerve
Femoral Nerve
Radial Nerve
Median Nerve
Tibial Nerve

Striking Points to AVOID	
Temple	Back of Neck
Eye	Collarbone
Upper Lip	Spine
Ears	Kidney
Hollow Behind Ears	Solar Plexus
Bridge of Nose	Tailbone
Throat	Groin
Jaw	

Use of force incidents are very stressful, highly dynamic events that are not a common occurrence for community corrections officers. It is possible that as you are attempting to strike an offender in one of the primary striking points you inadvertently end up hitting an area that you would normally try to avoid such as the head, neck, or spine. If this happens it becomes crucial to accurately, and with specificity, document the incident with great detail to explain that the situation was dynamic, fast, and that the offender moved during your attempt to strike causing you to hit the head instead of hitting primary striking point "__X__".

Conducted Energy Device

Conducted Energy Devices (CED) are less-lethal weapons designed to disrupt an offenders/subjects central nervous system. This is accomplished by deploying battery powered electrical energy sufficient to cause uncontrolled muscle contractions and override an individual's voluntary motor response. Such devices discharge a high voltage, low amperage jolt of electricity. An example is the TASER® X26™ Electronic Control Device.[xxiv]

Conducted Energy Devices (CED) are also referred to as:

- Electronic Control Device (ECD)
- Electro-Muscular Disruption Technology (EMDT)
- Electro-Muscular Incapacitation device (EMI)
- Electro-Muscular Device (EMD)

They all serve to describe this category of less-lethal weapons.

In a community corrections setting the use of conducted energy devices are mainly used with specialized units specifically tasked with apprehending probation and parole absconders. These specialized units are commonly known by the following names: warrants, fugitive apprehension unit, fugitive apprehension detail, warrant apprehension unit, absconder unit, absconder recovery unit, absconder search unit, special services unit, etc. Officers assigned to these high-risk units receive specialized training in the correct operation and application of these conducted energy devices when issued by the department. Depending on the department's policy and procedures for apprehending offenders with warrants, officers in these units can work alone and request backup once an offender is located, they may work in teams, or they may work in conjunction with local, state, and federal law enforcement agencies. Some probation and parole officers are assigned to be part of a task force.

Having a conducted energy devices is an important tool for officers who work in a high-risk fugitive apprehension unit because it provide another valuable tool to address non-compliant offenders. In addition, if a probation/parole warrants officer is armed with a firearm but no CED and they are working with police officers who do have CED's such as a TASER® the probation/parole officer will be limited to using deadly force while the police officers have access to their less lethal TASER®. This places the probation/parole officer in a situation when working with police where the police have their TASER® pointed at an offender and the probation/parole officer has their firearm pointed at the offender thereby completely eliminating an effective less-lethal option for the community corrections officer. If the offenders behavior require the use of lethal force it may very well be the probation/parole officer who fires his weapon and not the police officer. Probation and parole departments should really consider providing all officers who work on a fugitive apprehension detail to be issued a TASER® so that the community corrections officer is not solely responsible for using lethal force when working in conjunction with police officers who have a TASER®.

At this time most probation and parole departments are not issuing conducted energy devices to officers who are not assigned to a unit whose task is to apprehend absconders. Application to other units such as a specialized case load of high-risk violent offenders or domestic violent offenders who have a demonstrated willingness to use violence should be considered. Also to be considered are specialized search teams who are either a dedicated team or an "on call" team to conduct probation or parole searches of an offender's residence. In these cases issuing a conducted energy device can be an effective less lethal tool.

Currently many juvenile probation and juvenile parole departments have apprehension regarding the issuance of conducted energy devices to officers for two main reasons. First, is the medical implications of using such a device on a juvenile especially considering that testing has not been conducted on this population to see if there are specific health implications. Second, is public perception about the use of such a device on a juvenile.

Some of the benefits of using a CED, besides being less-lethal, is that some devices have the ability to download user data such as date of device activation, duration of application, temperature, and battery status. In addition, some models can provide a video and audio recording of the incident which provides accountability and an accurate record of the incident. Additionally, it is possible to be 12-15 feet away from an offender/subject when employing such a less-lethal device which is safer for the officer.

Firearm

One of the most common firearms used in law enforcement today is the Glock in either a 9mm or .40 caliber. Glock firearms are a very reliable weapon that is easy to shoot and maintain. Each firearm will come with two spare magazines and your department will provide an approved holster and magazine carrier. The preferred method for carrying your service weapon would be strong side hip holster although other carry options may be available such as utilization of a shoulder holster. The holster should provide some level of retention so that the weapon is not easily taken by an offender/subject and so that it does not fall out should you need to run, climb a fence or wall, or if you were to fall during an attack. You must be able to qualify with the department approved holster that you will be carrying on duty. In addition, your department may allow you to utilize a tactical flashlight that attaches directly to your firearm. In such cases you will need to utilize a holster that will accommodate the firearm and attached light.

Body Armor

Generally, body armor provided to officers will have the ability to stop handgun rounds but not rounds from a high powered rifle. It is important for officers to know the limitations of their equipment. Department policy will mandate situations when officers are required to wear body armor. At a minimum, it would be good practice to wear body armor in the following situations:

1. Field arrests
2. Probation/parole searches
3. Contact with high-risk offenders (High-risk is a term open to interpretation. If you think you need body armor then wear it.)

Officers can provide many excuses not to wear body armor. I believe it is better to wear it and have an added layer of safety than not wear it due to inconvenience.

Duty Belt and Keepers

Your duty belt is a piece of equipment that allows you to carry your safety gear to include firearm, magazines, baton, OC spray, handcuffs, flashlights, and other equipment such as gloves. The duty belt comes in many different styles and often uses belt keepers to attach the duty belt to your personal belt so that your equipment stays secured and does not move around. It is important to always use belt keepers to prevent your duty belt from sliding around especially during a crisis.

Radio

Officers should either be issued a handheld radio or have access to a radio. This is especially important for officers in the field. The radio should be part of a complete communications system that includes a dispatch center that tracks each officer's location and time on scene. The radio can literally be their lifeline. Many radios have an emergency button that when activated notifies dispatch. There must be a clear procedure that dispatch follows if the emergency button is activated or dispatch is not able to make contact with an officer. It is important to always provide dispatch with your location. It is critical to ensure that your battery is fully charged.

Use of Force Continuum

Use of force continuums have been around since the 1960's as a way of providing law enforcement officers a way to determine what level of force is appropriate based upon situations that police officers encounter. There does not exist one universal use of force continuum that all departments utilize and, in fact, there are dozens of different versions being utilized by agencies today. Some force continuums are very simple and basic while others are complex and difficult to understand. Considering that there are so many different versions of use of force continuums being utilized it would lead one to also conclude that not all of them are consistent, meaning that one continuum may require a different response from an officer as opposed to a different force continuum. It is possible that one force continuum would allow an officer to use an empty hand technique while another would allow use of a chemical agent such as pepper spray and yet another would allow use of an impact weapon such as an expandable baton. How much validity is there in this tool if different models allow for different responses to the exact same type of threat? Later I will discuss whether use of force continuums remain a valid tool and if not what might be the alternative.

Utilization of force by an officer is always in response to the actions of the offender or subject. I include the word "subject" because you should not assume that you will only be dealing with offenders. As a community corrections officer you will also interact with the offender's family, friends, employer, acquaintances, school, treatment provider, and the general public. Do not assume (faulty assumption) that the utilization of force will be limited only to offenders that you supervise in the community. Anyone can be a potential threat to your safety.

> **Use of Force must comply with federal law, state law, and department policy and procedure.**

The use of force continuum is designed to provide guidance to officers so that when confronted with condition "A" the correct response is "X". But real world violent encounters are typically very dynamic and occur under less than ideal conditions. Reacting and responding to the uncertainty of a violent situation is not necessarily as simple or clear cut as just choosing an option from the force continuum. It becomes very easy for administrators, investigators, and fellow officers to second guess an officer's decision to use a particular level of force. This can lead to unreasonable expectations being placed on officers who in the midst of a crisis are thinking about how others will perceive their actions as opposed to stopping a threat. It also becomes very easy for officers to doubt their own decisions. Let's examine a basic use of force continuum and see what levels of force it is composed of for officers to utilize.

Level Of Force	Subjects Actions	Officer: Type of Force
Officer Presence	Offender/Subject is cooperative and not a threat	No force is used or needed - Professional appearance - Identification of authority - Command presence - Interview stance
-Verbal Skills -Verbal Commands	Offender/Subject is compliant only in response to verbal directions or verbal commands	No force is used; only verbal communication - Verbal skills & de-escalation techniques - Verbal direction - Verbal commands
Empty-Hand Control	Offender/Subject actions may cause physical harm	Officer uses bodily force to gain control. Force may consist of: - Personal weapons such as punches, kicks, knees and elbow strikes - Control holds - Joint locks - Pressure points

Officer Survival for Probation and Parole Officers

Less-Lethal Methods	Offender/Subject actions likely to cause physical harm	<ul><li>Chemical spray such as OC spray</li><li>Impact weapon such as an expandable baton</li><li>Conducted Energy Device such as a Taser</li></ul>
Lethal Force	Offender/Subject actions may cause serious physical injury or death	Utilization of deadly force to include:<ul><li>Firearm</li><li>Edged weapon (Does your department have an edged weapon policy?)</li></ul>May include weapons not intended for lethal force such as:<ul><li>Personal weapons</li><li>Expandable baton</li><li>Weapon of opportunity</li></ul>

Examples of Use of Force Models

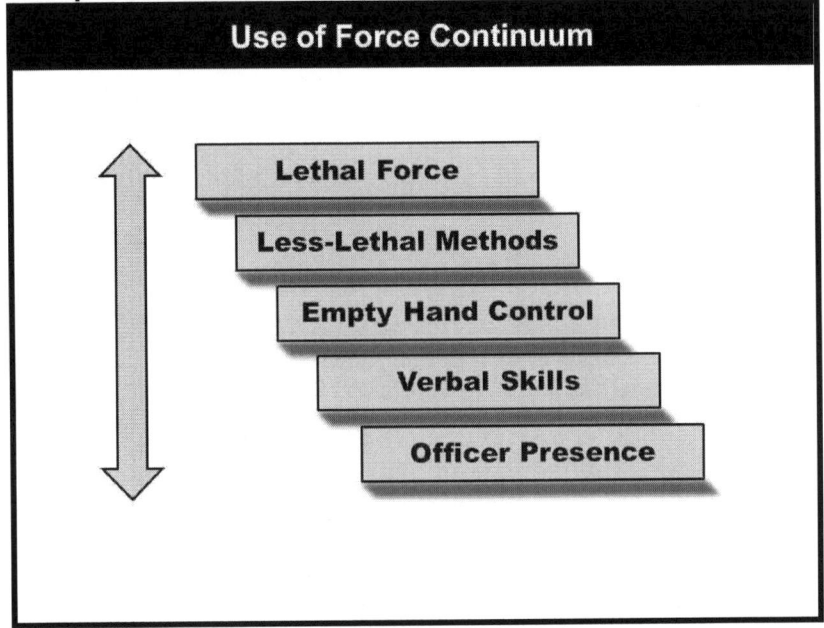

Figure 1: Example of a basic Use of Force Continuum

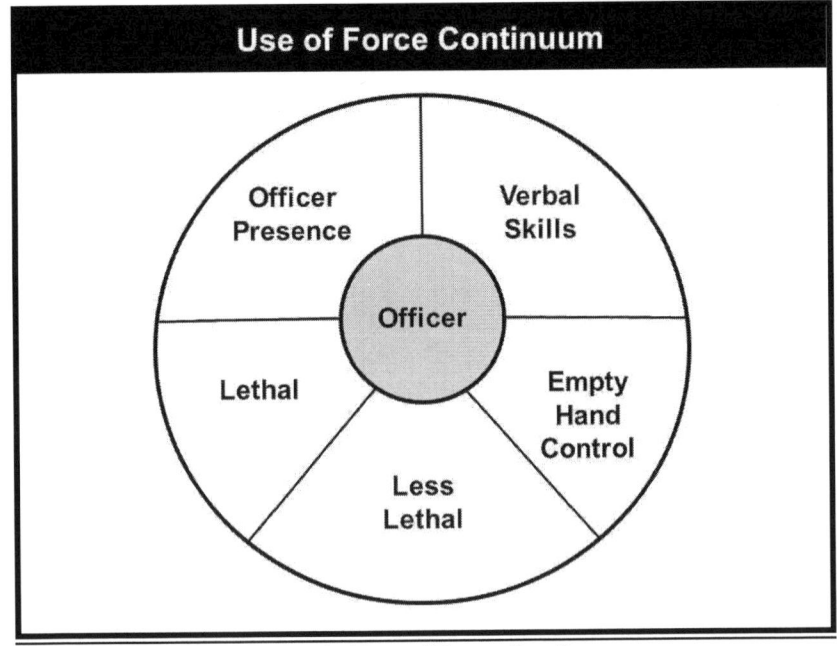

Figure 2: Example of a basic Use of Force Continuum

Understanding the Use of Force Continuum

Figures 1 and 2 are two basic examples of the use of force continuum. While the information contained in the continuums are the same they are formatted differently which can potentially lead to different interpretations of the same information. For example, Figure 1 is oftentimes interpreted as a "stair step approach" in which the officer must start at the bottom with officer presence and then progressively utilize each level of force until lethal force is used if necessary. Clearly, this is not the case as the officers response is based on the subject's actions. Officers are not forced to start at the lowest level of force and then progressively work their way up the continuum to the highest level of force. It is critical that officer survival instructors teach proper application of the use of force continuum so that new officers do not believe that a stair step approach is required before utilizing a higher level of force. Unfortunately, an illustration such as Figure 1 is very powerful and even though a use of force instructor teaches the continuum appropriately the new officer sees a visual image that becomes more powerful than the instructors words and instructions. Remember, different people learn differently and it becomes easy for a visual learner to look at an image and become "locked-in" on an incorrect interpretation and application of the model. This can lead to disastrous results for an officer who for example is clearly in a lethal situation but is trying to use verbal de-escalation skills against a lethal threat. ***It is important to understand that you can start at any level of force and end at any level of force. The force that you utilize is always based on the subject's actions. You are not required to start at the lowest level on the use of force continuum.***

The use of force continuum in Figure 2 has the same information as the continuum in Figure 1 but it is presented differently. This type of continuum may be referred to as a "wheel" or "circular" continuum. This model places the officer in the center and provides an array of options that the officer can use based on the subjects actions. There is no implication that the officer must use one level of force before progressing to a higher level of force. Regardless of which use of force model is being taught it is important for the use of force instructor to properly explain how the model is to be interpreted and provide numerous examples of its application.

There are many other versions of the use of force continuum which are significantly more complicated than the models just discussed. As the complexity of the model increases it becomes increasingly important to receive proper instruction and application of the model. It is critical that officers are so well trained on using force that during a use of force incident the officer is responding appropriately and reasonably based on the circumstances as opposed to trying to determine what level of force to utilize. Remember, in a use of force situation you more than likely will be nervous and feeling the psychological and physiological reactions to stress. Not knowing what level of force to use or trying to think about what your policy allows will only add to your level of stress at a time that you may already be maxed out. This is a recipe for disaster. Once again, I need to stress the importance of training so that if you are ever in such a situation you know how to respond and are confident in your abilities to successfully stop a threat. Next, we will review each level of the use of force continuum.

Officer Presence

Officer presence simply refers to your presence and identification of authority and has the benefit that no force is used. Never underestimate how you portray yourself to offenders and the public. When you meet someone for the first time they typically form an opinion of you within seconds. This does not give you a lot of time to make a favorable first impression so your presence really matters and will determine what an offender thinks about you as their probation/parole officer. Because many community corrections officers do not wear a uniform your presence may not have as strong as an impact as say a uniformed police officer. People have a tendency to view individuals who wear a uniform as an authority figure which increases the impact of presence. It is important for community corrections officers to have an attitude and demeanor that exhibits professionalism and is nonthreatening. Community corrections officers can utilize the following methods to improve presence:

1. Identify your authority as an officer

    From the very first time you introduce yourself to an offender you supervise you want to state your name and that you are their supervising officer. For example, *"My name is Officer Scott Kirshner and I will be your probation officer while you are on probation."* This sets that tone that the relationship is one of authority consisting of probation officer and offender. While it should be obvious to you, it needs to be clear to the offender that this is not a relationship based on friendship. As an officer you should never become friends with the offenders you supervise. Developing a friendly or personal relationship with an offender compromises your integrity and can lead to serious ethical violations.

    One significant advantage that community corrections officers have over police officers is that when supervising offenders you have the ability to develop a rapport over the time of their community supervision grant. Yes, police officers can interact with the same offenders over extended periods of time but this type of relationship is significantly different than that of a probation/parole officer.

2. Wearing your department identification badge

    Wearing your court issued or department issued I.D.

badge is a visual reminder to the offenders you supervise you are their probation/parole officer; not their friends and not their equals. Remember, as an officer you always maintain the majority of power and authority in your dealings with offenders.

3. Wearing your metal badge

   Many community corrections officers do not wear their metal badge displayed on their clothing. It is acceptable to not display your metal badge the majority of the time but there are times that you should wear the badge such as when you know you are going to be arresting an offender, when conducting a search, when working with other law enforcement officers, and if you carry a firearm while on duty. Your metal badge is a very clear visual indicator of your presence and what you represent as an officer.

   Not all departments issue metal badges to their staff. I have conducted training for probation officers who work for municipal courts who only supervise misdemeanor offenders and strictly work in an office environment. These officers do not conduct fieldwork and do not have arrest powers.

Typically, the offender you are supervising is cooperative and there are no problems. The offender is compliant and behaving appropriately. But, situations can rapidly deteriorate and problems develop causing a potential escalation in the amount of force necessary to maintain control or regain control of the situation. In these cases you want to display **command presence** which is body language that conveys authority, confidence, and respect. How you present yourself is an important aspect of command presence. It is important to dress professionally, carry your gear correctly, maintain your gear in good working order, and have grooming that is appropriate.

Remember, you have a very short time to make a lasting impression. First impressions last and will be based upon the offender's perception of you and how you present yourself. Whether the perception is true or not is irrelevant because perception is reality.

You will be supervising offenders that are experts in reading body language especially if they have done significant prison sentences or numerous jail sentences where their very survival can depend on being able to analyze people. Prisons and jails are notoriously violent places where an inmate can be brutally assaulted or killed for saying the wrong thing, giving a certain look to another inmate, or being disrespectful. The "prison code" is a strong motivator for inmates to play by inmate rules. These offenders will analyze and judge you very quickly as their supervising officer and make a determination if you are going to be "cool", a "push over" or a "hard ass" while they are on community supervision. Every time that you meet with an offender they are sizing you up and making an assessment of you. This is true whether the offender is male or female, juvenile or adult, low risk or high risk, or new to the system or institutionalized. To make matters worse these offenders talk to each other about you! How many times has an offender said to you, "*I heard you were cool.*" In such situations the offender has obtained this information from another offender. How do you feel knowing that an offender you supervise has sought out intelligence about you?

When utilizing command presence you want to use your authority to gain control of the situation, avoid escalation if possible, and prevent the need to utilize a higher level of force. Anytime a situation arises that causes you to use command presence you must maintain command presence throughout the entire incident regardless of the level of force that you utilize and until threat is neutralized or no longer a threat. Do not become lax or let your guard down as you do not know the intentions of the offender/subject you are dealing. Now is not the time to become complacent, relaxed, or comfortable.

Presence is also displayed when officers utilize an interview stance, also known as a field interview stance, when interacting with offenders/subjects. An interview stance is a non-threatening, non-aggressive stance that provides officers a basic level of safety when interacting with offenders. When utilizing an interview stance the officer's body will be bladed at a 45 degree angle to the offender with your firearm, baton, or chemical spray turned away from the offender. Feet are positioned about shoulder width apart with the knees slightly bent for balance and increased mobility in any direction. Body weight is to be distributed evenly with the non-dominant leg forward and the dominant leg back. Arms are kept close to the body and hands are positioned above the belt line with hands in an open position. The use of an interview stance allows you to keep your firearm (or baton, pepper spray) farther away from a potential threat whether offender or other subject. It allows you to have your hands in a position to respond if needed.

<u>Verbal Skills</u>

Verbal communications skills, in conjunction with presence, are tools that officers commonly utilize very effectively in community corrections on a daily basis. Verbal direction refers to commands of direction where you instruct the offender on what they need to do, or not do, based on your instruction. With proper training, practice, and experience, officers tend to develop an excellent verbal skill set that prevents many situations from escalating into potentially dangerous and violent incidents. The amount of compliance obtained from the use of verbal skills is very impressive and quite effective considering that community corrections officers supervise offenders that do not have the best communication skills and have oftentimes demonstrated a pattern of behavior that is not conducive to authority or following rules.

Officer Survival for Probation and Parole Officers

The goal of verbal skills is to get an offender to do something that they may not want to do without escalating the situation. Oftentimes, you will utilize verbal skills on offenders that are cooperative. At other times the offender will only be cooperative in response to your verbal direction. Officers can use a variety of verbal techniques to obtain compliance such as asking questions to obtain information, advising the offender/subject on what course of action to take, informing the offender of potential consequences, or issuing a verbal command. Verbal techniques also allow officers to de-escalate situations thereby preventing them from escalating. Verbal skills can range from an officer issuing a calm, nonthreatening command such as, "*Let me see you're your court paperwork*" to the utilization of a loud, clear, concise verbal command to gain compliance such as, "*STOP*" or "*DON'T MOVE.*" The latter example is used when a situation is about to escalate or already has escalated and requires immediate verbal intervention.

Asking questions:

- Specifically, what is causing you to be so upset today?
- I can see that you are visibly upset about receiving a positive drug test for meth. How is being upset going to get you to resolve the issue of your drug use?

Advising on a course of action:

- An option for you would be to discuss your anger with your therapist.
- When you feel the urge to use drugs call your sponsor.
- Discuss with your employer that your scheduled work hours are at the same time you are scheduled for domestic violence counseling which is a requirement of your probation. Try explaining that your work hours and treatment

hours were discussed prior to being hired and you were assured that there would not be a conflict between the two.
- Instead of directing your violence on other people you could use the skills that you learned in group classes.

Informing of potential consequences:

- If you act out on your thoughts you will end up back in prison.
- Being disruptive in the probation office and arguing with everyone will result in you being sent back to court to address your behavior.
- If you continue to have positive drug tests you may end up receiving more treatment hours to address your substance abuse. Also, you may end up with a new court date to explain your actions to the judge.
- If you decide to take off and abscond a warrant for your arrest will be issued. Your problems will not go away just because you stop reporting.
- If you come closer I will spray you! (As you are holding a can of OC spray at the offender/subject.

Issuing a verbal command:

- Stop!
- Don't move!
- Drop the weapon!
- Show me your hands!
- Get on the ground!

Utilization of verbal commands is not a difficult skill to learn or incorporate yet I have seen officers have difficulty in a training environment with this essential skill. As an officer survival instructor I have repeatedly seen officers in training that are hesitant, timid, or shy about using such commands. During scenario based training evolutions designed specifically to elicit verbal commands from an officer I have witnessed numerous examples where the volume of the officer's verbal command was literally a whisper! Trainers must ensure that officers have the ability to use proper verbal commands in training so that this skill will translate to a real incident. If an officer fails to be able to utilize proper verbal command in training there is a likely chance that the officer will not be able to utilize a proper verbal command during a real incident where the stakes are real and much higher than in a training environment. Trainers have an obligation to provide every opportunity to officers to develop proper verbal skills. Conversely, officers have to get to the point where they are not timid, embarrassed, or shy about using such commands. The officer's life may depend on their ability to provide a loud, clear, and concise verbal command.

LOUD, CLEAR, CONCISE VERBAL COMMANDS

During an incident it is vitally important that officers have the ability to give verbal commands that are loud, clear, and concise for the following reasons:

Loud: Just as you may experience psychological and physiological reactions to stress so may the offender or subject that you encounter. The offender may experience auditory exclusion or become so hyper-focused on what they are doing that they will not hear what you say if you fail to issue a loud command.

Clear: During a crisis the offender can become so worked up that it becomes difficult to comprehend what you are saying. As the officer giving the verbal command it is critical that you do not allow yourself to lose composure and provide an unclear message.

Concise: Short, simple verbal commands provide less opportunity for the command to be misinterpreted. Short and simple is best in this situation.

There are many effective verbal skill programs available that provide officers essential verbal de-escalation skills to handle offenders who are non-compliant and using threatening behavior. I have seen a trend over the last few years in which probation and parole departments attempt to use a specific program in a safety environment in which the program was not designed to be used. An example of this is the use of Motivational Interviewing. Community corrections departments all over the United States and even internationally are utilizing Evidence-Based Practices (EBP) and Motivational Interviewing (MI) as an integral part of their supervision strategy. I firmly believe that using EBP and MI as a method to facilitate behavioral change in offenders is the right path to take in order to reduce recidivism and have offenders engage in pro-social, law abiding behavior. Having said that I also have seen numerous examples where motivational interviewing is incorrectly incorporated into officer survival training programs. When I see an officer survival instructor incorporate motivational interviewing in an officer survival training curriculum it makes me doubt their abilities and their understanding of both motivational interviewing and officer safety. According to Miller and Rollnick, motivational interviewing is defined as:

> *"A client centered, directive method for enhancing intrinsic motivation to change by exploring and resolving ambivalence."*[xxv]

Motivational interviewing is about resolving ambivalence. Motivational interviewing is not designed as a verbal de-escalation program and is not related to officer safety. Yet, there are departments, organizations, and trainers that repeatedly throw out the buzz term of motivational interviewing relating to officer safety. This is like trying to put a square in a circular hole. Motivational interviewing as a whole has nothing to do with officer safety or de-escalation which is evident based on the definition of MI. Having said that it is important to understand that there are components of motivational interviewing that are similar to techniques used in some verbal de-escalation programs but departments, organizations, and trainers should not attempt to mix motivational interviewing with officer safety or verbal de-escalation.

Empty-Hand Control

Empty-hand control is the use of bodily force to gain control of a situation utilizing techniques that have a minimal chance of injury. Community corrections officers are highly effective in preventing the majority of incidents from escalating to high levels of force with their use of presence and verbal skills. Empty-hand control is different from presence and verbal skills in that the officer is now in physical contact with an offender or subject and is "hands on" in an attempt to resolve the incident. Anytime you are in close proximity to use an empty-hand technique you are in a dangerous situation as the offender is close enough to grab or punch you thereby placing you in jeopardy. Let's examine the tools that make up empty-hand control.

Many force continuum models break down empty-hand control into two categories often referred to as soft techniques and hard techniques.

Soft Techniques consist of grabs, pressure points, joint locks, and control holds with or without a takedown.

Grabs:

Grabs are utilized as a method to obtain control over an offender or to redirect an offender's movement. Grabs can be used in conjunction with a follow up maneuver such as handcuffing, initial move before implementing a control hold, or to maintain control while transporting a prisoner. It is important for officers to understand that for every grab there is a counter move. And there is a counter for every counter move. It is critical that when an officer uses a grab they not hesitate to immediately gain control or the offender may attempt to initiate a counter move.

Pressure Points:

Pressure points are considered a pain compliance technique that renders a nerve temporarily inoperable. Application of a pressure point should not cause permanent nerve damage and it provides the officer time to gain control of the offender.

PRESSURE POINTS

Important considerations and information when using pressure points:

- Always utilize in conjunction with loud, clear, and concise verbal commands.
- If you have not obtained your desired result after 5 seconds consider using another control technique. Do not try to force a technique that is not working.
- Release the amount of pressure that you are applying once the offender/subject begins to comply. BUT, do not lose control or you may need to fight to regain control. Once you have control never give it up as you might not be so fortunate the next time!
- Do not use objects such as a pen, flashlight, knife, keys, kubaton, baton, etc. to apply a pressure point. Use fingertip (digital) control or an appropriate strike depending on which pressure point you are striking.
- Depending on which pressure point you are utilizing be sure to use pressure and counter pressure to stabilize the location for greater effectiveness.

Again, it is important to emphasize that in order to use a pressure point technique you are in very close proximity to the offender/subject. If the offender is psychotic or under the influence of drugs or alcohol the use of a pressure point may not be effective and may only motivate the offender to become more aggressive to resist or injure you. When you make the conscious decision to go "hands on" with an offender or subject you must display confidence in your ability to control the situation. If you are hesitant or unsure you are fighting not only the offender but yourself.

Joint Locks:

Joint locks can be utilized as a method to obtain control over an offender such as to redirect an offender's movement or as an initial move to initiate a takedown technique. Joint locks can be used in conjunction with a follow up maneuver such as handcuffing, initial move before implementing a control hold, or to maintain control while transporting a prisoner.

Control Holds:

Control holds provide officers with pain compliance techniques to assist with offenders who are physically resisting arrest, offenders who are passively resistant, and as a method to transport a restrained offender from one point to another. Control holds can consist of escort holds, arm bar control holds, reverse wrist locks and takedown, and other wrist lock techniques.

Control hold techniques, *when applied correctly*, have a minimal chance of causing injury. However, the dynamics of an altercation with an offender who is resisting can lead to potential injury. For example, if you have an offender who is resisting being controlled in a wrist lock and the offender begins to actively fight there is a chance that the officer applies more pressure to the wrist lock resulting in a sprain, strain, or fracture to the wrist. In such cases the officer needs to accurately document the dynamic factors of the incident which resulted in an injury to the offender/subject.

Hard techniques consist of direct impact strikes such as punches, palm heel strikes, elbow strikes, kicks, knee strikes and heel stomps. These techniques are considered personal weapons as they are weapons inherent to the officer as opposed to external weapons such as pepper spray, baton, or firearm.

Less-Lethal Methods

Less-Lethal can be defined as application of force that meets a tactical objective with less potential for causing death or serious bodily injury than conventional more lethal tactics.

In a community corrections environment less-lethal consist of:

- Chemical sprays
- Impact weapons
- Conducted Energy Devices (CED)

Depending on the department that you work and your assignment you may be issued none, some, or all of the above listed less-lethal tools. If you work in probation for a municipal court where you do not conduct any field work you may not be issued any of the above equipment. If you work for a parole department in the absconder unit you may be issued all of the above equipment. Many departments only issue chemical sprays regardless of your assignment.

Lethal Force

Probation and parole officers may use deadly force against an offender/subject only if the officer reasonably believes that such force is necessary to prevent the offender/subject from inflicting imminent serious bodily injury or death to the officer or others. In such cases lethal force may be authorized by the use of deadly force tactics which may include the use of any means necessary such as a firearm, baton, personal weapons, or weapon of opportunity.

Under the stress of a deadly force encounter it is important for officers to know and understand federal and state laws regarding use of force, department policy, as well as the tactics and techniques that pertain to lethal force. Officers many not have a lot of time in a critical incident to think, analyze, or respond to events that are occurring at a fast pace under less than ideal conditions. Add into this mix the psychological and physiological reactions to stress and you will understand that you either know how to respond during such a crisis or you don't. The common thread is training. You must be trained so thoroughly well that you respond appropriately during a crisis instead of going into Condition Black (freezing) or by taking precious time to think about what the law allows you to do, what policy authorizes, or what tactics and technique to use to neutralize the threat. If an offender or subjects actions require you to utilize lethal force and you take their life it is important for you to know that you made the correct decision. When you lay your head on your pillow at night you do not want to second guess your own decision. There will be plenty of other individuals doing that for you. There will be a police investigation and an internal investigation. Fellow officers, the public, and even the media may judge your actions oftentimes without complete information. But, it will be comforting for you to know that you made the correct decision and that you followed law, department policy, and that your actions were appropriate and justified.

Department Policy: Use of Force

Many use of force policies that are implemented by probation or parole departments obtain their authority based upon state law, federal law, judicial code, and/or administrative orders. It is important for officers to understand that a department's policy can be more restrictive than what the law allows. For example, state law may allow you to defend yourself without having to retreat from the threat but department policy may require that you make every effort to retreat or withdraw before using force. It is possible for an officer to act appropriately within the confines of the law but outside the mandate of policy. In such cases the officer may face disciplinary charges for breaking department policy. The consequences for such a violation can range from verbal counseling to termination from employment. It is very important that officers have a definitive working knowledge on the application of department policy.

Common verbiage in many community corrections use of force policy include:

- The use of force is reserved for *defensive purposes only*
- Officers will resort to the use of force in the performance of their duties when necessary *and when defensive retreat is not available*
- The use of force must be *reasonable and necessary*
- Officers shall base use of force decision upon the facts known to them at the time of the incident and whether, under the circumstances, the use of degree of force is *reasonable*

In the above examples the use of italics and underlining is added to stress that many departments require their officers, when possible, to avoid situations that require using force and when force is used that it is reasonable. This reiterates the point that community corrections officers are not first responders with an obligation to respond to an incident such as a police officer. Use of force for community corrections is generally reserved for those situations where an officer has absolutely no other choice than to utilize force. The officer would be in a situation where they cannot physically leave the area and all other options for de-escalation and tactical disengagement are not effective or possible. A good analogy is to think of an animal backed into a corner with no avenue of escape; the animal has no choice but to defend itself from harm.

Remember, the law may allow you to legally use force but you may be breaking department policy in the process. It is very important for officers to have a working knowledge of policy to know when they can and cannot use force and under what circumstances. Failure to appreciate and acknowledge the differences between law and policy can lead to inappropriate actions resulting in disciplinary action. Let's examine, in general, when community corrections officers are authorized to use force.

USE OF FORCE

The use of force is reserved for defensive purposes only except for those circumstances in which an officer is:
- arresting,
- detaining, or
- preventing the escape of an arrested or detained individual.

The implication is that there are two instances where an officer is allowed to use force:

1. For defensive purposes only.

    As an officer you have the right to protect yourself and/or others. In a community corrections environment this generally includes the caveat that tactical disengagement is not possible. The officer has the right of protection when there is no avenue to leave or attempting to leave places the officer in further danger.

2. When an officer is arresting, detaining, or preventing the escape of an arrested or detained individual.

> This is not a "defensive purposes only" situation but a time when the officer is authorized to be proactive, as opposed to defensive.

At this point it is important to discuss the terms defensive and offensive. Many community corrections policies reiterate that use of force is for defensive purposes and that officers must retreat when possible. We tend to think about "defensive" as meaning to protect or defend. In community corrections we often link defensive with retreat which is then interpreted as the officer moving backward in order to retreat. On the other hand "offensive" is thought of as aggressive or an attack. Offensive is thought as moving in a forward direction. What about situation when the officer attempts to retreat but must move in a forward manner or toward and offender or subject? Moving in a forward direction is often misinterpreted as an offensive act. I have seen officer survival instructors in scenario based training classes chastise students for moving in a forward direction which the instructor perceives as an offensive movement. This forward movement is interpreted as offensive (aggressive) by the instructor. Yet, in these scenarios moving in a forward direction is the only option for the officer who wants to retreat. The direction of travel that an officer moves is not necessarily correlated to whether an officer's actions are offensive or defensive. Let's look at the following example:

> A parole officer is conducting a residential contact of an offender. While the parole officer usually attempts to maintain control of the front door the offender lured the officer into the apartment to prove that he did not have any alcohol in his refrigerator. The offender was on parole for an aggravated driving under the influence of alcohol (Agg DUI) charge in which he was

in an accident that seriously injured two individuals. The offender has a long history of substance abuse problems but claims that he has been sober for the last year despite a positive drug test for marijuana. During the last residential contact the parole officer noticed an empty 40 oz. can of beer on the living room couch. The offender said it belonged to his girlfriend and that it was not his beer.

After the offender proves that there is no beer in the refrigerator the parole officer reviews other aspects of the offender's parole. The officer is being polite and respectful but the offender is becoming agitated over the whole substance abuse issue. The offender is now standing between the front door and the parole officer and is verbally expressing his displeasure with the parole officer.

Questions to consider:

1. Would you consider the parole officers forward movement toward the door and the offender as an offensive (aggressive) move?

2. Is it possible for an officer to move in a forward direction and still be considered a tactical retreat?

In order for the parole officer to leave the residence (retreat) he must move forward in the direction of the front door which is also moving in the direction toward the offender. The officer is not being offensive and is in fact attempting to be defensive. Being offensive or defensive has more to do with the motivation of the officers' actions; not the direction of travel or movement. Moving back away from an offender is not necessarily defensive and moving forward toward an offender is not necessarily offensive. It is important for instructors to evaluate the big picture to see and understand what it is the officer is attempting to accomplish.

Officer Survival for Probation and Parole Officers

Elements of Force

Use of force policies will often discuss "Elements of Force" pertaining to when an officer is justified in using force. Elements of force include:

> <u>Ability:</u> An attacker is capable of injuring or killing. This power may come in the form of a <u>weapon</u> or through <u>disparity of force</u>.

Utilization of a weapon by an attacker clearly gives that person an advantage. Even items not designed as weapons can cause lethal injuries such as a baseball bat, screwdriver, tire iron and even rope.

Weapon:
- Gun
- Knife
- Sword
- Club
- Tire iron
- Baseball bat

Disparity of Force: Is a situation which places you at an overwhelming disadvantage in your effort to protect yourself against immediate and serious bodily injury.

Factors include:

- Age: Offender is 22 years old and the officer is 55 years old
- Size: Offender is a 6'2" tall male; officer is a 5'8" male
- Strength: Offender is a strong muscular bodybuilder
- Gender: Offender is large, in shape male; officer is a petite female

- Numbers: You are outnumbered; 2+ attackers verse you
- Skill Level: The offender is a martial artist, boxer, weapons expert, etc.

> <u>Opportunity:</u> An attacker is immediately capable of injuring or killing.

An attacker needs more than just the ability to injure or kill you they need the opportunity to cause you harm immediately as in right here and right now. Realistically there are many people with the ability to hurt, injure, maim, and kill you but they do not have the opportunity because they are not near you to inflict harm. Two components to opportunity are <u>distance</u> and <u>obstacles</u>.

Distance:

The attacker needs to be close enough to you to actually be a threat. This can be dependent on the type of weapon used. An attacker with a baseball bat that who is 50 yards from you is not much of a threat. An attacker holding a knife who is 30 feet from you may be considered a lethal situation. An attacker holding a handgun who is 10 yards from you may be considered a lethal situation. An attacker holding a tire iron and cursing at you from across a busy parking lot is probably not a much of a threat.

Obstacles:

If there is a barrier that prevents the attacker from immediately being able to injure or kill you then he is not an imminent threat. If the attacker is behind a secure and solid locked door (no firearm) then he would not be a threat.

Officer Survival for Probation and Parole Officers

> **Jeopardy:** An attacker is displaying behavior in a way that a reasonable and prudent person would conclude he/she intends to injure or kill.

If the offender/subject has the ability and opportunity to injure or kill you and is acting in a manner that leads you to believe that the person will act out then you are in jeopardy. The attacker/offender/subject is acting in a way that leads you to the conclusion that you are in danger.

Jeopardy can be very subjective in that you have to determine if you are in a "potentially" dangerous situation or "actually" in a dangerous situation. You do not have the ability to know what a person's intent as you are not a mind reader. You can only judge the attacker by his appearance, demeanor, actions, and statements that would be consistent with intent to harm you.

Each day we are surrounded by people who have the *ability* to cause us harm, they have the *opportunity* to cause us harm but they do not have the *intent* to hurt us which means that we would not be in jeopardy. The question becomes: Are you in immediate danger? As an officer you need the ability to clearly and accurately articulate why you were in imminent danger which resulted in you being in jeopardy of your life. Specifically, you want to document and articulate what the attacker saying, doing, and acting that led you to the conclusion that you are in jeopardy.

> **Preclusion:** Officer assessment to determine if a different level of force is an option; and retreat is not possible.

Preclusion means that you must have done everything within your power to avoid having to use force without placing yourself or other innocents in jeopardy. Officers are expected to use force as a last resort, when no other options are available, and when tactical retreat is not possible.

Questions to consider:

- What options are available to avoid the need to use force?

- Can you safely retreat without placing yourself in further danger?

Graham v. Connor, 490 U.S. 386, 396-97 (1989)

When it comes to use of force, specifically excessive force, the landmark case is Graham v. Conner which is the national standard that is utilized today. In this 1989 case the U.S. Supreme Court declared use of force to be a Fourth Amendment issue subject to an "objective reasonableness" standard. The ruling states the following:

- The "reasonableness" of a particular use of force must be judged from the perspective of a reasonable officer on the scene, rather than the 20/20 vision of hindsight.

- The calculus of reasonableness must embody allowance for the fact that police officers are often forced to make split-second judgments – in circumstances that are tense, uncertain, and rapidly evolving – about the amount of force that is necessary in a particular situation.

- The "reasonableness" inquiry in an excessive force case is an objective one: the question is whether the officers' actions are "***objectively reasonable***" in light of the facts and circumstances confronting them, without regard to their underlying intent or motivation. [xxvi]

Based on this information, when attempting to determine the reasonableness of an officer's use of force it must be done under the following conditions:

1. Judge through the perspective of a "reasonable officer at the scene".

    This reasonable officer is expected to view the incident based upon similar circumstances and with the same or similar training and experience.

2. Judgment must be based upon the totality of the facts known to the officer at the time the force was applied.

    One cannot use hindsight or base judgment on information that is found *after* the conclusion of the incident.

3. Based on the facts known to the officer without regard to the underlying intent or motivation.

    What was the information the officer had that lead to his/her decision to use a particular level of force?

The proper application of what is reasonable takes into account the facts and circumstances of each particular case to include:

- The severity of the crime
- Whether the suspect poses an immediate threat to the safety of the officers or others
- Whether the suspect is actively resisting arrest or attempting to evade arrest by flight
- The fact that officers are often required to make split-second judgments

It is important for officers to understand the standards that Graham establishes. For example, an officer's use of force that ends up in litigation may end up being resolved in the safety and comfort of a courtroom long after the incident. An attorney may try to present information to a jury that was not known to the officer at the time that force was used against an offender. It is easy to look back in time with "hindsight bias" and state that the officer 'should have' or 'could have' done this or that. Such a maneuver is not right or fair to the officer. Fortunately, Graham does not allow this to happen. Additionally, each particular case is judged on the facts and circumstances of that incident. Information that was not known to the officer cannot be used against an officer after the fact. Being that such litigation often happens years after the incident it is imperative that officers write a well written use of force report that accurately and factually explains exactly why the officer used force and that the level of force used was reasonable based on the offenders/subjects actions.

Is a "Use of Force Continuum" Necessary?

This chapter has looked at the use of force continuum, use of force policy, and the U.S. Supreme Court decision of Graham v. Connor. There are dozens of different models of the force continuum being utilized and different force continuums may allow for different levels of force based on the exact same incident. If different force continuums allow for different responses from officers to the same threat some might view that as problematic. Even if there was one universal force continuum being used by all law enforcement agencies the question remains whether it would be a valuable tool considering that the Graham decision sets the standard with the 'objective reasonableness" standard. Additionally, with Graham v. Connor the court makes the following important statement:

> *"the test of reasonableness under the Fourth Amendment is not capable of precise definition or mechanical application."*

That is a powerful statement and in some respects it shows that use of force continuums attempt to accomplish exactly what the Supreme Court says is not possible. _There is no precise definition or mechanical application!_ As stated previously the court states that "*proper application requires careful attention to the facts and circumstances of each particular case.*" The utilization of a force continuum attempts to categorize an offenders/subjects actions and the officer's response into narrowly defined and very subjective categories of a rigid force continuum model that does not accommodate *the facts and circumstances of each particular case* as stated in Graham. The force continuum can become ambiguous and unclear for officers to determine the correct response to utilize. Additionally, are force continuums capable of incorporating the following factors?

- Totality of circumstances

    As a probation or parole officer you normally have access to a lot of information about the offenders that you supervise. It is important to completely and thoroughly read all the information at your disposal.

    - Variables – Fitness level of subject, skill level of subject (such as martial arts, boxing, weapons experience, professional fighter, power lifter, body builder, etc.), environmental conditions (innocent bystanders, extreme heat or cold, rain, snow, slippery ground, road hazards, etc.), height and weight of subject, gender, age, etc.

    - Special Circumstances – Mental state of subject, prior knowledge of subject, suspect under the influence of drugs or alcohol, multiple subjects, ground fighting, injury to officer, exhaustion of officer, etc.

When talking about the "Totality of Circumstances" the officer must consider and take into account these variables and circumstances. A use of force continuum can look at the *subject's actions* but it does not take into account if the subject is a 6'1", 210 pound mixed martial artist with multiple violent felony charges to include assault and domestic violence, has a diagnosis of anti-social personality disorder, and is a methamphetamine user. It can be easy to see how you end up in court for an allegation of excessive use of force where the offender's attorney shows an uninformed jury that you violated your department's use of force continuum as listed in policy. Yet, it is very possible that your actions were "reasonable" force according to Graham. As an officer you have to understand how a continuum can be a liability due to its rigid structure that does not allow for analysis of the totality of circumstances. Graham v. Connor is the standard yet your department policy that includes a force continuum can result in disciplinary actions being taken against you.

- The need for split-second decision making in circumstances that are tense, uncertain, and rapidly evolving

Departments should consider eliminating use of force continuums and instead focus officer training on the reasonable officer standard as determined in Graham. Remember, there are dozens of different versions of the force continuum being utilized with different outcomes but the legal standard rests with Graham v. Connor. Administrators and officers alike may gasp at the thought of eliminating the utilization of a use of force continuum. Let's look at a scenario to put this into perspective.

Probation Officer Smith is conducting a residential contact at an apartment complex on an offender at

9:30AM on a Monday morning. Officer Smith knocks on the offenders door which is the last apartment tucked in the corner on the bottom floor of the complex. The offender does not answer the door so Officer Smith starts to leave. As he is leaving a person in the next apartment opens the door and exits. He looks directly at the Officer Smith and by chance notices that it is his probation officer and he has an active warrant for his arrest (this offender is not the offender that Officer Smith was just attempting to make contact). The offender, Mike McDonald, has a warrant for absconding and has a history of assaultive behavior towards law enforcement. McDonald is 6'1" tall and weighs about 225 pounds with a muscular build. Offender McDonald takes one step toward Officer Smith directly looks him in the eyes, with clenched fists and says, "I knew you would be looking for me but I'm not going to jail today and you are not arresting me so let's get it on."

Based on this scenario, where would offender McDonald's actions fall on the force continuum? Unfortunately, the answer can vary depending on what force continuum that you are using and who you ask the question. One officer who is a defensive tactics instructor may use an empty hand technique, another officer may decide to use OC spray, while another officer may utilize an expandable baton. Different answers to the same scenario so who is correct? Using the objectively reasonable standard as set forth in Graham all of those responses could be "reasonable" based on the totality of the circumstances especially during an incident that is tense, uncertain, and rapidly evolving. The key from this exercise it to see that having a "Use of Force Continuum" does not provide the ability to neatly categorize what level of force an officer will use which applies to all officers or all situations. Again, Grahams states, **"the test of reasonableness under the Fourth Amendment is not capable of precise definition or mechanical application."** Force continuum models are rigid and inflexible while real incidents are fluid and dynamic not to mention potentially lethal. If you are an officer sitting as a defendant in a courtroom facing an allegation of excessive use of force would you rather be held to the standard of a "reasonable officer" or a use of force continuum that is rigid, inflexible, and fails to take into account a host of variables and circumstances? Do you want to go against a slick attorney who knows how to "work" the force continuum model against you? Remember, force continuums are rigid yet we have seen how different officers can utilize a different levels of force based on the same incident. An attorney will not use this incongruity to your benefit but to the benefit of his client (the offender) who may have received injuries. The attorney will convince a jury that you, as the officer, must follow the force continuum to the letter regardless if doing so places you in jeopardy. Such a process would be greatly improved by educating the jury on the "reasonable officer" standard as described in Graham v. Connor and show that your actions were reasonable based on the totality of circumstances. Graham does not even require that you use the "best" level of force; only that the level of force is reasonable. Also, Graham does not say anything about "escalating" or "de-escalating" force, it does not say that you must use "minimal force" and it does not say use of force must be "progressive" where an officer is required to start from the lowest level of force and work up to lethal force. Yet, such statements are generally found in use of force policy and force continuums. Again, this differs from the Graham standard.

Back to my statement that departments should consider eliminating use of force continuums. The question then becomes: Is this possible to eliminate use of force continuums? Yes, it is possible to eliminate the use of a force continuum model and the Federal Law Enforcement Training Center (FLETC) did just that in 2005. FLETC replaced the model by focusing on Graham v. Connor and by providing training on mental preparation and use of force report writing to improve articulation of why an officers response to a subjects actions were reasonable and based on the totality of the circumstances. Departments should consider eliminating force continuums from policy and instead include language of the Graham Standard:

An officer's use of force shall be objectively reasonable based upon the totality of the circumstances known or perceived by the officer at the time force was used.

Such language breaks the officer free from the constraints of a rigid force continuum that handcuffs officers to unrealistic expectations when officers are faced with dynamic and violent situations that require split second decision making. Officers need training, to include scenario based training, on what "reasonable force" is so that they make appropriate use of force decisions. Officers also need to be able to write documentation that clearly articulates that the officer's response to the subject's resistance was reasonable.

Each department will need to assess if it will utilize a use of force policy with or without a force continuum model as part of the policy. I suspect that it will be very difficult for many agencies to eliminate the utilization of a force continuum model. Change always seems to be difficult for people and organizations. Even departments that are considered progressive tend to change slowly and usually as a result of a negative incident that forces change to occur sooner rather than later.

I would ask that all probation chiefs and department directors in conjunction with their executive management team conduct the following exercise. Departments should answer the following questions to see if using a Use of Force Continuum is in the best interest of the department *and* officers:

1. Is a Use of Force Continuum beneficial to the department? If so, specifically document how?

    a. List positive attributes that benefit the department when utilizing a Use of Force Continuum.

    b. List negative attributes that the department faces when utilizing a Use of Force Continuum.

2. Does incorporating a Use of Force Continuum decrease or increase liability to the department? Provide specific examples that justify your answer.

3. Is a Use of Force Continuum beneficial to officers? If yes, how?

4. Does incorporating a Use of Force Continuum decrease or increase liability to the officer? Provide specific examples.

5. How would the department benefit from focusing on the "objective reasonableness" standard as in Graham v. Connor?

6. Is it possible for an officer to use force that is "objectively reasonable" yet violates the department's use of force continuum?

    a. Does the department view this situation as an inconsistency that needs to be corrected?

    b. If yes, specifically what steps does the department plan on taking to resolving such a situation?

7. Is training officers on Graham v. Connor and a Use of Force Continuum providing a consistent message on the application of force?

Officer Survival for Probation and Parole Officers

a. Are there any inconsistencies that negatively impact:

  i. Training
  ii. Application of force during an incident
  iii. Legal liability

Now I completely realize that departments do what is best for the department and not necessarily what is in the best interest of the officer. But, in this exercise I want the department's leadership to specifically see how policy that includes utilization of a use of force continuum impacts the officer. When such issues are viewed from a different perspective then change might occur a little easier and faster.

For many officers the thought of dealing with policy, procedures, administrative rulings, memorandums, codes, and laws relating to use of force is an unpleasant experience that one tries to avoid at all costs. You cannot have this attitude when it comes to use of force because the consequences that you face from improper conduct can have significant impact on you and your family. It can destroy a career, ruin a family, and lead to civil liability and/or criminal prosecution. Right now as an officer if you do not understand policy to include its application then you will surely not know what to do during a crisis. This will get you in serious trouble if you over react and it may get you dead if you under react. Become an expert on policy and its application. It may just save you in more ways than one!

EXERCISE 1: Use of Force

This exercise will focus on adherence to the standard as set forth in the United States Supreme Court decision in Graham v. Connor. In this exercise each scenario can be reviewed individually or in a small group where officers can discuss their thought process on how they determined what level of force is appropriate. In these scenarios "you" are the officer so the goal is to determine how you as the officer take into account all the factors that contribute to the scenario. If you are working through these scenarios in a group setting then complete the same scenario but change the officer to each member of your group to see how impacts the totality of circumstances and use of force options that may be utilized. Due to the variances and inconsistencies of the multitude of Use of Force Continuums that are utilized this exercise will not consider any force continuum model.

Officer Survival for Probation and Parole Officers

During this exercise keep the following information in mind regarding the Graham court decision:

Graham v. Connor

The Supreme Court of the United States regarding use of force:

- Objective Reasonableness

- Based on Totality of Circumstances

- The calculus of reasonableness must embody allowance for the fact that police officers are often forced to make split-second judgments – in circumstances that are tense, uncertain, and rapidly evolving – about the amount of force that is necessary in a particular situation.

- The "reasonableness" of a particular use of force must be judged from the perspective of a reasonable officer on the scene, rather than with 20/20 vision of hindsight.

- The test of reasonableness under the Fourth Amendment is not capable of precise definition or mechanical application.

- Its proper application requires careful attention to the facts and circumstances of each particular case, including the severity of the crime at issue, whether the suspect poses an immediate threat to the safety of the officers or others, and whether he is actively resisting arrest or attempting to evade arrest by flight.

In this exercise you will be provided a scenario. If necessary, you can modify the scenario to fit your specific needs such as changing an offender from an adult to juvenile or by changing any of the factors that are included in the scenario. Also, you are encouraged to complete the scenario as described and then repeat the scenario after changing some of the variables to see how the changes impact force options. Graham clearly states that use of force will be impacted by the totality of circumstances so it is important that either individually or as a group you determine what factors or variables influence your force decision. Such variables may include the following:

Subject:

- Physical size of subject
- Mental state of subject
- Skill level
- Demeanor
- Weapons
- Under the influence of drugs or alcohol
- Other

Officer:

- Experience
- Level of training
- Physical size
- Injury to officer or exhaustion due to a physical confrontation
- Other

Environmental:

- Innocent bystanders
- Crowded location
- Location – isolated, rural environment, urban environment
- Night time – low light, no light conditions
- Extreme heat or cold conditions
- Rain, snow, or slippery ground
- Road hazards
- Other

Other Variables or Factors:

- Number of subjects
- Is the subject resisting?
- Is the subject fleeing?
- Is the subject's actions *not likely* to cause death or serious bodily injury?
- Is the subject's actions *likely* to cause death or serious bodily injury?
- Proximity of police assistance/response time

Scenario Example A:

You have been assigned a new offender to your caseload and are conducting your first contact at his residence. You have no safety equipment on you other than a department issued cell phone and you are alone. You met the offender once previously in your office to review his terms and conditions of probation along with a behavioral contract. During your initial meeting with the offender he was very quiet, polite, and did not have much to say.

The offender's residence is a single story home in an upper middle class suburban neighborhood. The offender was sentenced to probation for an Aggravated DUI. He was watching football on a Sunday afternoon when he ran out of beer. He drove to the store and brought his 9 year old son with him when he was pulled over by the police for speeding. The result was an arrest for Aggravated DUI. The police did a blood draw and the offenders blood alcohol content (BAC) was .28 and he admitted to drinking about 13 or 14 beers. He has no prior criminal history but an assessment did reveal alcohol abuse. No other areas of concern were noted on the assessment.

As you exit your vehicle and approach the residence

you notice the offender is standing in his front yard which consists of grass. The offender is with two other adult males and they are each holding a 40 oz. can of beer laughing and talking very loudly. As you get closer the offender and his friends begin to verbally harass you. The offender says, "*Here comes my po*" and in a condescending voice he says "*are you taking me to jail for drinking a beer officer.*" The offender's two friends laugh loudly at his comments. One of the offender's friends yells to the officer, "*Do you want a beer we have plenty?*" Again, they all laugh very loudly and continue to taunt the officer.

Totality of Circumstances:

Subject:

- Male offender
- DUI offender who is drinking beer
- No other criminal history
- Assessment indicates offender is addicted to alcohol
- Verbal harassment

Officer:

- Alone
- No "safety" equipment other than a department issued cell phone
- Limited knowledge or experience with the offender

Environmental:

- Upper middle income
- Suburban neighborhood
- Daytime hours
- Clear weather

Officer Survival for Probation and Parole Officers

Other Variables or Factors:

- Presence of two adult male subjects who are consuming alcohol
- Both adult males are verbally harassing officer

Officer Response:

Based on the facts that have been provided with this scenario, the officer may use one or more of the following:

- Disengage
- Presence
- Verbal commands

Scenario Example B:

You are conducting an office day and have seen a steady stream of offenders all day long. You have no safety equipment on your person. It is the end of the day and you are exhausted. You have one last offender to see who is on parole for possession of methamphetamine and possession of narcotic drugs for sale. The offender has been on probation 3 prior times and was unsuccessful each time due to continued drug use. On his last probation grant he received a probation violation and was sentenced to prison for 5 years. The offender is 5'9" and weighs 160 pounds.

Currently, he has been on parole for 4 months. He is not working and sporadically attending substance abuse treatment. The offender has refused two drug tests with the treatment agency and is about to be discharged for noncompliance. This week you received two anonymous phone calls that the offender is using methamphetamine again. Your plan is to conduct a U/A in the office once the offender arrives.

Scott Kirshner

You are supposed to be off duty at 6:00PM and it is 5:55PM when the offender arrives. Most staff have already gone home for the day and there are only a few other officers in the office. There are no supervisors in the office.

You inform the offender, who is in your office, that he will need to do a U/A in the restroom right now. The offender stands up and becomes agitated. Based on his nonstop hand movements, picking at his face and arms, and rapid talking you suspect that he is using drugs. You attempt to verbally calm him down and de-escalate the situation when he suddenly does a strong two hand push hard enough to knock you backward into a wall. You bang your head against the wall and become dizzy from the impact. The offender then grabs a pen off a desk and raises it above his head as he comes at you in an overhead stab position stating, "*I'm going to fucking kill you*" as his face turns bright red in anger.

Other officers working in the building do not hear anything and no one seems to be coming to your aid.

Totality of Circumstances:

Subject:

- Male offender
- Possibly under the influence of methamphetamine
- History of failing probation
- Refused two drug tests with the treatment agency
- Sporadically attending treatment
- Offender physically pushed officer, grabbed an improvised weapon (pen) and verbally stated his intentions to kill the officer

Officer Survival for Probation and Parole Officers

Officer:

- No safety equipment on your person
- Tired, end of the day
- Officer physically assaulted
- Officer hit head on wall due to assault, is dizzy and injured due to impact

Environmental:

- Office setting
- Office is about to close for the day

Other Variables or Factors:

- No supervisor in office
- Minimal staff who do not hear assault and do no aid officer

Officer Response:

Based on the facts that have been provided with this scenario, the officer may use one or more of the following:

- Presence
- Verbal commands
- Empty hand control
- Less lethal
- Lethal force

Scenario 1:

An offender reports to the probation office. The offender has an active warrant for absconding, failing to attend sex offender treatment, having contact with juveniles under the age of 18, and failing to pay fees. He was sentenced to lifetime probation for 12 counts of sexual misconduct with a minor. The defendant spent 15 years in prison and was assaulted numerous times due to his crime. The victims ranged in ages from 6 to 13 years old. The offender is 54 years old, 5'7" tall and weighs 245 pounds. The defendant is very out of shape and extremely overweight. The offenders previous work history is 10 years as an accountant for a prestigious accounting firm.

He states, "*I know I seriously messed up but I'm ready to do what I need to do. Please do not arrest me or put me in jail. I'm begging you, please.*" You inform the offender that you will see what you can do to clear the warrant and have him wait in the lobby. You immediately notify your supervisor who tells you to call the police to have the offender arrested on the warrant and transported to jail. The police dispatcher informs you that there is a major police incident in your area and it will be a minimum of one hour before a police officer will arrive to the probation office. Your department does not transport offenders.

The offender is becoming very agitated in the lobby and the supervisor brings the offender back to your office. On your person you have OC spray and handcuffs. The offender sits quietly for about 5 minutes then jumps out of his chair demanding to know if he is getting arrested or not. The offender turns to you and screams, "*Are you taking me to jail? I need to know now. Don't you realize what they do to child molesters in jail! They will kill me.*"

Officer Survival for Probation and Parole Officers

Totality of Circumstances:

Subject:

1. _____
2. _____
3. _____
4. _____
5. _____

Officer:

1. _____
2. _____
3. _____
4. _____
5. _____

Environmental:

1. _____
2. _____
3. _____
4. _____
5. _____

Other Variables or Factors:

1. _____

2. _____

3. _____

4. _____

5. _____

Officer Response:

Based on the facts that have been provided with this scenario, the officer may use one or more of the following:

____ Presence

____ Verbal commands

____ Empty hand control

____ Less lethal

____ Lethal force

Officer Survival for Probation and Parole Officers

Scenario 2:

You are a juvenile probation officer assigned to a local high school. At the high school you have a very small office in the corner of the administration building. The school also has a School Resource Officer (SRO) who is a police officer. The SRO has a small office next to your office but he called in sick today. The principal and school counselor want you be involved in a meeting today with an offender who is assigned to your caseload who has excessive absences, failing grades, and is being disruptive in class. The school prohibits you from carrying any safety equipment including handcuffs. All you have is a department issued cell phone.

The offender is 17 years old and on probation for committing a drive-by shooting when he was 15 years old. He is 5'11" tall and weighs 185 pounds with a muscular build. The offender is a gang member and says the drive-by was his initiation into the gang. He has been on your caseload for 2 months. The offender spent 9 months in juvenile detention and was then released to a residential treatment facility for substance abuse treatment. While in juvenile detention he was involved in three fights. In one of the fights he assaulted a detention officer but claims it was an accident. He has a tattoo on his back that says "hardcore" across his shoulders. On his chest is a tattoo that says "Live by the sword, Die by the sword." He currently lives at home with his divorced mother who has prior criminal history of drug charges and prostitution. The offender's father is currently in prison serving a 15 year sentence for running a criminal syndicate, aggravated assault on a law enforcement officer, and resisting arrest.

The meeting with the offender is being held is a small conference room in the administration building. In the room is a rectangular conference table with eight chairs around the table. In the meeting are the following individuals: principal – 57 year old female, school counselor – 40 year old female, teacher – 26 year old male, probation officer –

you, and the offender.

Everyone sits down in a chair and the principal begins the meeting by telling the offender that they want to find out why he is disruptive in class and why he has so many absences that are negatively impacting his grades. The offender sat perfectly still in his chair with his hands under the table as he stared directly at the table. The offender never made eye contact with any of the participants. When asked a question the offender did not answer and continued to stare at the table. Despite efforts from the principal, counselor, and teacher the offender never moved. The principal continually attempted to get the offender involved in the meeting but all efforts were unsuccessful. The principal then raised her tone of voice to get the offenders attention and told him that he needs to start answering questions regarding his actions. At this point the offender began to breathe deeply and begins to clench his teeth. The principal continues to tell the offender he needs to start talking. Explosively the juvenile offender stands up while grabbing the chair he was sitting on as he swings it at the principal hitting her in the face. The principal is knocked out unconscious on the floor and bleeding profusely from her face. The juvenile begins swing the chair wildly at others in the room. He never said a word during the meeting.

Totality of Circumstances:

Subject:

1. _____

2. _____

3. _____

4. _____

5. _____

Officer Survival for Probation and Parole Officers

Officer:

1. _____
2. _____
3. _____
4. _____
5. _____

Environmental:

1. _____
2. _____
3. _____
4. _____
5. _____

Other Variables or Factors:

1. _____
2. _____
3. _____
4. _____
5. _____

Officer Response:

Based on the facts that have been provided with this scenario, the officer may use one or more of the following:

____ Presence

____ Verbal commands

____ Empty hand control

____ Less lethal

____ Lethal force

Scenario 3:

You receive a phone call from an ex-girlfriend of an offender who is under your supervision. She tells you that she was at the offender's apartment last night and that she saw a gun tucked between the cushions of the couch that is located in the living room. The ex-girlfriend said she has never seen the offender with a gun and did not know if it was his or if it belongs to someone else. She also said that he was acting weird and saying that things are not going well right now but he was never specific with what he was talking about. The ex-girlfriend believes that something bad is about to happen and she wants you to go to his place and check on him. She requests that you keep this information confidential and not tell him that you called. The ex-girlfriend is very worried and has a bad feeling.

The offender is on 3 year's probation for Theft of Means of Transportation. He has been on your caseload for 9 months without incident. He has no prior criminal history and no history of violence or

Officer Survival for Probation and Parole Officers

substance abuse. He completed community service, is current on all fees and has completely paid restitution to the victim. He did five random drug tests of which all had negative results for drug use. He has been employed with the same company for the last 5 years as a welder and his boss says he is his best employee.

You staff the case with your supervisor and ask if you and another probation officer can conduct a residential contact to see what is going on with the offender. The supervisor asks if you want to do a probation search instead but you said that you were not sure what the motive of the ex-girlfriend is and that the offender has been extremely compliant. You feel a search at this point is premature. Your supervisor approves your request and informs you to take all of your safety gear and be careful. You ask another officer to go with you to check on the offender. Both officers have a firearm, two spare magazines, tactical flashlight, baton, OC spray, radio, and body armor.

It is 5:45PM when you arrive at the offender's apartment. He just got home from work and did not expect to see you or your partner. The offender appeared very nervous and let both officers in the apartment after confirming that no one else was in the apartment. Your partner maintained control of the front door to the apartment which leads directly into the living room. As you are talking with the offender he glances at the couch where the ex-girlfriend said the weapon was located. You look at the couch and see a gun between the cushion. As you look at the offender he is looking directly at you and sweating profusely. You yell the word "gun" to your partner to let him know that you saw the weapon. The offender is now staring directly at you and is pale as a ghost.

Totality of Circumstances:

Subject:

1. _____
2. _____
3. _____
4. _____
5. _____

Officer:

1. _____
2. _____
3. _____
4. _____
5. _____

Environmental:

1. _____
2. _____
3. _____
4. _____
5. _____

Other Variables or Factors:

1. _____

2. _____

3. _____

4. _____

5. _____

Officer Response:

Based on the facts that have been provided with this scenario, the officer may use one or more of the following:

____ Presence

____ Verbal commands

____ Empty hand control

____ Less lethal

____ Lethal force

Scenario 4:

You supervise a specialized caseload of seriously mentally ill offenders. Today is your office day and you have handcuffs and OC spray on your person. It is 10:15AM and the office is fully staffed. An offender is in your office who is diagnosed with paranoid schizophrenia. You are both about the same size. The offender is on psychotropic medication which was verified through blood tests one month ago. The offender has a case manager through a state agency for his mental health issues and he has been doing well in treatment and has been compliant on probation.

The offender is on probation for 3 counts of Trespassing. The offender has a history of misdemeanor assault for hitting a crisis counselor who was attempting to help him during a psychotic episode. While in your office the offender appears to be distracted and keeps looking into space as if he is having hallucinations. You ask him if anything is wrong. Suddenly, the offender begins to scream and then tackles you to the ground where he repeatedly strikes you in the face.

Totality of Circumstances:

Subject:

1. _____

2. _____

3. _____

4. _____

5. _____

Officer Survival for Probation and Parole Officers

Officer:

1. _____
2. _____
3. _____
4. _____
5. _____

Environmental:

1. _____
2. _____
3. _____
4. _____
5. _____

Other Variables or Factors:

1. _____
2. _____
3. _____
4. _____
5. _____

Scott Kirshner

Officer Response:

Based on the facts that have been provided with this scenario, the officer may use one or more of the following:

    ____ Presence

    ____ Verbal commands

    ____ Empty hand control

    ____ Less lethal

    ____ Lethal force

Scenario 5:

You are making a residential contact on a juvenile offender who lives in a very remote location. It takes you approximately one hour on a fairly well maintained dirt road to get to his residence. Cell phone service ends approximately thirty minutes prior to arriving at the residence and you will not be able to receive cell phone service again until approximately 30 minutes after leaving the residence. You have a department issued radio but it will not work at this remote location. The only safety equipment that you are issues is OC spray and handcuffs. The average response time for the local sheriff is 45-50 minutes because the location is so remote. At night there are no signs or road markings.

The juvenile offender is a 16 year old male who is on probation for transporting 250 pounds of marijuana in his parent's truck. The juvenile said he did it for the money to help out his family because his father was recently laid off from his job. The offender states that he transported the drugs between two cities for a drug cartel and was paid $3000 per load. He states he made 6 trips before getting arrested. A member of the drug cartel assured the offender that he would only get a slap on the wrist if caught with the drugs because he is a juvenile. He has no prior criminal history, is a "C" average student in school, and smokes marijuana about twice a month but stopped since being place on probation.

You normally inform your supervisor when you are going to this offender's residence due to the remote location but you forgot to let him know this time and you are already out of cell phone range. When you arrive at the offender's residence only the offender and his father are home. You enter the residence and notice the juvenile offender has a huge black eye and that the left side of his face is bruised and swollen. You ask the juvenile what happened but he just looks at his father. The father tells you, "*It ain't not of your business so quit asking.*" You tell the father that it looks like he needs medical attention. The father says, "*Did you just not hear me? Now mind your own damn business before I kick you out of my home you damn cop!*" The father is now visibly angry and appears to be getting very mad that you inquired about the injury. The father is pacing back and forth in the living room with both fists clenched. He is mumbling something to himself that but you cannot understand what he is saying. You believe that the father abused the juvenile offender. You sense an uncomfortable level of tension and decide to leave. The father is now glaring at you with a 1000 yard stare.

Totality of Circumstances:

Subject:

1. _____
2. _____
3. _____
4. _____
5. _____

Officer:

1. _____
2. _____
3. _____
4. _____
5. _____

Environmental:

1. _____
2. _____
3. _____
4. _____
5. _____

Officer Survival for Probation and Parole Officers

Other Variables or Factors:

1. _____

2. _____

3. _____

4. _____

5. _____

Officer Response:

Based on the facts that have been provided with this scenario, the officer may use one or more of the following:

____ Presence

____ Verbal commands

____ Empty hand control

____ Less lethal

____ Lethal force

    By conducting these scenarios and changing different factors you can get a good idea how modifications to the scenario can change your response and the level of force that you use. Again, I must reiterate the importance of attending training that is dynamic, scenario based, and on-going. A thorough understanding of your safety equipment, department policy, judicial code, laws, and case law is absolutely critical. These may not be the most fun subjects to learn but failure to do so can have significant implications.

Scott Kirshner

Chapter 5: Office Safety

There is no imaginary safety bubble around your office that magically protects you from harm

It is not uncommon for many probation and parole officers to spend a lot of time working in the probation or parole office. They are having contact with offenders, completing paperwork, writing numerous reports, checking phone messages, filing faxes and other paperwork, calling treatment providers, schools, and employers. Essentially they are attempting to keep their head above water so that their caseloads are being properly supervised. New files are constantly being assigned as officers try to get rid of current files preferably with successful completions of the community supervision grant. Officers are constantly juggling responsibilities and tasks on a daily basis. You may arrive at work with a well-intentioned "to-do list" that gets put on the back burner because of one phone call stating that offender Smith, a sex offender, was just seen talking to children at a local elementary school. So much for your plans as you now have a new priority to address. Despite the change in plans your other tasks still need to be completed when you arrive back at the office. A typical day in the life of a community corrections officer. When referring to an "office" it is a place that probation or parole officers normally perform their work related duties and is typically owned or leased by the municipality, county, or state. This chapter will focus on officer safety in the parole or probation office environment.

In an earlier chapter it was established that some community corrections officers strictly work in an office environment and are prohibited from doing any field work. This means that all of the offenders on their caseload report to the probation or parole office on a regularly scheduled basis. Whether field work is authorized or not most officers have an "office day" in which offenders are provided specific reporting instructions such as:

> "You are to report to the probation office located at 123 N. 1st Ave., on the second Wednesday of each month at 2:15PM to meet with your probation officer."

But, there will also be times when offenders report

unannounced and you do not know the reason for their unscheduled contact. Many of these unscheduled contacts are a result of a problem that the offender is experiencing. Once again, your "to-do list" is put on hold and you are adapting to the call for assistance.

Department Responsibility: Physical Security Measures

Before delving into office safety from a probation/parole officer perspective it is important to first discuss physical security measures that departments must consider in order to make the office environment as safe as possible for all staff. Due to the enormity of the field of physical security this will be a very rudimentary overview of the basics.

Physical security is the utilization of a comprehensive security system designed to protect people, prevent damage or theft to assets, and to prevent unauthorized access to the building and/or property. This security process begins well before an offender, member of the public, or employee ever enters the building. These measures can include: physical barriers/site hardening, access control, security lighting, alarm systems, video surveillance, security personnel, and signage. The level of security that will be implemented varies depending on many factors such as the risk level, what is being protected, and what the threats are to both people and property.

Physical Barriers / Site Hardening

When possible the building should be surrounded by a barrier such as a metal fence that is 6-7 feet tall which creates a perimeter around the office and property. Such a fence will define territorial boundaries and discourage unauthorized access to the building or its property. It clearly sends a message that if you do not belong on the premises then you are to remain outside the boundary of this fence. Another benefit of a physical barrier is that is has the ability to direct people or vehicles into authorized areas.

Doors can be hardened by having a door frame that is structurally secure, using a steel plate for reinforcement, kick plates, and using set screws in hinges. Departments should consider using bullet-resistant windows to prevent someone from shooting into the office from a position outside of the building. While these windows are expensive they should be considered based upon the population of offenders that are being supervised.

Access Control

Access control is designed to only allow authorized personnel to enter the facility and to prevent entry of unauthorized persons. There are many different types of access control security systems. Many probation and parole departments utilize swipe cards or access control cards that are presented to a card reader to allow entry into the building and to access restricted areas within the building. Depending on your status you may be allowed full access to all areas within a building or you may be restricted only to certain areas. Many of these security access systems will document the date, time, and location of each place within the building that you accessed. It will also record when you attempt to access a location that you do not have access. Some systems will send an automated alert when you attempt to repeatedly access an unauthorized location or when you make a predetermined amount of attempts to access an unauthorized location. These cards can also prohibit your access to the building before or after business hours.

Weaknesses of these types of cards include losing the card, allowing unauthorized individuals to "tailgate or piggyback" and enter into a restricted area, or not ensuring that the door is closed and secure once you enter a restricted area. Lost cards should be immediately reported and deactivated.

Security Lighting

Security lighting provides deterrence, improved surveillance, and enhanced observation of the property. It is used to augment other security measures to create a comprehensive security system. All lights should be on continuously during hours of darkness. Lighting should be checked on a regular basis to ensure that they are working and that they have not been vandalized, tampered, or broken. Parking areas that are inside the secure perimeter should be well lit. There should be no place that is dark which could hide an unauthorized individual.

Alarm Systems

Probation and parole offices should be equipped with a monitored alarm system to detect unauthorized access. All doors and windows must be equipped to detect attempted or unauthorized access into the facility. Internal areas should be equipped with motion detectors. Restricted areas where officers have contact with offenders should be equipped with panic alarms.

Video Surveillance

Video surveillance provides a deterrent effect and can aid in the apprehension and conviction of suspects that engage in illegal activity. Cameras should cover the parking area, all entrances and exits, lobby, and internal areas as deemed necessary. Cameras must also have the ability to take quality video in low light environments. All video must be digitally recorded and have quality resolution.

Security Personnel

The utilization of security officers is an important aspect of a comprehensive and effective security system. Departments should use security officers to perform a security screening process of all offenders and non-employee personal that enter the facility to check for weapons and contraband. Security should also conduct daily patrols of the area to check for unauthorized individuals, contraband, property damage, and suspicious activity. Security officers are to be well trained and versed in policy and procedures as it relates to their job duties. It is highly advisable that security officers are armed with a firearm and less lethal weapons in order to properly respond to a worst case scenario such as an active shooter.

Signage

Signs should be displayed in appropriate locations stating any prohibitions. The perimeter fence should have signs stating "no trespassing" and "under video surveillance." All exterior doors should have a sign stating that weapons are prohibited and all persons and belongings are subject to search. Restricted areas within the facility should also have appropriate signs such as authorized access only or restricted area.

These basic physical security measures are critical to deter, detect, and delay unauthorized or illegal activity at the workplace. All staff, officers and non-officers, will approach safety and security more seriously if the department fosters a culture that takes safety seriously by implementing a comprehensive physical security system. Physical security of the property and building is a complex area that requires planning, expertise, and resources. What I have covered is the tip of the iceberg as physical security is a comprehensive subject. The focus will now shift to the officer's perspective.

Mindset

Too many officers believe that their day starts as soon as they enter the office or worse just before seeing their first scheduled offender contact of the day. Nothing can be further from the truth. You should consider yourself "on-duty", at least mentally, before you leave your residence. In chapter 2, I outlined the process that I use before leaving for work to mentally prepare and fight complacency. Even if you are a community corrections officer that never leaves the office to conduct field work or has no department issued safety equipment provided to you it is imperative that you mentally prepare and have the correct mindset before leaving your residence. At a minimum read the officer survival creed that you wrote in chapter 2 as a method to mentally prepare for the day and any threats that may present danger to your safety. Before you leave the safety and comfort of your residence the last thing you say to yourself is:

"I'm on duty now and I will remain in Condition Yellow."

You are now in the proper mental state to leave for work. Do not underestimate the importance of having such a mindset. In the information age and the availability of the Internet it is extremely easy for offenders to find out where you live. If you own a home many counties now provide free online access to your residential information which provides your home address. The offender can then type in your address to a host of websites that will not only provide a map of your address but a photograph as well. Even if you have this information redacted from the county website there is an assortment of other websites that have your information some for free while others will sell it to anyone very inexpensively. Remember, once your information is on the Internet it is impossible to remove as it will be stored and backed up on a server. Even if you do not own a home there are many ways to determine where you live. All an offender has to do is just follow you home.

Some officers will ask if this is really necessary. These officers feel that if they treat the offenders on their caseload with respect and dignity they don't need to worry about such topics. It is not only necessary it is critical that you have the right mindset. Do not assume (faulty assumption) that how you supervise a caseload will directly correlate to you being safe from an offender. It is about the offender and how they perceive you or your supervision techniques. You, as the officer, can never assume how an offender perceives your actions. What you consider "doing your job" they may consider a threat to their freedom. Do not take this lightly and do not make assumptions on how offenders perceive you or your actions. Your mindset is the prerequisite of all other activities that you perform as a community corrections officer. At the risk of sounding crass, if you cannot or are not willing to obtain this mindset then you may be in the wrong profession. Yes, it is that important! Having the correct mindset is not about being paranoid. It is about being open to the possibility that some offenders may want to do you harm for reasons that we simply cannot understand.

Once you leave your residence and you are in your vehicle it is important to scan your environment for anything that is out of the ordinary. Treat anything that is suspect as a potential threat to your safety. Do not ignore warning signs that you observe until you have verified that it is not a legitimate threat to your safety. Vary your routine on a daily basis by knowing alternate routes to and from work. Predictability is your enemy. When you leave the house the same time every morning and travel the same route it will be easy to determine your pattern. There are many cases of public officials being assassinated because they followed the same routine on a daily basis. Complacency and routine kills!

It is also a good idea to speak with your spouse and children of an appropriate age about the potential, yet remote, dangers of your profession. The manner in which you present this information to your family is very important because you do not want to cause panic or undue fear. There is no benefit to anyone if your spouse and children worry about your safety each day that you leave for work. Present this information in a relaxed, calm manner. Reiterate that the chance is remote that something would happen at your home. While this family discussion is precautionary let family members know that they are to immediately inform you of any situation that is out of the ordinary such as a suspicious person, vehicle, or package on or near your residence. If you are not available then discuss situations when the police should be notified. This is also a good time to teach your family about situational awareness which is a very beneficial skill. If you are facing a specific work related threat then inform your family of the threat, what precautions to take, and if there will be any changes from their normal routine. Communication in a way that is not alarming is key.

Community Corrections: The Office Environment

As indicated in an earlier chapter:

> **25.5% of assaults to officers occur at the office and these assaults are committed by offenders 41.3% of the time.**

Statistically speaking, the office is the second most dangerous place for you as an officer. The offenders who are reporting to see you as part of their community supervision requirement pose a threat to your safety. Yet, this is where officers spend much of their time and do so with a feeling of safety. There is a reason to take adequate safety precautions while working in the office environment. Let's examine the office environment from your arrival to your departure.

Office Arrival

As you approach the probation/parole office building it is important to scan the environment. Pay particular attention to anything or anyone out of the ordinary. Immediately report an unattended backpack or similar item to security or your supervisor. Observe offenders or other subjects who are in the parking lot or standing around the building especially if they are acting suspiciously. Most of the time these offenders are just having a cigarette or they are on their cell phone as they wait for their scheduled appointment. There should be clearly identified designated waiting areas both inside and outside the office where offenders may wait until their appointment time. These areas should be under video surveillance that is recorded. Offenders or other subjects should not be allowed to wander the premises.

Parking

Ideally, you will be provided a secure parking area for your vehicle that offenders will not have access. If you do not have such a parking lot or garage you must vary where you park each day to minimize routine. Unless you have a secure parking area avoid assigned parking spaces and never have your parking space identify you by name. Most community corrections offices will not have secure parking. As you exit your vehicle continue to be in Condition Yellow and maintain situational awareness. Do not have earphones in your ears as you listen to your iPod and try not to be on your cell phone. Note anyone that seems to be keying in on you. If you notice a person is paying too much attention to you then look at their hands to see if they are holding anything such as a weapon. Scan their clothing to look for signs of a hidden weapon. Also, notice if the person is dressed appropriately for the weather conditions. If necessary, alter your path to avoid this person. Be prepared to run for cover or defend yourself if the situation dictates. If an unknown subject is rapidly approaching your location and you cannot alter your path or you are unable to run then give a loud, clear, and concise verbal command of "STOP" for this person to stop their approach. If the potential threat stops then inquire as to what they want. If they do not stop then consider this person a threat and defend yourself accordingly. Not a good start to your workday!

Officer Survival for Probation and Parole Officers

Entrance/Exit

Community corrections staff should have a separate and secure employee entrance when entering or exiting the building. Secure doors should be opened with key card access that is linked to your department issued ID card. If your department ID card also functions as a key card used for building access it is important to maintain control of this card at all times as offenders may find a lost card or steal your card and then have unrestricted access to the building. Immediately report lost/stolen ID cards or key access cards. Unfortunately, many offices do not have key card access or a separate employee entrance so it is possible that officers, offenders, and members of the public will be entering the building through the same entrance. This is a less than ideal situation because an offender will know exactly which door you will be entering and exiting the building. Anyone who wants to do you harm just has to monitor this door and wait. They may even be able to accomplish this from the office parking lot especially if it is not monitored by security. Before you leave the building it is a good idea to scan the outside through a window or a glass door to see if you notice anything out of the ordinary. This can be an individual, a group of people, or a suspicious vehicle.

Identification Badges

All staff should be required to wear their department issued identification (ID) badges while in the office. Typical identification badges will include the department name, your name, photograph, and an expiration date. Because community corrections officers generally do not wear uniforms this is a visual way to identify an employee. ID badges must be worn appropriately to be an effective method for identifying staff. Staff often wear their ID badge turned around so that their photograph is not visible. This should not be an acceptable practice. It is not uncommon for officers to travel to different offices to pick up a file, meet a co-worker, or attend training. Your identification badge may be the only piece of identification that informs other employees that you are also an employee. In a small department this may not be an issue but some departments are very large where you may not know officers who work out of a different office. Also, it is possible that an offender creates a fake identification badge and turns it around to appear like an employee in order to access unauthorized areas. It should be the obligation of every employee to question anyone who is in a secured area without an ID badge.

Safety Equipment in the Office

When permitted by policy officers should wear department issued safety equipment in the office. Do not be lulled into a false sense of security and think that you are safe because you are in the office which is oftentimes considered your own territory. Your office environment does not come with an impenetrable safety shied that protects. Even if your facility has excellent security measures it is still possible for it to be breached. Safety equipment is only valuable if located in a place where it is readily available for use. Generally, this will be on your person where you have immediate access should a situation arise. Do not be concerned with how other officers perceive you or comments that they make to you regarding your safety practices. I have seen situations where one officer will give another officer a hard time about wearing their safety equipment in the office implying that the officer wants to be a cop or is scared of the offenders. This is unprofessional and should not be tolerated. Additionally, it shows the mindset of the officer who refuses to carry safety equipment. Departments that buy and issue safety equipment spend a lot of time, money, resources, and training to provide you this equipment. It does you no good in your desk, gear bag, the trunk of your vehicle, or worse, at home. It is important to maintain your safety equipment and immediately exchange any expired or faulty equipment.

Officer Survival for Probation and Parole Officers

Armed Security Officers

All community corrections offices should have armed security officers equipped with a firearm, Taser, OC spray, handcuffs, body armor, and radio. Many departments who utilize security officers are hesitant to provide these officers with firearms because of the expense, training, and perceived liability. Instead they may be provided a Taser or other less lethal item. Unfortunately, if a dedicated threat comes into the office with the intention of causing harm the security officer will not have a viable safety tool to provide an appropriate response if they are not equipped with a firearm. In fact, the security officer will more than likely be one of the first victims targeted and killed by the dedicated threat. A Taser, OC spray, baton, or other less-lethal item is no match for a dedicated threat brandishing a handgun, rifle, or shotgun. **Security officers must be more than a visual deterrent. They should be provided the necessary tools and training to effectively and efficiently stop a dedicated threat from wreaking death and destruction throughout the community corrections office.**

Magnetometers

Security officers should also have a magnetometer (metal detector) to check for weapons. Magnetometers detect the presence of metals but would not detect weapons that do not contain metal. Do not get pulled into a false sense of security because your office utilizes a magnetometer. Deadly weapons can be made from polymer plastics capable of inflicting deadly injuries. These items will not show up with a magnetometer, are easy to conceal, and can pass through a security screening process. Some companies make and sell "plastic" knives that are designed to pass airport security.

In reality many offices have no security and this is not acceptable. Yes, security is expensive but again there is a clear level of foreseeability considering the offender population being supervised. Fortunately, most offenders do not have any intention of shooting up an office or killing staff. Yet, this does not diminish the need for effective security measures. One incident resulting in the deaths of an officer or officers will surely result in significant, prompt, and costly security changes. Departments that are proactive instead of reactive can not only save money in the long run but lives as well.

If your probation/parole office has no armed security officers, magnetometers, or security screening process then you must assume that at least some offenders are bringing both weapons and contraband into the office. Typically, offenders will be waiting in a lobby area where you will greet the person and then escort him back to your office. With no security process in place it would be wise to first visually observe the offender in the lobby through a window to see if the offender is acting suspicious, wearing appropriate clothing based on the weather, and if there is any visual indication they are in possession of a weapon. Always perform a visual scan of the hands and waistband. When greeting an offender at the lobby door, but before allowing entry into the restricted area, ask the offender if he is in possession of any weapons, contraband, or prohibited items. Do this every time with every offender. At a minimum it lets the offender know that you are serious about safety. If the offender states he is in possession of contraband then follow your department's policy in your response. If your department does not have a policy for such situations one needs to be created.

The importance of an established protocol to include policies and procedures for handling prohibited items cannot be overstated. Officers need to have clear guidelines for the appropriate response to such situations. Training classes should include a scenario of an offender bringing in a firearm or other contraband into the office.

Prohibited Items

There should also be a policy that prevents anyone from bringing weapons, drugs, contraband, backpacks, luggage, food, drinks, and possibly even purses into the building. This means that such items will either need to be left in the person's vehicle or stored in a locker under the control of security. There should be signs posted that all persons entering the building are subject to searches including their belongings. If an offender or other person enters the building with a backpack or similar item but does not have a vehicle to secure it in then security must conduct a thorough search of the backpack before storing it in a locker. If the person refuses to submit to a search they must immediately be escorted off the property. If it is an offender that refuses the screening process then security must obtain the offender's name prior to being escorted off the property and inform the probation/parole officer of the incident. Security must be trained to look for weapons, explosives, and other contraband. Imagine the devastating result of securing a backpack in a locker that was not properly searched and the backpack contains an improvised explosive device. Such incidents routinely occur in other parts of the world and the United States is not immune from such violence. Think back to the devastation caused at the Boston Marathon bombing from a pressure cooker hidden inside of a backpack. There must also be a process to ensure that any item secured in a locker is removed by the owner when they leave the property.

Lobby Area

The lobby is a waiting area where offenders wait to be called by their supervising PO. On both the main entrance door and the door leading from the lobby to the restricted area of the building there should be signs posted stating:

> **NOTICE**
>
> No weapons allowed.
>
> All persons who enter this facility are subject to search.
>
> Any person who refuses to submit to a search of his or her person or personal belongings shall be denied entry.

The lobby should be visually checked by security in the morning and evening for any contraband, suspicious items, or items that were inadvertently left by an offender. The lobby should be under recorded video surveillance. Officers should have access to a security monitor for situations in which the officer wants to observe an offender prior to bringing him back into a restricted area. The door between the lobby and the work environment should have a lock that prohibits the offender from opening the door and gaining entry to restricted offices. The waiting area should be a relatively sterile environment with minimal items that can be thrown or utilized as a weapon. When possible, chairs and furniture should be bolted to the floor to prevent them from being thrown. When an offender enters the lobby they typically are required to sign-in and fill out some paperwork. Generally, there is a support staff worker available to assist offenders. There should be bullet resistant glass between the support staff and offender.

Working in Conjunction with Support Staff

Support staff are an integral part of every community

Officer Survival for Probation and Parole Officers

corrections office. In a sense they are the eyes and ears of the office especially when they interact with the same offenders on a regular basis. Support staff often has a feel of the office as well as offenders. If something in the office is not right or an offender is acting different than usual a member of the support staff will key in on this discrepancy. Support staff should immediately notify their supervisor of any activity that is out of the ordinary. If an offender is acting different the support staff person should immediately notify the supervising PO <u>before</u> the PO initiates contact with the offender.

Anytime an offender acts inappropriately with a member of the support staff team the supervising PO needs to address this issue with the offender along with potential consequences. Support staff wants to know that the supervising PO will not tolerate inappropriate offender behavior.

Support staff are typically responsible for monitoring sign-in boards to track the location of officers. Such boards provide the officers name and whether they are 'in' or 'out' of the office. If out of the office it may list that the officer is in the field, training, court, sick, vacation, etc. These boards should never be placed in a public location that an offender can view. This information needs to be for internal use only and located in a secure location not visible to offenders.

Support staff should never provide information about an officer to an offender no matter how innocuous it may appear. Again, do not underestimate the offender's ability to gather intelligence to obtain information on an officer with the goal of harming the officer. Additionally, offenders will work in conjunction with another offender to gain information on an officer. This may require that the offenders ask different employees seemingly innocent question but when put together the information provides a lot of detail. Support staff should never release the following information to an offender:

- Personal information such as birthday, family information about a spouse or child, type of vehicle the officer drives, etc. I once heard a support staff employee tell an offender, "Officer Smith is off today to celebrate his 35th birthday." Too much information for an offender to know!
- That you are off due to illnesses, injury, training, or vacation.
- Schedule – never provide information as to the current or anticipated location of the PO or return time back in the office.

When in doubt do not provide information and take a message. Less information is definitely best in this situation.

Office Code Word or Phrase

Each community corrections office should have a code word or phrase to alert co-workers of an emergency situation or a potentially escalating incident. All staff members must know and understand the process to follow including officers, supervisors, support staff, counselors, educators, or any other employee that works in the building. The word or phrase should be unique and not common otherwise it may inadvertently trigger a response. When a code word or phrase is "activated" it is important that staff members respond and not assume that it was an accident, a drill, or a test. Failure to respond can lead to officer or employee injury. Remember, not all offenders will yell, scream, or carry on loudly in the office which would allow other staff members to hear and immediately respond. Some offenders will remain calm, cool, and collected yet say something that is threatening or abusive without raising the volume of their voice.

Escorting Offenders

When retrieving an offender from the lobby you must then escort him either back to your office, interview room, or other location. When your contact is complete you will also escort the offender back to the lobby to exit the building. Always ensure that the lobby door is closed and secure when you retrieve the offender from the lobby and when the offender is leaving. Never leave an offender unattended in a restricted area even for a brief period of time. The first time that you meet with an offender you should inform him of the escort process. Tell the offender that every time he reports to the office he is to always walk in front of you and you will follow him to your office or interview room. Never walk in front or beside the offender that you are escorting as this is not a tactically sound position if the offender decides to do you harm. When the offender is in front of you it is a good practice to create some distance between you and the offender. Even with this distance it would not take long for an offender to turn around to attack you. Always maintain situational awareness, observe the offenders body language, visually scan the hands and waist area, and be ready for a potential surprise attack.

First Office Contact with a New Offender

The first meeting with a new offender assigned to your caseload is one of the most important contacts that you will conduct. Do not rush through this initial contact and give it your undivided attention. Do not answer your cell phone, work phone, or allow other people to interrupt you unless it is an emergency. This is an opportunity for you to set the tone of your supervision style so that the offender knows exactly what is expected. From your initial introduction you want to exhibit command presence and be professional, polite, and respectful. Remember, the offender is sizing you up to see what you will be like and if you exhibit any weaknesses. Also, it is a very common practice for offenders to talk with other offenders that you supervise to see what you are like as a PO. Offenders will gather intelligence to see if you are going to be a "push over" or a "hard ass." Remember, the offender may be a transfer from another PO who had a very different supervision style than you have so you will need to set the tone for your supervision style.

Topics to cover during your first office contact:

- Escort – describe the escort process as previously discussed.
- Terms & Conditions of Community Supervision and Behavioral Contract – Review terms & condition in detail so that the offender completely understands the requirements of community supervision. Have the offender sign a behavioral contract. Review potential consequences for non-compliant behavior.
- Arrest – inform the offender that you will not provide advance notification that you are going to initiate an arrest. You can inform the offender that anything negative that happens while he is on community supervision is a direct result of something the offender did or did not do.
- Warrant - inform the offender that you will not provide notification that you will be requesting a warrant for his arrest.
- Support Staff – offenders are to be informed to treat support staff respectfully.
- Skills – Ask the offender if they have specialized training or skills in martial arts, firearms, explosives, or other related skills.
- Hobbies – Inquire about the offenders hobbies and note if any are a potentially a safety risk.

If you receive a transfer case from another PO inevitably you will have an offender say something like, "but my last PO never made me…" It is important to quash this immediately as it is a form of offender manipulation. In a professional manner clearly let the offender know that your supervision style is different than the previous PO who supervised you.

Case Management is Part of Officer Safety

Juvenile and adult probation and parole officers generally have access to an abundant amount of information regarding the offenders assigned to their caseload. When a new case arrives you get a file with information that may include: terms and condition of supervision, prior criminal history both adult and juvenile, presentence investigation report, probation/parole assessments, medical records, psychiatric records, psychological records, employment history, prior prison/detention disciplinary history, etc. I cannot stress enough the importance of completely reading all new files to obtain as much information as possible regarding the offender that you are going to be supervising. All too often an officer will receive a new file and only look at the crime that the offender is being supervised and maybe review the presentence report. It is too easy to make assumptions and think: It's just another burglary, possession of dangerous drugs, theft, aggravated assault, domestic violence, child neglect, sexual assault, manslaughter, elder abuse, drive by shooting, arson, fraud, embezzlement, driving under the influence, drug trafficking, human smuggling, possession of marijuana or fill in the blank with a crime. We lump all offenders into a non-existent framework and prophetically assume that the offender will somehow neatly fit into all of our preconceived notions. ***This is called complacency, which leads to false assumptions, which can lead to inappropriate supervision, which can lead to officer safety issues, which can lead to serious injury or death...of you!*** Read the file. All the information contained in the file is there for a reason. I know that there are many reasons you can come up with justifying why you can't read the file. You are too busy, you have too many cases, you have training classes to attend, you read the files and never find anything of concern, no one else reads their files, the information is old and outdated, etc. Rationalize all you want but the reality is that you are responsible for knowing the information in the file and you are responsible for administering appropriate supervision strategies. Failure to know the content of the file puts you at risk. Let's review items in a file that may provide valuable information:

Terms and Conditions of Supervision

The Terms and Conditions of Supervision often provide information on what will be required of the offender during the supervision grant. This may include:

- The criminal offense committed by the offender. Again, it is important to refrain from having a preconceived notion about the offender based solely on the listed criminal offense. Additionally, many offenses are plea bargained down from a more serious offense.

   > One time I supervised a case where the offender was sentenced to probation for "Disorderly Conduct" but the original charge was "Aggravated Assault with a Deadly Weapon." Quite a difference between those two charges! The offender stabbed his girlfriend in the back with a knife. He received a plea agreement which lowered the original charge from a very serious and violent crime to disorderly conduct.

- Special terms or conditions such as: sex offender, domestic violence, mental health, DUI/Drug court, etc.
- Prohibitions such as: curfew, not to possess weapons, not consume alcohol or drugs, etc.
- Maintain full time employment or attend school.
- Pay restitution, fines, and fees

Prior Criminal History both Adult and Juvenile

The best predictor of future behavior is past

behavior. Valuable information can be obtained from an offender's criminal history. For example, you may have an offender who is on probation for possession of marijuana which is a relatively minor offense. Yet, this offender's criminal history shows convictions for domestic violence, simple assault, and aggravated assault. This information should raise some red flags and lead you to take precautionary measures when dealing with this offender who has a documented record of violence. From an officer safety perspective this is information you want to have prior to supervising the offender.

Police Report

Many officers skip reading the police report and instead read the presentence investigation report. In my view this is a serious mistake. The police report provides much more detailed information than a presentence report. Oftentimes the police report specifically details the offender's actions during the arrest which can provide you with valuable information such as if the offender resisted arrest, made threatening statements, used racial slurs, or was under the influence of drugs or alcohol. Police reports often provide text of the offender's interview or interrogation. Such information can provide you with important insight into the offender you supervise. Take the time to read police reports.

Presentence Investigation Report

The presentence investigation report is a report written by a probation officer and used by the court to assist with the offenders sentencing. The presentence report will briefly summarize the police report but leaves out significant amounts of detail (as it should.) The presentence report includes information on the offender's criminal history, probation or parole assessment, family history, school history, employment history, substance abuse, and provides a sentencing recommendation for the court to consider.

Violation Reports

If the offender was previously on probation or parole and was violated due to noncompliant behavior then the violation report may provide valuable information as to the offender's actions that prevented him from being successful on community supervision status.

Probation/Parole Assessments

An accurate and valid assessment is the foundation of an effective supervision plan with the goal of obtaining pro-social, law abiding behavior. The assessment should clearly report problematic areas that need attention. Common domains covered in assessments include: vocational, educational, social, residential, alcohol, drugs, mental health, attitude, and behavior. Problematic areas are to be addressed in a case management plan.

Medical Records

Typically medical records are only provided if there is a circumstance in which the offender states that he cannot abide by one or more terms and conditions of supervision due to a medical issue. In such cases the offender will either sign a medical release of information or provide medical documentation to support his complaint. Even with medical documentation do not make an assumption that the offender will not pose a safety risk. For example, an offender may say that they cannot work because they injured their back. Yet, the offender looks and acts as if there is no issue with his back.

During your last residential contact the offender was lifting heavy boxes while cleaning out his garage. The medical documentation from his doctor states he cannot work, lift any item over 10 pounds, he is not to sit, bend, or stand for longer than 45 minutes at a time, etc. It is not uncommon for offenders to "doctor shop" until they find a doctor who will provide them the documentation, or medication, they want.

Medical documentation can also include information on communicable diseases such as HIV/AIDS, hepatitis, tuberculosis, meningitis, etc. Officers should always use universal precautions when indicated. According to the concept of universal precautions, all human blood and body fluids are treated as if known to be infectious for HIV/AIDS, hepatitis, and other bloodborne pathogens.

Psychiatric and/or Psychological Records

These records can provide you with mental health history, diagnosis, treatment plan to include patient progress/regress, and medications.

Employment History

An offender's job can provide insight into special skills that they may possess. For example, you may have offender's on your caseload that are professional fighters, gunsmiths, prior military with explosives experience, former law enforcement officers, security camera installer, pharmacist, etc. These offenders may have a unique skill that could be used to harm you either overtly or surreptitiously. Many offenders enjoy talking about their job so ask probing open ended questions to obtain relevant information. Document relevant information that may relate to officer safety issues.

Prison or Detention Disciplinary History

Detention facilities and prisons, whether adult or juvenile, are very regimented institutions. It is good practice to obtain the disciplinary history of an offender who is locked up in such an institution. If they cannot behave appropriately in a secure and confined facility it may be an indicator that the offender will not behave appropriately on community supervision. Typically the disciplinary action report will provide the violation date, type of infraction, and verdict. When reviewing the disciplinary history look for patterns. Oftentimes, there is disciplinary action shortly after the offender arrives to the facility. This seems to be due to a period of adjustment for new offenders that break the rules in the beginning of their sentence but then complete the remainder of their sentence with no more disciplinary action. Other times, offenders have an ongoing consistent pattern of disciplinary problems.

Office Set Up and Configuration

Probation and parole departments vary dramatically and there is little standardization especially when it comes to office set up for offender contact. Office set-up can include the following:

- Interview Rooms
- Office with a single officer
- Office with multiple officers
- Cubicles
- Large open area that has between 10-15 officers. The open area has a desk for each officer and chairs for offenders

Unfortunately, officers typically have to make do with whatever type of configuration is possible based on the office structure and layout. Oftentimes, buildings are used that were not designed with offender contact in mind and are built in a way that is not conducive to a safe office environment. In such cases you have to do the best with what you have. Typically, the only fix is renovating the office to create an environment that is safe for officers to conduct offender contacts.

Following are some general principles and guidelines to follow when configuring an interview room, office, cubicle, or other set up to conduct offender contact.

- Officers should have access to a duress alarm/panic button should a contact escalate to the point where additional assistance is needed.
- If your office is an interview room or single person office the safest configuration is for the officer to sit closest to the door in case a rapid exit is needed. Maintain a clear path to a door or exit that does not require you to have to pass by the offender.
- Doors should be removed from offices. If this is not possible, doors are to remain open at all times during offender contact. Doors should not have locks to prevent the offender from taking the officer hostage and then locking the door. The idea is to minimize a hostage/barricade situation.
- Lights must remain on at all times during offender contact. Consider having the light switch on the outside of the office so that an offender does not have the ability to turn off the lights.
- Other officers and staff should be able to maintain visual contact on you and the offender. If you have an office or interview room there should be an unobstructed window so that others can see what is occurring.
- Other officers and staff should be able to hear you if you utilize a code word or phrase.
- When possible, the chair that the offender uses should be bolted or secured to the floor so that it cannot be used as a weapon of opportunity.

- Extra chairs, furniture, or office equipment should be kept to an absolute minimum and secured to the floor. This will prevent objects from being moved to block a door during a potential hostage situation.
- Walls should be painted white to maintain an easily identifiable environment.

Office Content

Offices should be a sterile environment with two specific areas of concern regarding the availability of:

1. Personal information
2. Potential weapons or weapons of opportunity

In an office environment it is your responsibility to protect your personal information from offenders. Offenders should never have access to items such as family photographs, calendars with notes, magazines that have labels with your home address, mail with your home address, business cards of your doctor, personal email address, etc. Too many times I have seen officers who "decorate" their office with items that are completely inappropriate such as:

- Bulletin board hanging in the office which has family photos to include spouse, children, and pets. Even pictures of pets should be discouraged. An offender may not want to physically hurt you but they may injure or kill your pet to get revenge on you for a perceived injustice. Remember, it really isn't too difficult for an offender to find out where you live. And, the offender will be able to figure out some of your work schedule especially because he knows you will be in the office on office day. This provides an opportunity for an offender to break into your home to steal your belongings, kill your pets, or destroy your home.
- Picture frames on the officers desk with her partying at a bar with friends.

- Post-it notes with appointment dates, time, and location listed for all to see.
- Personal emails laying on the desk.
- Training confirmation letter with date, time, and location of the training.
- Work related telephone list on the desk similar to a rolodex. Oftentimes these contain items that are not for public release so offenders should not have access to this information.
- Women who leave their purse "hidden" under their desk and then leave the offender in the office alone. Offenders should never be left alone in the office even for a brief period of time. I knew an officer who stepped out of her office for less than 20 seconds to obtain a piece of paper off the printer. During this brief time span the offender stole her cell phone out of her top desk drawer.
- Candles, aromatic incense, and burning aromatic oils.

These situations are unacceptable and provide the offender with too much access to your personal life. Fortunately, the majority of offenders may never use any of this information to harm or stalk you. But, there is always the very real possibility that an offender does have evil intentions. Having photos of your family to include children and pets provides details about you that should remain confidential. The department should provide you the ability to lock personal items in a locker or in a desk that locks. Purses should always be locked and never hidden under a desk or in an unlocked draw as many of the offenders you supervise will have a history of burglary, theft, and shoplifting. They are aware of your hiding places.

The availability of "weapons of opportunity" should also be of concern to all officers. A weapon of opportunity is anything in your immediate environment that can be used by an offender to injure or kill you. Examples include: stapler, pens, pencils, metal hole-punch, scissors, coat rack, broom handle, hot liquids, hazardous materials such as cleaning chemicals, flammable liquids, fans, space heaters, candles, books, metal garbage can, electrical/power cord extension, glass or metal bottles, ceramic or glass mugs, picture frames on desk or wall, desk lamps, potted plants, bottles of anti-bacterial liquid containing alcohol, etc. All of these items should be kept away from offenders. Your desk should be clear of all objects. When having an offender sign a document use a pen that is shorter in length than normal to prevent him from using the pen to stab you.

The majority of office days and office contacts with offenders will go without incident. Each work day that you complete without incident reinforces your belief that the next day will be the same. This is the gradual process of complacency. While most days are uneventful and maybe even a bit boring it is critical to start each shift with the perspective that today may be the day that is something goes wrong. This is the mindset that "safety conscious" officers maintain. Such officers do not let routine lead to complacency. It only takes one incident to change your life dramatically and you will not get advanced warning. An offender is not going to call you with the following warning:

> "Officer Smith, I am not happy with you. Actually, I have never liked you. So, today when I report to your office at 2:15PM, I am going to stab you in the left eye with the pen that you will graciously provide me to sign some stupid document. Then I am going to repeatedly stab you in the neck until you die. Once you are dead on the ground like a lifeless sack of potatoes I am going to spit on your bloody face. By the way, anyone one of your crappy co-workers who tries to save your sorry ass will get the same treatment. See you at 2:15PM sharp. And I do mean sharp! Have a great day and I'll see you soon."

Sarcasm aside, if you were to get some type of advanced notice I'm sure it would lead you to do something different to prevent such a situation. Realistically, you don't get an advanced notice so be prepared all of the time with every offender that you supervise. Do not let the routine of the daily grind suck you into becoming a complacent officer. Routine can be a harmful trainer if you do not combat its insidious impact on a daily basis.

Attire

When it comes to dress use common sense and dress in a manner that is professional, appropriate, and provides you the ability to run or fight if necessary. If your department has a dress code policy then you will be held to that standard. Too many times I have seen officers dress in a manner that is not conducive to the work environment or offender contact. At any time you may be involved in a situation where you are required to either run to get away from an offender or fight off an attack from an offender. One way to solve this problem is for departments to institute a uniform for officers that foster a professional appearance yet allow the officer to be able to function in an officer survival capacity. A standardized uniform consisting of a long or short sleeve polo shirt along with cargo pants is an option. A button down shirt can be substituted for the polo shirt. Uniform shirts should have a department logo, badge, or insignia that is easily identifiable. While in uniform, officers should wear their duty belt along with any issued safety equipment to include handcuffs. Another benefit of a uniform is that it will be easier to identify who the officers are during a critical incident. While you may know officers who work in your particular building you may not know officers who work at a different location. A uniform will make these officers more easily identifiable.

Without a uniform following are some basic guidelines for your dress and appearance:

- Hair – avoid long hair that can easily be grabbed and pulled. Officers who have long hair should wear it in a style that prevents it from being grabbed.

- Earrings – avoid wearing earrings that are long or hang low on the ear that can easily be grabbed.

- Piercings – officers should not have any visible piercings that can be aggressively pulled out. These include nose rings, eye piercings, and lip piercings.

- Clothes – should be clean and pressed to present a professional appearance. Clothes should be conducive to running and fighting.

- Neck Ties – avoid wearing a neck tie which can be used as a strangulation device. Even clip on ties should be avoid because they can easily be pulled off and then used as a strangulation device.

- Shoes – should be comfortable, non-slip, and provide the ability to run. Female officers should not wear high heels due to the difficulty of running in this type of shoe. Additionally, open toe shoes, sandals and flip flops should not be worn.

Functionality should take priority over fashion. Working in a probation or parole environment is not the place to make a fashion statement.

Active Shooter in the Probation/Parole Office

Active shooter incidents are becoming increasingly more common and it seems that no one and no place is immune. Victims can be infants, children, adolescents, elderly, male or female, or physically or mentally challenged. These horrific incidents can occur at: schools, government facilities, military bases, movie theaters, private businesses, malls, shopping centers, hospitals, medical offices, nursing homes, religious facilities, day care centers, and public sporting events. Many active shooter incidents result in a high death count and numerous serious injuries.

> An **_Active Shooter_** is an individual or individuals who are actively engaged in killing or attempting to kill people and the shooter is not contained, controlled, or restricted in his actions.

The typical weapon of choice is a firearm which can include a handgun, rifle, or shotgun. The shooter may carry more than one firearm or multiple types of weapons. Oftentimes the shooter will carry hundreds of rounds of extra ammunition. The shooter may attempt to lock or barricade doors to prevent escape. Generally, the shooter will not stop their rampage until the shooter:

1. Is killed by law enforcement
2. Commits suicide
3. Gives up when confronted by law enforcement with overwhelming force
4. Is controlled by a group of non-law enforcement individuals usually at great risk to their safety
5. Runs out of ammunition or has a weapon malfunction that they cannot clear or do not know how to clear

One important aspect when referring to an active shooter incident is that it is happening now and any delay in stopping the shooter will generally result in additional deaths and injuries. If there was ever a situation where time is of the essence it is an active shooter incident. When a shooter is actively engaged in hunting down and killing people any delay in waiting for a police response means that people are going to die or be seriously injured. Departments who have armed probation/parole officers and/or armed security officers must seriously consider developing policy, procedure, and training to allow officers and security the ability to respond to the active shooter. Failure to do so will result in death as demonstrated in past active shooter incidents around the world. An active shooter situation is one time where it is appropriate for a probation or parole officer to be a first responder. Departments must embrace this concept and provide quality training to their armed officers so that they are provided all of the necessary tools and training to respond. Failure on the part of a department means that additional officers may needlessly be killed by a shooter if the department prohibits a response from armed officers. Probation and parole departments can work in conjunction with local police to obtain necessary input, guidance, and training.

Currently, the mantra for dealing with and responding to an active shooter situation for non-law enforcement is to: Run > Hide > Fight. There is a short yet high quality video available on the internet titled, *"Run > Hide > Fight: Surviving an Active Shooter Event,"* discussing this process. Essentially, the first and best option is to run and get out of the area especially if you are not an armed officer. If you do not have the ability to run or it is not safe then hide. The last option is to fight. This is only done when the options of running and hiding are no longer available.

The following information is from the Run > Hide > Fight video[xxvii].

Run:

- If there is an escape path, attempt to evacuate
- Evacuate whether others agree or not
- Leave your belongings behind
- Help others escape if possible
- Prevent others from entering the area
- Call 911 when you are safe

Hide:

- Lock and/or blockade the door
- Silence your cell phone
- Hide behind large objects
- Remain very quiet

Your hiding place should:

- Be out of the shooter's view
- Provide protection if shots are fired in your direction
- Not trap or restrict your options for movement

Fight:

- Attempt to incapacitate the shooter
- Act with physical aggression
- Improvise weapons
- Commit to your actions

The Run > Hide > Fight video is an excellent concept especially for people who are not trained to deal with active shooter situations. But, a probation/parole office may have armed officers and/or armed court security that have the ability to respond. Departments should evaluate the possibility for providing Active Shooter Intervention training to these officers. Granted, having probation/parole officers respond to an active shooter situation is one that is normally outside the scope of their duties. But, this is a true life or death situation in which seconds matter. Failure to take action will almost certainly result in a higher death count. Deaths that may have been avoided with properly trained community corrections officers.

When law enforcement officers arrive on scene of an active shooter their first priority is to stop the shooter. Everything else must wait including aid to injured victims even if the injury is life threatening. Police officers will not know who you are or whether you are the shooter trying to mix in with the crowd. Following are items to do when police arrive on scene:

- Remain calm
- Follow all commands and instructions provided by the police
- Raise your hands above your head and keep your fingers spread
- Keep your hands visible at all times and do not have any object in your hand
- Avoid quick or sudden movements and do not reach for items on your body
- Do not grab or hold onto a police officer
- Avoid pointing, yelling, and screaming as the scene will already be chaotic
- Do not attempt to stop a police officer

<u>If you are an armed officer be sure that your weapon is holstered when police arrive</u>. In an active shooter situation I do not recommend that you hold your badge or ID in your hand in an attempt to identify yourself as a probation/parole officer. Be like everyone else and have your hands in the air with nothing in them and fingers spread apart. Police officers are trained to look at the hands. There will be so many people around that holding your badge in your hand will attract an officer's attention to you. If you have an object in your hand the responding officer then must identify what is in your hand and if it is a threat to anyone's safety. In the police officers mind you are a threat until proven otherwise. This means that you may be handcuffed and secured. Do not resist and follow all commands and instructions provided by the police. The bottom line is that you need to keep your hands empty. Because probation and parole officers generally do not wear a uniform the police officer may not know that you are a community corrections officer. Keep in mind that the responding police officers will be under stress and will be putting their life at risk attempting to neutralize the active shooter. Do not do anything that will make the police officers job more difficult.

Virtual and Satellite Office

Many probation and parole departments encourage officers to maintain a presence in the community by having a "virtual or satellite office" where probation and parole officers supervise offenders in the community close to where the offenders reside. Virtual offices are sometimes referred to as satellite offices. Technically there is a difference between the two but most agencies use the terms interchangeably therefore I will not go into the specifics that make up the differences between the two. For consistency I will use the term virtual office. These alternative work locations are touted for increasing productivity and efficiency all while saving money for the department. In some cases departments completely close down their traditional office as a cost savings benefit. Virtual offices force probation/parole officers out of the traditional office environment to a more mobile arrangement where they essentially work out of their vehicle or an alternative location with the assistance of a cell phone, laptop, and borrowed space. Virtual offices can be at locations such as: police stations, court buildings, schools, community centers, treatment agencies, hospitals, fire stations, libraries, churches, YMCA's, etc. Community locations should be utilized for <u>limited</u> offender contact. The virtual office should not become an "unofficial" office. When acquiring space at a virtual office all that is generally needed is an empty office or space that meets safety criteria for the probation/parole officer to utilize one or two times per week for offender contact.

Officers who are removed from a traditional office environment to a virtual office often feel a sense of anxiety as they lose their "home base" of operations. Working as a virtual officer requires some essential qualities for the officer to be successful. These qualities include:

- Ability to work independently
- Time management skills
- Organizational skills

- Ability to prioritize
- Flexibility and adaptability
- Communication skills
- Remain focused
- Officer safety practices

There will be a transitional period as officers adapt to not only a new work environment but modification of their practices. To be effective departments must facilitate a smooth transition from an office environment to a virtual environment. Each department must have clearly defined policies and procedures for utilizing a virtual office that considers officer safety, community safety, and officer accountability. Additionally, the location being considered as a virtual office must approve the allowance of probation or parole officers to use their facility. Some places may welcome community corrections officers while others will never entertain the thought of "criminals" reporting on their property. Some organizations do not want to take any liability risks.

Virtual Office Considerations

Officer Safety:

Any approved location must meet well defined criteria regarding what constitutes an acceptable "virtual office" in relation to officer safety. Officer safety should never be sacrificed for a presence in the community.

Community Safety:

Safety to the public is paramount and some virtual office locations will not be suitable based on the crime committed by the offender. For example, sex offenders should never be permitted to report to a location where children are present such as a public library, YMCA, or community center. Such a location would clearly not pass a "headline test" and should never occur.

Officer Accountability:

Since officers will not be in a traditional office environment there must be a fidelity management tool to ensure that officers are completing assigned tasks. Out of sight should not be out of mind.

Two of the most common reasons for having a virtual office are:

1. Increased community presence which provides positive public relations while being more convenient for offenders to report to a virtual office which is often closer to the offender than a conventional office.
2. Departments no longer have to rent or lease office space because officers no longer work out of a traditional office.

Other benefits of being a virtual officer include:

- Increased interactions with offender, family, schools, treatment providers, employers, and community
- Provides additional opportunities to develop positive neighborhood relationships
- Increased opportunities to utilize local resources such as treatment agencies and potential employers for offenders
- Ability to network with stakeholders such as local police officers, schools, business owners, etc.

But, virtual offices can pose safety related problems that must be considered and officer safety must never be compromised for the sake of public relations, offender convenience, or cost savings.

Virtual Office Safety Considerations

When transitioning from a traditional office environment to a virtual or satellite office it is imperative that safety remain a paramount consideration when choosing a location. Departments must have a process in place to review all potential locations to verify if it is safe for the officer and so that potential risks to the community is minimized. Following are safety related concerns that departments must consider when approving the use of a virtual office:

Officer Survival for Probation and Parole Officers

1. Location

    a. Overall, is the location a safe place for officers to have contact with offenders?
    b. Is the officer in an isolated location away from other people?
    c. Are the community corrections officers permitted to wear all of their safety equipment to include a firearm if the officer is armed?
    d. Has the probation/parole department contacted the police department to see what crimes, if any, have occurred at the location?
    e. When driving to the office is the facility in a location where there is only one way in and one way out such as on a dead end street?
    f. Is the parking lot well lighted?
    g. Is the internal lighting satisfactory?
    h. Is there a lobby or waiting area for offenders?
    i. Is there an emergency exit available to both officers and offenders?
    j. Is there a way to ensure that offenders will not have any contact with victims that may be employed at the location?
    k. Is the location next to a school or other prohibited area where a sex offender on your caseload may report?
    l. The probation/parole department must obtain prior approval from the appropriate party for using the location.

2. Safe Office Set-Up

    a. Is it possible to have the office set-up and arranged in a manner that is safe for the officer?
    b. Is there more than one exit available in case the officer needs to rapidly leave or escape an attack?

c. Is the location capable of being secured in case of an emergency or if the officer needs to leave for lunch or to use the rest room?
   d. Will the department provide basic first aid supplies?

3. <u>Communications</u>

   a. Does the officer have access to a department issued cell phone, department issued radio, or a landline phone?
   b. Will the cell phone or radio receive consistent and reliable reception at the location?
   c. Is it possible to have an emergency button/panic alarm installed?

4. <u>Security</u>

   a. Is there any on-site security?
      i. Is security an internal security team or contracted through a private company?
      ii. Is security issued safety equipment such as OC spray or a firearm?
      iii. Is security responsible for conducting security screenings on all visitors?
         1. If yes, do they use a magnetometer or an x-ray machine?
         2. Do they have authority to conduct pat down searches?
         3. Will security work in conjunction with community corrections staff and inform the officer of any problems with offenders?
   b. Is the location under video surveillance?
      i. If yes, is it recorded?
      ii. If yes, how long is the video surveillance kept before it is deleted?

       iii. Are security video cameras located both outside and inside the facility?
       iv. If the department needs to obtain a copy of the surveillance tape will this be possible and what is the process?
       v. If the location does not have video surveillance can the department install its own surveillance at its own expense?

5. <u>Privacy</u>

    a. Does the community corrections officer have an environment where offender contact can be conducted in a private, yet safe, manner?

    Each department must individually evaluate the suitability of a virtual/satellite office to determine what is an acceptable location. Again, officer safety must never be compromised for convenience or cost reductions. Officers should never be allowed to work alone in a virtual/satellite office for safety reasons. When working in a virtual capacity one of the main considerations is how offenders are going to be screened for weapons or other contraband *prior* to being seen by the probation/parole officer. Departments must consider securing a virtual office in a location that already has a security screening process. Without this process an offender can easily bring weapons or other contraband to the contact. If an offender has intentions to harm the officer it will be easy to carry out such intentions if there is no security screening process to check for weapons. If an offender is a dedicated threat he will search and find the weak link with security and that will be the area that is attacked. This is why virtual/satellite offices must be adequately vetted for officer safety. If it is not possible to find a suitable virtual office for offender contact in the community that utilizes a security screening process then other options must be considered but it must be clearly stated that these options are less than optimal.

Office Arrests

One of the most dangerous and high-risk duties an officer will perform is the arrest and detention of an offender. Office arrests are preferred to field arrests as you have the ability to control more variables. Obviously, arrests will only be a factor for officers that have powers of arrest. Some departments can perform arrests but do not have a method of transporting offenders to jail while other departments will do the offender transport and complete the booking process.

There are a host of reasons to conduct an office arrest based on offender non-compliance such as positive drug tests, possession of a weapon, new criminal charges, violating special terms and conditions such as sex offender or domestic violence, evidence that the offender is going to abscond, etc. When conducting the arrest it is best to staff the case with your supervisor for approval. Also, plan out the details of the arrest to ensure that there are enough officers available if the offender resists, know specifically where in the office that the arrest will occur, complete violation paperwork ahead of time, ensure that you have all of your safety equipment, know who is transporting the offender (you or police), etc. Consider if the local police department needs to be involved. Anytime that there is information indicating that the offender has a weapon or is going to resist arrest then obtain police assistance.

Optimally, the arrest process will be as follows:

1. As the supervising PO, you obtain reason to arrest the offender.
2. Staff the case with your supervisor and obtain approval for the arrest. This step should be completed well before the offender is to arrive to the office.
3. Complete violation paperwork prior to the offender's arrival.

Officer Survival for Probation and Parole Officers

4. Gather an arrest team to assist with the arrest. If police assistance is required you will make the call once the offender arrives to the office.
5. The arresting PO must notify support staff that the offender is going to be arrested and they are to immediately report any suspicious behavior to you. Support staff is NOT to inform the offender of his impending arrest.
6. The offender will sign-in as usual and wait in the lobby area.
7. If police are going to be called to assist with the arrest then the supervising PO will now place the telephone call for police assistance. When making this call it is critical to provide relevant information such as the reason for the arrest, prior criminal history, if you suspect that the offender will have a weapon, prior history of violence, if the offender appears to be under the influence of drugs or alcohol, etc. If you are requesting a specific number of officers in anticipation of resistance then inform the dispatcher. Always obtain an estimated time of arrival for police arrival as you may need to stall the offender. When the police arrive they should enter through an employee entrance preferably out of sight from the offender. If the police are going to be delayed have the offender complete paperwork saying that you need updated information. Or you can tell the offender you are running late and will be with him as soon as possible.
8. If police assistance is not required then have the arrest team stage to assist with the arrest.
9. Ask support staff if the offender is acting unusual.
10. If police are assisting with the arrest then provide a briefing on the offender. When the arrest team is ready you will meet the offender in the lobby and properly escort him to an empty office. It is best to arrest the offender in an empty room so that the offender cannot use any objects as weapons of opportunity.

11. Once in the "arrest room" inform the offender he is under arrest and immediately apply handcuffs to secure him. Now is not the time to debate or talk but to show command presence. Immediately applying the handcuffs on the offender is the priority. Once the offender is secure you can state the reason for the arrest and then complete a thorough search. Do not engage in talk at this point until the offender is secured. The longer the offender remains unsecured the more potential there is that he will resist arrest. Remember, once the offender is told that he is under arrest he may decide to resist which is why it is critical to handcuff immediately. It also helps to have a lot of officers present to show overwhelming presence to the offender. If the offender decides to resist he is aware that there are a lot of officers available and his chances of a successful resistance are significantly diminished by the sheer number of officers.
12. Once the offender is handcuffed and searched then you can transport to jail, detention, or if a parole violator back to prison. Always be sure to visually check the vehicle used for transportation to look for possible contraband that was left in the vehicle from a previous transport.

Avoid arresting offenders in the lobby because there will be other offenders who may cause problems. Also, you do not want to cause a scene that offenders will talk about with other offenders.

Conclusion

Far too often officers become complacent when working in the probation/parole office environment. Even if you have security procedures in place the human element of the offender can decide to initiate violence against you or others. It is important to stay in Condition Yellow, maintain situational awareness, fight complacency, and accept that something can go wrong.

Officer Survival for Probation and Parole Officers

Officer Safety Considerations - OFFICE

Following are considerations that all officers should be cognizant of when having contact with offenders in an office setting.

Office Considerations:
Are you in the proper mind-set and are you ready for the unexpected?
Are you in Condition Yellow?
Did you inspect all of your safety equipment prior to leaving your residence?
Do you have equipment either on your person or have access to such equipment? (*Remember, in an emergency situation you will not have enough time to access equipment that is not on your person*)
Are you visually scanning the environment as you approach the front lobby?
Do you visually scan the offender upon contact?
Does the offender have prohibited items? If "Yes", What are you going to do with such items?
Do you escort offenders correctly?
Do you know where all exits are located?
Do you know where cover and concealment are located?
During offender contact is the offender in a location that blocks your exit in an emergency?
Is all your personal property in a location that the offender cannot see?
Is the offender asking you personal questions or questions that are not appropriate?
If in an interview room with an emergency button do you know where the button is located?
If conducting an "in-office arrest" do you have enough assistance?
If conducting an "in-office arrest" do you have handcuffs on your person?

If conducting an "in-office arrest" who is transporting the prisoner? (You or police department)
If conducting an "in-office arrest" do you have a department vehicle available and ready to transport?
Is your paperwork written out ahead of time?
Are you more focused on paperwork, your computer, or what the offender is doing?
Never schedule to meet an offender at the office during non-business hours.

Chapter 6: Field Safety

Conducting fieldwork is one of the most dangerous aspects of the job for a community corrections officer with 92% of officers killed in the field

Working in the field, often alone, to monitor and supervise convicted felons is a dangerous aspect of being a community corrections officer. Conducting fieldwork means that you are having offender contact in such locations as the offender's residence, place of employment, school, treatment provider, half-way house, placement facility, etc. Such contacts can take place in a busy urban environment or a very remote area. Contacts are made during the blistering heat of summer and the cold windy days of winter. Contacts are done during the day and in some cases during the middle of the night especially with high-risk offenders. The offenders that you contact are statistically the ones who are going to do you harm and who pose the greatest threat to your safety.

Mindset

When conducting fieldwork your mindset is a critical safety component. Unlike a piece of gear that you attach to a belt your mindset must be an integral part of who you are and helps to determine what you are made of especially during a violent encounter. The topic of mindset comes up repeatedly because of its importance. You may forget to carry a piece of safety equipment but there is no excuse to not have a winning mindset. When it comes to mindset you have it with you all of the time and you can't forget it at home or the office. If you have taken the time to properly develop your mindset you should take comfort in knowing that it is with you all of the time. Never underestimate this aspect of your training and never underestimate the importance of having this unseen tool with you. If you skimmed through chapter 2 and failed to do the exercises then go back now and re-read that chapter. More importantly complete the exercises; all of them. At this point in the book you must have written your own "Officer Survival Creed." I will not accept excuses from you for not having an officer survival creed. Do not read any further until you have your own written personalized officer survival creed. Do not be lazy, do not accept complacency, and do not allow false assumptions to allow you to rationalize or minimize the threat. The possibility for violence being directed at you is real. If you do not want to create an officer survival creed for yourself then do it for your family and loved ones. Following is my officer survival creed from chapter 2:

Officer Survival Creed:

- I will not allow routine to lead to complacency.
- I will remain in Condition Yellow.
- I have trained for the worst case scenario; oftentimes at my own expense.
- I will never give up and winning is not enough; <u>I WILL prevail.</u>
- I owe it to myself, my family, my friends, my co-workers and my department to not only survive but prevail.
- I am prepared to respond to any act of violence that is directed toward me or a fellow officer.
- I know and understand department policies relating to the use of force.
- I am confident in my officer survival knowledge, skills, and abilities that I honed and I have trained hard to prevail in a violent encounter.
- I will use lethal force if necessary and understand that if I am forced to take a life today it is because the adversary left me no other option.
- I am confident and prepared.

If you cannot take the time to develop and write down your own officer survival creed then this is not the book for you. This book is for officers who not only want to win but prevail when violence is directed at them. ***It is one thing to want to prevail in a violent encounter it is another to prepare for that encounter.*** If you are not willing to prepare then give your copy of this book to an officer who will. It just might save their life one day.

Community Corrections: Fieldwork - The "Offenders" Environment

When conducting fieldwork it is important to remember that you are now in the offender's environment. You are in their territory, their neighborhood, and their home. For many offenders this is empowering. The offender may believe that he "controls" this domain and you are an unwelcome guest. In the mind of an offender he may believe that you control the office but the field is not yours to control. In an earlier chapter we learned the realities of officers killed and assaulted in the line of duty:

Officers **Killed** in the Line of Duty:

Of the 13 officers killed in the line of duty 12 of these officers or 92% were killed in the field.

Officers **Assaulted** in the Line of Duty:

50% off assaults to officers occurred in the field and the offender was responsible for the assault in 41.3% of the cases.

These statistics clearly demonstrate that conducting fieldwork is dangerous and requires a safety oriented officer with a winning mindset. Officers must remain in Condition Yellow and maintain situational awareness of their environment. Failure to know who is in your immediate environment and what is happening around you can result in a disastrous outcome. In the field you must maintain your focus and concentration. Now is not the time to be thinking about all the work that is piling at the office, the fifteen voicemail messages that you have to return, problems at home, how you dislike your supervisor, how you keep getting new cases assigned to you, how you are overworked and underpaid, etc. Put all of these distractions on hold until you have completed your tasks in the field.

Each field contact must have a clear objective and should never be done just to complete a required monthly statistic. Field contacts should be meaningful and productive. Each department will have its own contact standards regarding how often an officer must have face-to-face contact with an offender in the field. A low risk offender may only be seen one time every three months while a high-risk offender may be seen anywhere from 1-4 times per week. Let's look at an example where you are required to see an offender one time per month for a face-to-face contact which lasts 20 minutes. For this example we will assume that the month has 30 days. There are 43,200 minutes in a 30 day period. When you calculate a 20 minute contact with an offender you are only seeing the offender for .046% of the time that they are in the community.[xxviii] This equates to less than ½ of 1% of face-to-face contact with the offender in the community! The majority of offenders are capable of being on their best behavior for this extremely brief period of time. When contacting an offender for such a brief period of time it is important to make the contact meaningful. Following are reasons to conduct offender contact in the community:

- Verify compliance, monitor, and supervise offenders
- Verify residence
- Verify employment
- Verify school status and progress
- Verify attendance at treatment groups
- Meet with collateral contacts such as spouse, family, friends, employer, neighbors, acquaintances, etc.
- Provides an opportunity to see the environment that the offender lives. For example, is the residence clean, how the offender interacts with collateral contacts.

Community corrections officers should avoid confronting the offender with issues of non-compliance such as positive drug tests, missing treatment groups, violating terms or conditions, etc. These matters are best discussed in an office environment where the probation/parole officer has more control. It is important that officers avoid the following situations in the field:

- Do not get in the middle of a domestic violence situation. If one develops during a contact do not try to become the peacemaker or referee. It is not uncommon for both parties to turn their aggression on you.
- Do not get into a power struggle with an offender or family member
- Do not get into conflict in the field

In the profession of community corrections avoidance of potential safety problems is the best course of action. No one benefits from purposefully placing yourself in a dangerous situation with the risk of becoming seriously injured or killed. If you are ever in a situation where you think another person is in jeopardy of beings seriously injured or killed then you have to decide whether to intervene if there are exigent circumstances. If the situation is not an emergency then retreat and call the police. One thing you must never do is leave and not call the police if there is a chance that another person may be in danger. You have an obligation to call the police and have a police officer, at a minimum, conduct a welfare check.

A residential contact may start out fine but once in the residence the situation can rapidly change and become unsafe or dangerous. Following are times when you should immediately leave when conducting a home contact:

- Verbal threats from:
    - Offender
    - Family member to include spouse, children, parents, or other relatives
    - Friends

- Aggression from dangerous animals
- Body language from the offender that is not appropriate or typical for the offender
- Weapons: knife, gun, rifle, explosives, etc.
- Weapons of opportunity: baseball bat, golf clubs, letter opener, etc. These items may not be a problem unless their presence is in conjunction with other indicators that the residence is no longer safe.
- Presence of drugs, drug paraphernalia, or alcohol.
- Evidence of a crime is present, i.e. methamphetamine lab
- Anytime that you feel unsafe

Working with a Partner

Of all the safety precautions that a community corrections officer can utilize, working with a partner is one of the most effective and proactive steps that can significantly increase officer safety. According to the Federal Judicial Center[xxix] an officers odds of being attacked are reduced by:

70% with 1 additional officer present, and
90% with 2 or more additional officers present

Working with a partner provides the following benefits:

- Additional visual presence of another officer
- Early warning of a potential problem that you do not notice or because your attention is purposefully being distracted by an offender or others
- Additional situational awareness
- Ability to utilize the "Contact/Cover" principle

There is one significant factor that cannot be overstated when choosing a partner. Find a partner that is both safety conscious and skilled. Your partner must have an unbeatable mindset, know department use of force policy, have excellent verbal de-escalation skills, be proficient in defensive tactics, be proficient in firearms (if armed), and understand officer safety principles and tactics. Simply having a warm body with you is not enough and can cause more problems than it prevents. Get a well skilled partner which significantly makes both of you much safer.

Contact / Cover Principle:

The <u>Contact Officer</u> handles the contact with the offender as the <u>Cover Officer</u> provides over watch from the offender and other subjects who are present or may arrive latter.

The <u>Contact Officer</u> is responsible for interacting with the offender and does the talking.

Random and Unscheduled Contact vs. Scheduled Contact

Overall, random and unscheduled field contacts tend to be more meaningful in that the offender is not expecting his probation/parole officer to arrive at their residence. Random contacts provide the officer an opportunity to see what the offender is doing and how he will react to an unscheduled contact. Such a contact is also more risky for the officer especially if the offender is engaging in activities that violate their terms and conditions such as drinking alcohol, using illegal drugs, having unapproved contact with a victim, etc. In such cases you can never assume how the offender is going to respond when you unexpectedly show up and catch him in the act. Such contacts can be classified not only as high-risk but unknown risk. In your mind you may view the violation as very minor violation but the offender may view it as an imminent risk to his freedom. If the offender thinks that he is going to be arrested or taken back to prison he may attempt to flee the scene or he may fight you for his freedom. Make no assumptions and be ready for anything to happen. What you believe is a "regular" or "routine" contact may be viewed very differently by the offender you are contacting especially when caught in the act of non-compliant behavior.

Scheduled contacts should be used sparingly and generally occur when there is a specific reason for meeting with the offender. For example, you may be delivering a travel permit to the offender for an out of state trip, you need the offender to sign a document, or you are meeting with a juvenile and his parents to discuss how community supervision is going. While scheduled contacts are generally considered low-risk they are still also considered an unknown risk. For example, an offender may request that you come to his residence at a specific time under a guise to conduct a normal task. Yet, the offender may use this as a ruse to injure or kill you.

Some officers use the term "surprise" contact when referring to an unscheduled contact. I do not use the term "surprise" because it give the impression that you are actively looking to "catch" the offender doing something that he should not be doing. If this is the case then the appropriate term to use is surveillance. Conducting surveillance on an offender is a perfectly legitimate tool to use when indicated.

Field Contact

Random and Unscheduled	Scheduled
- Higher-Risk Contact Unknown Risk Contact	- Lower-Risk Contact but still unknown risk
- Can find offender engaging in non-compliant behavior	- Offender tends to be on their best behavior
- Opportunity to see home environment as it may normally be situated	- Home environment may be cleaned and sterilized of inappropriate items prior to contact
- Collateral contacts may be around especially family members	- Friends will typically not be around for a scheduled contact
- Offender may be anxious, agitated, and surprised by the contact	- Offender may be more relaxed because the contact was scheduled
- Can provide more information about the offender who was not expecting to see his probation/parole officer	- Never assume a scheduled contact will be a safe contact

Basic Officer Safety Principles for Conducting Field Work

1. Slow Down or Stop When Necessary

    - Do not rush into a situation
    - Remember: Nothing is routine
    - Use your senses such as vision, hearing, and smell

2. Perceive

    - Scan the environment for potential or actual threats to your safety
    - Observe the environment before proceeding to your contact
        - Who is around?
        - What are people doing?
        - Do you observe any suspicious activity?
        - Are there signs of illegal activity?
        - Do you notice gang graffiti or drug paraphernalia?
        - Are you being observed?
    - Maintain "situational awareness"
    - Actually "see" what is in the environment
    - Target Identification – Is what you are "seeing" a threat to your safety?

3. Analyze

    - What is happening?
    - Weigh your options

4. React

    - React appropriately based upon the situation
        - Make contact with offender
        - Utilize verbal de-escalation skills
        - Leave
        - Tactical disengagement

- Observe from a safe distance
- Call 9-1-1

Dangerous or Potentially Dangerous Contact:

There is no field contact so important that you should willingly place yourself in harm's way. If you believe that making the contact is not safe or places you in jeopardy then immediately leave.

Thoroughly document all safety issues and notify your supervisor.

Call 9-1-1 if indicated for criminal activity.

It is highly recommended that you develop a relationship with different police officers who patrol your supervision area. Patrol officers know the area very well and can provide valuable information and intelligence especially relating to officer safety issues. The relationships that you develop must be a two way street and you must be willing to provide relevant information that can aid the police. An absolutely critical element of your relationship with police officers is that you never divulge confidential or law enforcement sensitive information to offenders. Doing this will immediately destroy your relationship with local law enforcement officers or worse it can put officers lives in danger. When building a relationship with local law enforcement it is important to:

- Attend shift briefings
- Provide warrant bulletins of offenders who have an active warrant
- Conduct ride-alongs which provides an excellent opportunity to develop a professional relationship and you can obtain valuable information regarding the community that you supervise

- Educate police officers to your role as a community corrections officer. Many police officers do not understand what authority you have, your capabilities, and what type of training that you receive. Many police officers incorrectly believe that you have similar training like they receive in the police academy.

Also, do not hesitate to develop relationships with federal law enforcement officers from agencies such as: Federal Bureau of Investigations (FBI), Drug Enforcement Administration (DEA), Bureau of Alcohol, Tobacco, Firearms and Explosives (ATF), and U.S. Marshals Service.

Utilization of Field Book

Field books are portable notebooks or binders that contain relevant information on each offender that you supervise. There are many varying opinions about the use of a field book as some officers like them while others do not use them at all. There is no right or wrong way to utilize a field book and they can take time to keep current and up to date. If you choose to use a field book it is important to develop a method so that you actually use it and keep it up to date. A lot of confidential information may be placed in your field book so it is critical that you do not lose this book. Also, follow all department policy regarding the use of confidential or law enforcement sensitive information such as an offender's criminal history. Following is a list of information that you may choose to keep in your offender field book:

Offender Information Face Sheet

Includes: name, date of birth, social security number, other law enforcement identification numbers such as a FBI number or state ID number, driver's license number, home address, home phone, cell phone, pager, email address, gang affiliation, tattoos, scars, or other identifying information, recent offender photo (offender photos should be updated every 6 months or when the offenders appearance changes), type of vehicle offender drives to include license plate number and picture.

Residential Information

Includes: address, who the offender lives with to include dates of birth and social security number when possible (note relationship to offender), layout of the residence to include a diagram (see Figure 1), map to the residence, aerial photo of neighborhood from Google Earth, Google Maps, MapQuest or other service. Aerial photos provide a birds-eye view of the neighborhood, allows you the ability to zoom in for more detailed information, and provides you with familiarization of the area. Keep in mind that some aerial photos may be dated and no longer accurate. When looking at aerial photos you want to pay attention to what is in the photograph, if there are any potential problems or hazards that you can identify, what is your plan of approach, and what is your emergency "get out" plan in case something goes wrong. Do not underestimate the value of this information. It does take some extra time to put into a field book but it may provide very useful information.

Officer Survival for Probation and Parole Officers

Residential Diagram

Information

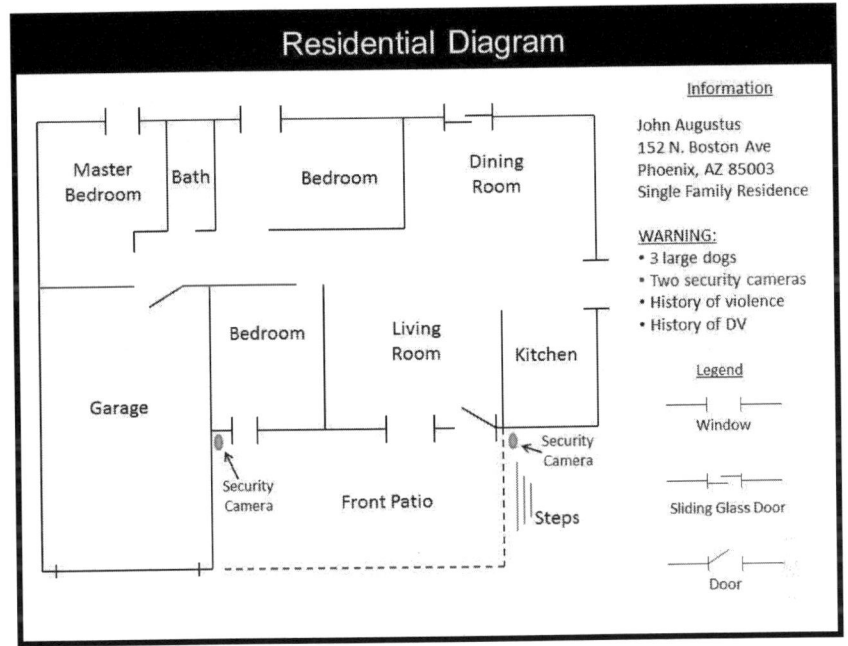

John Augustus
152 N. Boston Ave
Phoenix, AZ 85003
Single Family Residence

WARNING:
- 3 large dogs
- Two security cameras
- History of violence
- History of DV

Legend
- Window
- Sliding Glass Door
- Door

Figure 1: Residential Diagram

Terms and Conditions of Community Supervision

This will inform you what crime the offender committed to be on community supervision along with any specialized terms such as: Sex offender, domestic violence, gang, mental health, drug court, intensive probation, etc.

Assessment and Case Management Plan

Many assessments provide a graph highlighting problematic areas. This is a good reference to carry in your field book along with any behavior contracts and case management plan.

Officer Safety Information

One of the most critical parts of your field book is information pertaining to any officer safety issues. This information should be highlighted and easily visible for review. In this section you may include information on: history of violence, prison disciplinary record, history of drug use, weapons violations, vicious animals, special skills such as boxing or mixed martial arts, security camera posted outside the residence, gang affiliation, terrorist affiliation, threats made to police officers or community corrections officers, relevant criminal history, etc.

Warrant Bulletin

Carry warrant bulletins for all offenders on your caseload that have an active warrant for their arrest. These can also be distributed to law enforcement officers that you have a relationship.

When an offender transfers to another officer because he moves out of your supervision area be sure to take out their information from your field book and send a copy to the new supervising officer. The new supervising officer may not use a field book but you should always provide all relevant information that you have obtained. Also, keep a copy for your records in case the offender moves back to your area of supervision. I also recommend keeping a copy for your records even if the offender is successfully discharged or violated and sent to jail or prison. File these records in a cabinet alphabetically and purge them every few years or if you move on to a different assignment. The information that you comprise may be of value in the future.

Field contact can be broken down into three distinct phases

1. Pre-Contact: The time period prior to offender contact.

2. Contact: Actual contact with the offender and/or collateral contacts.

   If the offender is not home then this would be an attempted contact.

3. Post-Contact: The time period after offender contact is complete.

Pre-Contact

The more prepared you are for conducting field work the more confident and focused you will be to function effectively and, if necessary, at peak performance during a crisis.

Before you head out to conduct fieldwork consider the following:

- Have a plan of which offenders you are going to see and in what order. Have a map in your vehicle in case you get lost. Also, your field book, if you use one, should have a map printout of the offender's residence.
- Whether you drive a government vehicle or your personal vehicle carry an extra set of vehicle keys for your partner. Should something go wrong both you and your partner will be able to access the vehicle.
- Bring only what is necessary such as your driver's license, health insurance card, a limited amount of cash, and one debit or credit card for emergencies. I also recommend that your driver's license does not have your home address but instead has a PO Box

address or an address to a private business such as The UPS Store which has mailbox services and provides a street address.
- Wear comfortable clothes and shoes. Be able to run or fight if necessary.
- During hot weather drink plenty of water to stay hydrated.
- During cold weather wear appropriate layers of clothing to stay warm. You can then remove layers if you become too hot.
- Have a personal first aid kit or "go bag" with you for emergencies. I will discuss this in more detail in another chapter.
- Make sure your department issued cell phone and your personal cell phone is fully charged. Consider purchasing a spare battery for your personal cell phone or have an external backup battery.
- Always have a pen and notepad in your vehicle to document information
- Conduct a visual inspection of the vehicle that you will be driving to make sure that all lights are working, gas tank is full, no warning lights are on, tire pressure is good, etc. If you have to drive your personal vehicle make sure that you keep it properly maintained so that you don't break down at the worst possible time. Avoid keeping personal information in your private vehicle in case it is stolen.
- It is imperative that you have all of your department issued safety equipment with you to include: body armor, handcuffs, handcuff keys to include a hidden key, pepper spray, baton, firearm, spare magazines, ammunition, department issued radio with a fully charged battery, metal badge, and department identification. Your department may not issue all of this equipment but carry what you are provided. Do not get into the habit of storing safety equipment in your vehicle as you will not have time in a crisis to get your gear.

Officer Survival for Probation and Parole Officers

Vehicular accidents are a major cause of both injuries and deaths to probation and parole officers. Always wear your safety belt and follow all traffic laws whether in your personal vehicle or a department vehicle. Avoid talking on your cell phone or texting while driving which can be a distraction from potential hazards. It is also good practice to make sure that you are well rested and had enough sleep the previous night as driving while tired can be a factor leading to an accident.

As you approach the offender's location it is imperative to scan the environment. Consider driving by the location to get a feel for the neighborhood and to scan the residence you are about to contact. If there are any signs of potential danger then avoid making contact until a safer time even if this means that you need to come back another day. Again, there is no contact which is so important that you should willingly place yourself in harm's way. Document this incident in the computer database that your department utilizes for documenting offender contact. This information is important because you may be transferred to a new unit and another officer may take over your caseload. Once you scan the environment and determine that it appears safe you must then consider where you are going to park your vehicle. The goal is to park in a location that is tactically advantageous in case you must leave in a hurry. When parking your vehicle consider the following:

- Under no circumstances should you ever park in an offender's driveway.
- Avoid parking directly in front of the residence and instead park one or two houses away.
- Avoid parking where you can be blocked in or prevented from leaving.
- If you are on a dead end street park your vehicle in the direction that you would need to exit. This prevents you from having to turn your vehicle around during a crisis.

- Back into parking spaces when possible to avoid having to back out. This is especially important in apartment complex that may have a lot of undesirables roaming the property. When it is time to leave you want to exit as fast and safely as possible.
- When possible, park in a location that will not require you to drive past the house, apartment, or residence that you just made contact. If the offender wants to harm you it is best to avoid driving by the residence where you may be shot at from the offenders house or apartment.

Contact

The contact phase is potentially the most dangerous aspect of field work as this is the time that you are generally in close physical proximity to the offender, collateral contacts, other individuals as well as dogs or other potentially dangerous animals. Not only are you in close contact with the offender but you are often in the offenders home where he can have hidden weapons and is familiar with the layout of the residence. The offender may have contraband such as alcohol, drugs, drug paraphernalia, weapons, or pornography in plain view when you unexpectedly show up. How the offender reacts to your presence may be unpredictable regardless of how long you have been supervising the offender or how well you think you know the offender. Again, an offender who believes that his freedom is in jeopardy may act very unpredictably. Even low risk offenders can be dangerous and violent under the right set of circumstances. It is important for you as the officer to fight complacency and not make false assumptions. Next, we will look at different aspects of the contact stage.

Vehicle

Driving a department vehicle may give people the incorrect impression that you are a police officer especially if you have a "G" plate or government license plate on the vehicle. In neighborhoods that do not have a high regard for law enforcement you may find yourself in a potentially dangerous and hostile environment. If your area of supervision has drug infested neighborhoods then realize that many drug dealers utilize lookouts to spot police officers. These lookouts will spot you before you exit your vehicle and may incorrectly assume from your department vehicle that you are either an undercover or plain clothes police officer. Many drug cartels and drug dealers will go to extraordinary lengths to protect their drugs and their profits including using extreme violence.

First Residential Contact

Good officer safety protocol dictates that you always conduct field work with a partner. Practically this is not always possible especially with small departments or officers that supervise remote locations. When possible always conduct field work with another officer. During your first residential contact with an offender it is essential that you conduct this contact with another officer for safety reasons. Having another officer with you provides a significant added measure of safety. The back-up officers role is to keep his eyes and ears open especially relating to any potential safety issues. Officers must use the contact/cover principle. The presence of a second officer sends a very loud message to the offender that officer safety is paramount. The great aspect of this message is that you do not have to say anything to the offender. This is a great example of the old saying: Action speaks louder than words. In future contacts to the residence the offender will never know if you are coming alone or with another officer. Generally, your first residential contact is to verify the address and to ensure that the offender is residing at an approved location. It is during this first residential contact that you want to diagram and/or photograph the location. If the offender lives in an apartment complex you can contact the property manager to obtain a floor plan of the apartment that the offender lives. Place the floor plan in your field book and write notes on the floor plan if necessary. Also, be sure to conduct a thorough walkthrough of the premises to include the backyard for homes. A thorough walk through of the backyard of Phillip Garrido, a convicted sex offender, may have saved victim Jaycee Lee Dugard from 18 years of rape and imprisonment. Dugard was abducted at the age of 11 back in 1991 in Lake Tahoe. Garrido fathered two children with Dugard while holding her captive. Dugard lived in Garrido's backyard in tattered sheds and tent like structures. In June 2011, Garrido was sentenced to 431 years to life in prison.

Approaching the Residence

As you approach the residence slow down, remain alert and focused, and scan the environment for potential threats or hazards. Observe the yard for signs of drug use to include: used needles, empty bottles of alcohol, drug paraphernalia, baggies to hold drugs such as meth, marijuana, cocaine, heroin, etc. Look for dogs, weapons, loose rounds of ammunition, knives, security cameras, fortifications to the property, security doors, security bars on windows, booby traps, and anything that appears out of the ordinary based on your experience. Document all safety issues.

The "Front" Door

Consider the following when at the front door of an offender's residence:

- Before you knock on the door or ring the doorbell listen to see if you can hear anything inside the residence such as arguing or fighting. The last thing you want to do is get in the middle of a domestic dispute. If there is loud arguing or fighting leave the area and if necessary call the police for a welfare check. When calling the police identify yourself as a probation or parole officer and inform dispatch of what you heard or saw. Tell the dispatcher that you will stage at a location away from the residence where you can meet the responding police officer. Notify your immediate supervisor if required by policy. Document the incident.

- Before you knock on the door or ring the doorbell smell to see if there are any odors that should concern you such as the smell of gas which typically has an additive to give a rotten egg smell. Ringing the door bell, using your cell phone, or radio can be a fire or explosion hazard in the presence of gas. Smell for the presence of marijuana or chemicals that are often used in methamphetamine labs. If you smell natural gas immediately leave and contact the fire department. If you smell drugs such as marijuana leave. Depending on your department policy you can report the odor to the police. At a minimum document the odor and have the offender immediately report for a drug test.
- If you approach the front door and it is partially or fully open do NOT enter. First scan the inside of the residence to see if anything is out of the ordinary. Look for signs of a struggle. Listen for any noise that would not be considered normal. If the residence does not look right or you have a feeling that something is wrong then immediately leave. Consider the following options:
    - Get in your vehicle and drive to a new location.
    - Call the offenders residence and see if anyone answers. If they answer ask if everything is okay but don't say you were just there so that you can see what information the offender provides you.
    - If anything does not seem normal then call the police to conduct a welfare check. Do not go back to the residence until it has been cleared by the police.
- When you knock on the door or ring the doorbell, stand to the side of the door and not directly in front of

the door. If someone on the inside of the residence has a firearm and shoots at the door it will easily penetrate the door and possibly hit you.
- For doors that open inward position yourself on the side of the door closest to the doorknob and not by the door hinges. The reason for this is so that whoever opens the door will have to open it wide to see you. This will provide you a better position both tactically and to have a better field of view inside the residence.
- For doors that open outward position yourself on the side of the door that has the hinges. The reason for this is so that whoever opens the door will have to open it wide to see you. This will provide you a better position both tactically and to have a better field of view inside the residence. Be sure to stand back a few feet so that if the door is forcefully swung open you will not be hit by the door.
- When possible, avoid standing in front of a window when waiting for someone to answer the door.
- Before entering the property ask if anyone else is home. If other people are in the residence ask how many are there and who they are.
- Before entering the property ask if any pets such as dogs are in the home. If necessary provide instructions to have the animals secured in a safe location.
- If the offender is a juvenile follow department policy about being alone in a house with a juvenile. If your department's policy does not address this issue it is highly recommended that you have another officer with you especially if the offender is of the opposite sex.
- Before entering look through the crack where the door is hinged to the frame to see if anyone is hiding behind the door. Attempt to open the door all the way to the door stop prior to entering. Once inside immediately look behind the front door for potential weapons.

- Scan inside before entering. If it is dark inside have the offender turn on lights before you enter. If you are going from a bright outside environment to a dark inside environment your eyes will not have enough time to adjust so that you will see well. Have the offender turn on lights. If they do not have sufficient lighting or their electricity is turned off then you will need to use a flashlight if you choose to enter. This is another reason why officers should always carry a flashlight even during the day.
- Do not enter the residence if you feel unsafe.
- If you feel it is safe to enter the residence do not allow the offender to lock the front door, security door, or a screen door. Have the offender step away from the front door when you enter so that you maintain control of the front door.
- If the front door has a dead bolt visually examine at the lock from the inside of the door. Be cautious of dead bolts that require a key to open from the inside. If the offender locks the door you will not be able to exit the door in an emergency. This is a security red flag.

Inside the Residence

Once you enter the residence you are now in a confined space that the offender is more familiar with than you are in regards to layout, hazards, hiding places, and potential weapons to include weapons of opportunity. You are at a tactical disadvantage when inside an offender's home or apartment. If the offender has weapons hidden in the house he will know where they are located and you do not. The same goes for other contraband such as drugs and drug paraphernalia. Each time you are in the residence you want to scan the residence to see if anything is out of the ordinary or if anything has changed since your last contact. If the residence has significantly changed since your first contact where you created the residential diagram you will need to update any relevant changes.

Once you are inside the residence politely ask that loud items are turned down or off such as the television, radio, or computer. Attempt to keep yourself between the front door and the offender's location in case you need to leave in a hurry. When possible have the offender sit down which will reduce his ability to be a threat without telegraphing his move. One of the most troubling and potentially dangerous aspects of conducting a random and unscheduled contact is finding contraband inside the residence. If this happens you have a few options:

1. If you notice contraband but the offender does not notice that you saw it then the best course of action is for you to immediately leave. One good method to get out in a hurry is to look at your phone and say that you got a text from your supervisor and he needs to talk with you immediately. Have a set of excuses you can use to get you out of difficult spots such as you are late for a meeting or training.

2. If you notice the contraband and the offender is aware of what you saw then you can try to downplay its significance. Tell the offender, "*Hey, I see the bag of pot tucked in the couch. I'm sure it belongs to a friend of yours so get rid of it. I don't want to see this next time I come back.*" Again, immediately leave for your safety. Document this situation, staff with your supervisor, and take appropriate actions to include a drug test of the offender. You can also ask your supervisor permission to conduct a search of the residence and/or arrest the offender.

3. If you notice the contraband such as a firearm and the offender is aware of what you saw this can be a potentially very dangerous situation especially if the offender attempts to gain control of the weapon. You must assume that the weapon is loaded and because you cannot run faster than a bullet you have to use judgment on the best way to remain safe based upon

Officer Survival for Probation and Parole Officers

the situation. At no time can you allow the offender to obtain control over the weapon because you do not know what actions he will take once he has possession. Following are possible options:

- Give a calm but firm verbal command for the offender to not move toward the firearm, to back away, and, if necessary, to get on the ground in the prone position. The reason for providing a calm verbal command is to attempt to keep the offender calm and not escalate. If your radio has an emergency button activate the button. Calmly reassure the offender that this does not have to be a big deal and that you will take possession of the weapon and leave. Keep in mind that when you find one weapon that there may be others in the residence. When you leave you must leave in a hurry in case the offender attempts to obtain another weapon that may be hidden.
- If you are an armed officer you may need to draw your firearm and give a loud, clear, concise verbal command for the offender not to move. Have the offender get on the ground with his head facing away from you, arms spread out to the side with palms facing upward, and legs crossed at the ankles. If your radio has an emergency button activate the button. Obtain the firearm and secure it on your body. Now you have more options to consider at this point:
    - If you are alone then you can decide to leave and immediately contact the police. In such a case the offender is going to be arrested as a prohibited possessor.
    - If you are with a partner then you can handcuff the offender, search the offender for other weapons or contraband, and contact the police.

Depending on the situation you can: 1. remain inside the residence if no one else is home or 2. if others are home and are a potential problem then leave the residence.

4. If the offender attempts to obtain control of the weapon you must use whatever force is reasonably necessary to stop this from happening.
    - If you are an armed officer this means that you may have to shoot the offender to stop him from getting control of the firearm. Your goal is to stop the offender from obtaining the weapon. Your goal is not to kill the offender although this may be the end result. As an armed officer you must be willing to pull the trigger without hesitation when necessary. Are you willing to shoot the following if necessary:

        - Juvenile
        - Elderly
        - Physically challenged
        - Female
        - Pregnant female
        - Male

    - If you are not an armed officer this means that you may need to use empty hand techniques or a weapon of opportunity to stop the offender from gaining control of the weapon. Are you confident with your defensive tactics skills? Are you willing to take a pen that is in your hand and stab an offender in the neck or eyes to prevent him from getting the gun?

        Imagine that you are a female officer who sees a firearm tucked between the cushion of an offenders couch. The offender looks at you and says, *"You should not have seen that gun. I'm not going back to jail (or prison). I'm going to rape you and then kill you.*" What actions are you willing to take to stop this offender? I realize this is not a pleasant scenario but it is not outside the realm of possible. Now is the time to think not only about what you are *willing* to do and what you are *capable* of doing to stop such an offender. You may be willing to do anything to stop such an offender but if you are not capable then you have some training to do to increase your skill level. Always train for the worst case scenario. Anything less is unrealistic.

Fortunately, the majority of field contacts occur without incident. The vast majority of offenders have no intention of causing you harm. The problem is that you probably will not know the difference between offenders who are willing to harm you and those who have no such intention. This is why you must be consistent with each offender that you supervise. During a residential contact it is important to be professional, polite, and respectful while maintaining command presence. You do not want the offender or collateral contacts to think that a contact is equivalent to a social call and no one should interpret your role as a "friend" who is just visiting. As a community corrections officer you are in a position of authority that should not be viewed or construed as a friendship with the offenders that you supervise. When these lines get blurred, especially for the offender, trouble can ensue.

Family Members

Anytime that you are dealing with family members the dynamics of supervision can dramatically change. At times family members may fully support your supervision strategies and constantly contact you regarding the offender. But, when it comes time to arrest the offender for violating their community supervision grant the family member may

now turn on you. This is especially true if the offender is the only person in the household working to pay the bills and provide for the family. If you arrest this person and he is sent back to jail or prison the spouse/partner will now be in a financial bind without money to pay bills, buy food, or provide for children. If you are supervising a juvenile the parents may expect you to enforce parental rules which are outside the limits of your authority. At times community corrections officers have to be very diplomatic with family members and not get caught between family member dynamics.
Sometimes the family member is a victim of the offender such as a wife who was the victim of domestic violence. If the offender is authorized to live with or have contact with their spouse who is also the victim you must realize that the spouse/partner may provide you information that she does not want the offender to know that she reported. For the safety of the victim/spouse it is critical that you never inform the offender that the spouse provided you with information that may negatively impact the offender's ability to remain in the community. To do so may place the victim/spouse in serious jeopardy.

When interacting with family members consider the following:

- How do members of the family respond to you as the probation/parole officer? Are they:

    - Uninvolved
    - Cooperative
    - Respectful and polite
    - Verbally abusive
    - Irritated
    - Hostile
    - Belligerent
    - Violent
    - Passive-aggressive

- Are members of the family under the influence of alcohol or drugs?
- Are members of the family threatening you either overtly or through a veiled threat?
- Are other members of the family on probation or parole? If yes, obtain the name and phone number of their supervising officer. Remember, you may have multiple family members on some form of community supervision such as:

    - Dad is on state parole
    - Wife is on county probation
    - Adult son is on federal probation
    - Juvenile daughter is on juvenile probation

- If you feel that the family is a threat then leave, document, and inform your supervisor to determine what further action is necessary. Options may include going to the residence with another officer, having the offender move to a different residence, having the family member not be home when you report (difficult to do with unscheduled contact), or report to the house with a police officer.

Friends of the Offender

When conducting a random and unscheduled contact with an offender there is a possibility that there will be a friend or friends at the residence. Remember, before entering the residence you are to ask if anyone else is home before entering. If you determine that it is not safe to enter then do not. If you believe it is safe to enter then use good judgment. An option that you can utilize prior to entering the residence if you are issued a radio is to ask for a radio welfare or status check in 15 minutes. If you do not have a radio you can use the same technique with your cell phone. If you fail to respond to the status check then the communications center can follow established procedure to contact you. This procedure may include attempts to reach you on the radio, call your work cell phone, call your personal cell phone, and if necessary, have the police respond to your last location to conduct a welfare check.

When interacting with the offenders friends consider the following:

- How does the offenders friends respond to you as the probation/parole officer?
- Do the friends appear to be a positive or negative influence on the offender?
- Are any of the friends on probation or parole? If yes, are they authorized to have contact with the offender that you supervise?
- Do the friends appear to be under the influence of alcohol or drugs?
- Are the friends attempting to distract you? If yes, what is their motivation?

If the offender's friends are causing problems during the residential contact then immediately leave. As you leave the residence attempt to obtain license plate numbers of the vehicles that belong to the offender's friends. You can then run the license plate to verify if the friends have a criminal record or outstanding warrants. The next time the offender reports to the probation/parole office have a discussion regarding the previous contact stating that the offenders friends either need to behave appropriately or leave when you conduct a residential contact. If the friend(s) have a criminal history you may need to discuss whether it is appropriate for the offender to have contact with this person(s) while on probation or parole status.

Friends and other collateral contacts can be a valuable source of information. At times this information may be about positive aspects of the offender while other times it may be related to serious issues of non-compliance. If a collateral contact provides you with confidential information regarding the offender you have an obligation to keep this information private and not inform the offender of the source. Doing so may put the collateral contact in serious or even life threatening danger.

Food or Gift Offers

Community corrections officers are in a position of authority and must refrain from engaging in any activity that gives the appearance of impropriety. It is not uncommon for offenders or the family members of an offender to offer food or gifts around the holidays. Typically the gifts would be of nominal value yet the officer must not accept even a small gift. Also, many offenders have specialized skills such as carpentry, plumbing, electricians, or a mechanic and may offer their services to you for free or at a significantly discounted price. Again, it is not acceptable to accept such services. Food should never be accepted because it may be contaminated, distracts you from your task, or the family may consider it an "unspoken" favor. Food offerings are common in some cultures and refusal to accept the food can be interpreted as disrespectful. It is important to be respectful of cultural factors and explain that department policy does not allow you to accept food although you appreciate the gesture. Most offenders and their family will understand and respect you for following the rules of your department.

Animal Encounters

During the course of conducting fieldwork officers are in the community and entering residences so it would not be uncommon to come into contact with animals. The offender may own the animal or it may belong to a roommate. It is also possible to encounter stray animals. Dogs will probably be the most prevalent animal encounter. During your initial first contact with an offender at the probation/parole office it is important to inquire whether the offender owns any pets or if anyone living at the residence owns pets. Do not focus only on dogs but ask if the residence has cats, birds, pigs, snakes, ferret, rabbits, chinchilla, wolf or wolf hybrid, fox, skunk, rodents, iguana, or any type of an exotic pet such as a poisonous snake or monkey. It is amazing what kind of pets some people own. Questions to ask offenders include:

1. How many pets do you or anyone in the residence have and what types?
2. How are the pets secured? Are they in a cage or do they roam freely about the residence?
3. Do you have a veterinarian that regularly treats your pets? If yes, obtain the name, address and phone number of the vet.
4. Are dogs, cats, or other pets current with vaccinations?
5. Is your dog current with the rabies vaccination?
6. Have any of the pets exhibited signs of aggression towards humans?
7. Has your dog or other pets ever attacked anyone?
8. Has your dog or other pets ever bitten anyone?
9. Do you have a license or permission to own an exotic animal? (Requirements vary from state to state.) If they do obtain proof from the offender.

Upon arrival at a residence it is good practice to look for clues that indicate a dog is at the location. These may include: "Beware of Dog" signs, dog house, crate or kennel, animal toys, food and water bowls, bones, and dog waste. Dogs often regard their property where they live as their own territory and may defend it by barking, growling, or assuming aggressive body language. Signs of potential hostility and aggression in a dog include growling, showing their teeth, flattened ears, erect tail, stiff legs and showing their hackle which is hair on the back which raises. Do not attempt to make contact with an offender or collateral contact if you encounter a potential dangerous dog or other type of animal.

All dogs can be fearful of unfamiliar people, things, and situations they perceive to be threatening. Following are tips that community corrections officers need to be aware of to avoid being bitten:

Officer Survival for Probation and Parole Officers

- Ask permission before approaching a dog you don't know
- Don't pet a dog without letting him see and sniff you first
- Ask the owner to put the dog in a secure location when necessary
- Do not stand between the dog and its owner
- When possible keep distance between yourself and the dog
- Injured or scared dogs may bite out of fear
- Never corner a frightened dog and always provide and escape route
- A mother dog may be aggressive and bite to protect her pups
- Never turn your back on a dog or run away from a dog as their instinct will be to chase you
- Do not make fast or jerky movements around the dog
- Do not take food or toys away from a dog
- Do not surprise or disturb a sleeping dog
- Do not try to break up a dog fight

If you are approached by a dog follow these steps:

- Do not scream or run as the dog will instinctively chase you and can run faster than you
- Remain motionless and keep your hands at your sides and avoid eye contact with the dog
- If the dog loses interest in you, slowly back away until he is out of sight and leave the area

Defensive Measures Against Attacking Dogs

Voice Commands: Look directly at the dog and in a loud and firm voice state, "NO" or "DOWN."

OC Spray: When sprayed in a dog's face the OC spray may stop the attack. The stream is typically effective for ranges from 3-12 feet. At a range closer than 3 feet the OC may not become fully activated thereby decreasing it effectiveness.

Expandable Baton: When voice commands and OC spray are ineffective in stopping a dog attack officer may need to utilize an expandable baton. An officer can utilize a forward strike at a 45 degree angle and reverse strike at a 45 degree angle (figure 8 motion) to keep a safety zone that may allow an officer to retreat to a safe location. If necessary, the dog can be struck on sensitive areas such the nose or throat to stop the attack.

Another option is to hold the baton in your non-primary hand and extend the baton straight out. The day may focus its aggression on the extended baton and not the officer. If this does not work your primary hand remains free to use a firearm for armed officers when lethal force is necessary.

Lethal Force: An officer is authorized to use lethal force when it is reasonable to protect him/herself or other person(s) from immediate threat of death or serious bodily injury. Officers must understand that the ferocity of the attack, along with the speed, size, and strength of the dog can significantly impair your ability to accurately hit the target resulting in a missed shot. There is the possibility of a bullet critically injuring an innocent third party. Consideration should be given to the background and the possibility of a ricochet of the bullet. The primary target on the dog is the body.

Fire Extinguishers: Many government vehicles are required to have functioning fire extinguishers in the vehicle. A CO_2 fire extinguisher can be an effective deterrent when directly sprayed at the dogs face.

If you are not issued any safety equipment or do not

have your safety equipment on your person you may need to resort to utilizing empty hand techniques to stop a dog attack.

- Offer the dog your jacket, clipboard, purse or anything that you can put between yourself and the dog. If you do not have anything on you then consider extending your non-primary arm for the dog to attack.
- With your primary hand forcefully strike the dog on the nose
- If you fall or are knocked down, curl into a ball with your hands over year ears and remain motionless. Protect your neck and face. Try not to scream, thrash or roll around.

Working Safely at Night

All of the safety procedures used during the day apply to night time or low-light field contacts. The cover of darkness can attract a different group of people which are quite opposite of the day time crowd. Neighborhoods can change as darkness arrives and take on a completely different presence. People who group together can be under the influence of drugs or alcohol and have the intention of committing criminal activity. Street gangs may also take control of their "turf" during the night so that they can conduct illegal business to enhance their criminal enterprise. Officers working at night are encouraged to team up with a partner.

At night officers need to utilize a few extra precautions. It is important to ensure that your vehicle is in good working condition and that your headlights are functioning. Confirm that your department portable radio and cell phone batteries are fully charged. If possible have a vehicle charger as well. It is best to avoid groups of people especially if they are part of a gang. As you scan the environment pay particular attention to places that individuals or people can hide due to the cover of darkness. Such locations may not be effective hiding spots during the day but become highly effective at night. Conducting fieldwork at night takes on a new dimension.

If you rarely conduct fieldwork at night and randomly show up at an offenders door he is going to be wondering what is going on. The offender will be surprised to see you and may think that you are there to arrest him or that something is not right. If the offender is engaging in illegal activity or non-compliant behavior you may just have walked into the hornets nest. Even if you know nothing about the offender's illegal or non-compliant activity the offender will believe that you do know and are there to "get" him and possibly affect an arrest. What turned out to be just a night field contact may become a fight of your life. Even if the offender is compliant with his community supervision grant he will be wondering why you are at his house/apartment/trailer at night if you have never been there at night before. This may cause him to appear nervous and anxious. During your initial contact with the offender which you conduct in the probation/parole office it would be a good practice to inform offenders that you can show up at any time day or night. But again, if you usually conduct field contacts during the day and then show up one night the offender is going to be nervous and concerned as to why you are breaking your routine. Each offender you supervise will pick up on whatever routine you follow. Anytime that you deviate from the routine will raise a red flag for the offender. This is one important reason why you should avoid developing a routine and continually alter any contact patterns with offenders. Be as unpredictable as possible with field contacts.

Working at night also requires that you have a high quality flashlight. Actually, you need two high quality flashlights because inevitably one will fail when you need it the most. The flashlight market has exploded with a host of great flashlights offering a lot of choices. When choosing a flashlight I recommend that you look for the following qualities:

- LED – High quality, long lasting, and very durable.
- Aerospace-grade aluminum alloy, Mil-Spec Type III-hard anodized body or a polymer body.
- Lumens – Minimum of 120 lumens. It is now common to find LED flashlights that have a lumen output of 1000+ lumens.
- Variable Output – High output for a tactical environment or search mode and a low output for conducting paperwork or when you do not require high output.
- Activation switch – I prefer a tail cap switch for momentary on or constant on mode. Depending on your requirements you can also obtain flashlights that has a switch toward the head of the flashlight.
- Strobe Function – The ability to strobe is an excellent and effective feature.
- Batteries – I recommend AA batteries preferably ones that are rechargeable such as Eneloop rechargeable batteries. There was a time when it was not possible to obtain a high lumen output with AA batteries but technology has improved to the point where this is no longer an issue. Also, AA batteries are readily available and are reasonably priced. CR123's are another option but they tend to be very expensive and are not as easy to obtain.
- Programmable – The ability to program the flashlight for brightness levels or to pre-arrange a setting for when the light is initially turned on.
- Lanyard – Must have ability to attach a lanyard.
- Anti-Roll – In case you drop it the flashlight will not roll away.
- Waterproof – In case you work around water or in a wet environment.

If you are an armed officer having a high quality tactical flashlight is an essential piece of gear. If your department does not provide you with a tactical flashlight then spend your own money and get one as there is no substitute for an illumination tool. Additionally, it is imperative that officers receive low-light training and instruction on the use of a flashlight. Understanding the principles, tactics, and techniques for effectively using a tactical flashlight in a low-light environment takes time and practice to develop.

Post-Contact

Once contact with the offender is complete it is time for you to leave the location. Now is not the time to let your guard down. Remain in Condition Yellow, scan your environment, and maintain situational awareness. The contact may be concluded but the potential for danger has not. Remember, the contact that you just completed is "routine" for you but may be viewed very differently by the offender. The offender may decide to get a hidden weapon and come after you. He may get a butcher knife from the kitchen and follow you outside. The offender may decide to get in his car and follow you. Make no assumptions and be prepared for the unexpected. Not to the level that you are paranoid but to the level that you habitually practice officer safety tactics.

As you approach your vehicle scan the environment to look for potential threats and signs of tampering. Look to see if anything was placed under the tires to give you a flat tire when you run over the object. Have your keys in your hand ready to unlock the door. The majority of cars now have keyless entry so you will not need to insert the key into a door lock. Before entering the vehicle look in the back seat to see if anyone entered the vehicle and is waiting to carjack, assault, or hold you hostage. After you are safely in your vehicle drive to a location where is it safe to write down notes or use a digital recorder for later documentation of the contact to include what occurred, where it occurred, time, safety issues, offender progress or regress, etc. If there was anything unusual that occurred you can contact your

Officer Survival for Probation and Parole Officers

supervisor and if necessary write down notes for an incident report.

Once you have your notes written or digitally recorded the next step is to debrief yourself on the contact from an officer safety perspective. Ask what went well, what did not go well, and what you can improve upon and do different next time. This is what will make you a more safety minded officer. Experience alone will not make you a better officer. Evaluating, examining, and improving what you do is what will make you better and safer.

After you have evaluated your previous contact it is now time to mentally prepare for your next contact. Items to consider are safety concerns, the purpose of the contact, recent incidents of non-compliance, and progress of the offender. As you approach the location of the next contact it is important to scan the environment, remain in Condition Yellow, and maintain situational awareness. I know that this information has been repeated numerous times but it is through constant reinforcement that you will begin to use and develop these necessary officer safety skills.

Officer Safety Considerations - FIELD

Following are considerations that all officers should be cognizant of when having contact with offenders during field contacts.

Field Considerations:
Are you in the proper mind-set and are you ready for the unexpected?
Are you in Condition Yellow?
Did you conduct a vehicle check? (i.e. gas, oil, lights, tire pressure, etc.)
Is it possible to do field contacts with a partner?
If you are working with a partner do you have a code word or phrase for an emergency?
Do you and your partner use the "contact" and "cover" principle?
Are you dressed appropriately for fieldwork? (i.e. proper shoes)
Do you have equipment either on your person or have access to such equipment? *(Remember, in an emergency situation you won't have enough time to access equipment if it is not on your person)*
Do you have an extra set of vehicle keys for your partner?
Is your radio battery charged?
Do you have an organized plan of your contacts (i.e. list of contacts and directions)?
Do you have written documentation prepared ahead of time?
Do you have and maintain situational awareness?
Are you visually scanning the environment?
Is your vehicle parked in a good location that provides easy exit in an emergency?
Do you know where cover and concealment is located?
What is the best way to approach the front door?
Did you stop, look, listen and smell before knocking on the door?
Did you visually scan the offender upon contact?
Do you have control of the front door?
Do you ask if anyone else is in the residence before entering?
Do you utilize a field interview stance?
Once inside the residence are you conducting a visual search?

(Don't forget to look up)
Do you know where all the exits are located?
Do you have a "hidden" handcuff key on you that is accessible?

Chapter 7: Probation – Parole Searches

Guns and Drugs

Commonly found at probation/parole searches

Conducting a probation or parole search is one of the most invasive actions that a community corrections officer can perform. It is also a high-risk task in that it is difficult to predict how the offender, family members, friends, or associates may react to such a lawful invasion of privacy and belongings. The Fourth Amendment to the United States Constitution addresses the topic of unreasonable search in seizure and states:

> *The right of the people to be secure in their persons, houses, papers, and effects, against unreasonable searches and seizures, shall not be violated, and no Warrants shall issue, but upon probable cause, supported by Oath or affirmation, and particularly describing the place to be searched, and the persons or things to be seized.*

Case law has held that warrantless searches of offenders placed on probation and parole are legal. Additionally, many states have a condition stating that offenders agree to a warrantless search and seizure for the duration of their probation or parole grant.

Departments may have offenders sign a separate Search Acknowledgement Form stating that the offender is subject to search or seizure by a probation/parole officers at any time of the day or night, with or without a search warrant and with or without cause. The focus of this chapter is not the legal justification or case law surrounding probation or parole warrantless searches but rather officer safety practices when conducting a search. It is assumed that you have legal authority to conduct a probation/parole search and are within the guidelines of department policy.

Officer Survival for Probation and Parole Officers

Types of Community Corrections Searches

Essentially there are two types of probation/parole searches that can be used by community corrections staff. These searches are:

1. Plain view search
2. Planned warrantless search

A plain view search can turn into a planned warrantless search depending on what contraband may be found, department policy, and whether or not your department authorizes the use of warrantless searches.

Plain View Searches

Plain view searches differ significantly from planned warrantless searches which will be the focus of this chapter. A plain view search in relation to community corrections refers to a visual scan of the offender's property during the normal course of your job duties which result in observing contraband. Such a search does not involve moving or physical contact with objects other than room doors. A plain view search can become a very dangerous officer safety event especially when you notice contraband such as a weapon or drugs and the offender notices that you saw the prohibited item. In an earlier chapter it was discussed on possible courses of action to take should you find contraband inside a residence. This can be a very dangerous, unpredictable, and possibly violent situation as the offender may fight you to avoid arrest and returning to jail or prison. Your number one priority is your safety as there are so many variables involved in responding to a situation where you find contraband. Factors include what safety equipment you have on your person, whether you are working with a partner, your level of training, skill, and fitness level, the location, if other subjects are around, and factors relating to the offender. Factors determining how the offender may react can include:

- Is the offender under the influence of drugs and/or alcohol?
- Has the offender ever made a remark that he will never go back to jail or prison?
- Does the offender have a history of violence?
- Does the offender have a mental health diagnosis with or without a history of violence?
- Is the offender on psychiatric medications?
- Has the offender resisted arrest in the past or assaulted law enforcement officers?

Unfortunately, like many officer survival situations, there may not be a clear cut prepackaged response that will guarantee your safety and security in dangerous situations.

Depending on the offenders response to you noticing the contraband you may be able to downplay the incident and talk your way out of the residence or you may end up in a fight for your life especially if the offender believes that he will end up back in custody. If you see contraband during a plain view search the best course of action is to immediately leave and then decide if a planned warrantless probation/parole search is indicated. If there is evidence of a new crime you may need to contact your local police or sheriff's department to respond where the responding police officer may submit a subpoena requesting a warrant for the police to conduct a search. When you see contraband during a plain view search the offender will either:

1. Not notice that you saw the contraband, or
2. Notice that you did see the contraband

If the offender does not notice that you saw contraband then come up with an excuse to immediately leave. It is always a good idea to have a mental list of "pre-made excuses" that you can use when you need to rapidly leave such as:

- I got a text from my supervisor. I need to leave now.
- I'm late to a meeting. I need to leave now.
- I'm late to a mandatory training class. I need to leave now.
- I forgot I have scheduled maintenance on my vehicle. I need to leave now.

When possible have an excuse where the offender will believe that you have to meet with another person who is expecting you at a certain time. This way if the situation escalates the offender may believe that someone will come looking for you when you do not arrive. It is also a good idea to plant the seed that whoever is expecting you knows your exact location and will send help to that location should you not arrive.

If the offender does notice that you saw the contraband then attempt to use your verbal skills and rapport with the offender to try to prevent the situation from escalating. It is important to stay calm and relaxed. Remember panic is contagious and if you show signs of panic or fear then the offender may respond based upon how you are handling the situation. Your brain might be screaming *"OH SHIT! THERE IS A GUN TUCKED IN THE COUCH"* but your outward appearance needs to be cool, calm, and collected. Always be ready for the fight that you may not be able to avoid. Even when you remain calm and it appears that the offender is calm you do not know what he is thinking. He may try to come across as calm to provide you a false sense that it is no big deal. Then, all of a sudden he conducts an explosive attack. Cool, calm, and collected goes out the window and you must then switch to survival mode. Show command presence and if necessary fight for your life and don't just win but prevail.

If the contraband is a firearm many officers will not feel safe attempting to leave the residence without taking the weapon. This is a judgment call that you alone must decide based upon the facts of the situation. Exiting the residence without the firearm means that the offender, or other occupant, can then grab the weapon and come after you. Personally, I would always prefer to seize the weapon and take it with me so that the offender or anyone else in the residence does not have access to the weapon. Once you see the weapon hit the 'emergency button' on your radio if your department issues such a radio. If your plan is to seize the weapon remain calm but exhibit command presence from a field interview stance. Look and act like you are in control but do not be aggressive. Use a short, clear, non-threatening verbal command to direct the offender not to move or to back away from the weapon. For example, you can say the following to the offender:

> "Stop and do not move. _We_ can get through this but I'm going to take control of the weapon for _our_ safety."

In this situation you are letting the offender know:

1. He needs to stop

    > If the offender does not stop you need to respond appropriately which may include using physical force or lethal force if the offender is attempting to obtain control of the weapon. If you are an armed officer then drawing your firearm is an acceptable response.

2. Not to move (or have the offender take some steps back to create more distance and create a larger reactionary gap)

    > Again, if the offender moves toward you or the weapon you will need to respond accordingly.

3. When you state, "_We_ can get through this" you are attempting to obtain buy in from the offender. It does not create an adversarial situation where it is you verse me.

Your goal with obtaining buy in is to make the offender believe that this situation does not have to escalate or that he will be violated and sent back to jail or prison. (Yes, you may have to lie to the offender to keep yourself alive. If the offender is in possession of a weapon he is getting arrested and going to jail or prison.)

4. That you are going to, "*take control of the weapon for our safety.*" Again, by using the phrase "our safety" you minimize an adversarial situation and let the offender know that you do not want the situation to escalate or anyone to get hurt.

Once you obtain control of the weapon you would immediately leave the residence and drive to a safe location where you can secure the weapon and make it safe. If you are not familiar with the operation of the weapon do not attempt to unload it or make it safe. Point the weapon in a safe direction so that if a round is fired no one will get injured. Also, keep your finger off of the trigger at all times. If you are familiar with the weapon system then unload all ammunition and make it safe to transport. Now that you have the weapon in your possession and you are away from the residence you need to decide what action to take which may be dictated by department policy. At this point you should immediately notify your supervisor to obtain direction on the next step. This is a time to consider conducting a planned warrantless search of the residence since you already have firsthand knowledge of contraband. Another option is to contact local police so that you can go back to the residence and arrest the offender for a violation of probation/parole and possibly have the police charge the offender as a prohibited possessor. If you are going to conduct a planned warrantless search you will more than likely need assistance in putting together a search team. Also, you will be away from your office so you will need to rely on someone to bring a search kit and all other required items. Your supervisor would be a valuable resource to assist with these tasks. This is a great example of a situation where an up to date field book is a very valuable resource to have with you so that you can provide important information to the police. If approval is obtained to conduct a planned warrantless search then two probation/parole officers should be assigned to conduct surveillance on the residence from a safe location to see if the offender attempts to leave the location. This activity can also be coordinated with the police using an undercover vehicle.

Now, in a perfect world it would be great if an offender lets you take possession of the weapon and leave without incident. This is how we would want this situation to work out. But, offenders are not predictable and they may have another plans. Many offenders have learned to solve problems through the use of violence so an officers attempt to verbally de-escalate the situation may not be effective. In fact, the offender may not hear a word you say because they are conducting their own internal dialogue on how they are going to hurt you rather than go to jail or prison. As an officer you need to be prepared to fight for your life at any minute that you are dealing with an offender. Situations can deteriorate in a micro second. The training that your department provides must prepare you for the worst case scenario otherwise you will not be prepared. Remember:

Complacency is your enemy and faulty assumptions can get you killed!

The remainder of this chapter will focus on planned warrantless searches.

Planned Warrantless Searches

Planning a Search

Some departments encourage the use of planned probation/parole searches when indicated while other departments rarely, if ever, conduct a planned warrantless search even when there is indication that a search is warranted and justified. Departments should be proactive in conducting searches especially when reliable information is provided by family, friends, or collateral contacts that the offender is in possession of contraband such as weapons, drugs, child pornography, etc. Contraband is any prohibited property, item, or substance that cannot be possessed or produced by any probationer or parolee. Most, if not all, searches that I have participated resulted in the seizure of weapons and/or drugs. One search that I conducted on an offender with a history of misconduct involving weapons turned up a completed employment application for the probation department. The offender's roommate was attempting to get a job as a surveillance officer with the department to obtain access to confidential and law enforcement sensitive information. This individual is now serving a prison sentence for conspiracy to commit first degree murder of a law enforcement officer. This roommate would always report with the offender to the probation office and attempt to intimidate staff. He was 6 feet tall and 350 pounds. Before being sentenced he absconded and led law enforcement on an international manhunt. The U.S. Marshals issued an Interpol Red Notice and he was tracked through Europe and arrested in Iraq. He was brought back to Arizona, convicted, and sentenced to prison. The offender that was the target of the probation search was the leader of a criminal syndicate responsible for or accused of: forgery, theft of vehicle, burglary, money laundering, aggravated assault, robbery, armed robbery, misconduct involving weapons, probation violations, drug rip-offs, threats to probation officers, conspiracy to commit murder, conspiracy to murder a police officer, conspiracy to murder a county attorney, attempted murder, and murder. A total of six individuals were arrested as part of this criminal syndicate to include a former police officer. I was the supervisory probation officer that was threatened in this case and was granted authorization by the Chief Probation Officer to carry my department issued firearm off duty. Additionally, the probation officer in my unit who directly supervised this offender was also threatened. She had to be transferred to another unit for safety reasons. Members of this criminal syndicate went so far as to have a grave dug in the desert for the police officer they planned on killing. The police officer and his wife had to move from their residence twice, in the middle of the night protected by a SWAT team, for safety reasons. The offenders conducted surveillance on the officer's house and even had photographs that they had taken. Many of the members of this criminal syndicate are currently in prison. The leader of this criminal syndicate who threatened me and the officer I supervised was sentenced to life in prison in January 2013. I went to the sentencing and was very impressed how the county attorney prosecuted the case and how the judge sentenced the offender. It was also very touching to hear the police officer and his wife provide their victim impact statement outlining the living hell they went through for years while this case was going through the system. The offender was convicted of:

- Two counts of Misconduct Involving Weapons
- Two counts of Leading a Criminal Syndicate/Gang
- Two counts of Conspiracy to Commit 1st Degree Murder

    The offender will need to serve a minimum of 25 years before being eligible for parole. The day we conducted the probation search on his residence and arrested him was in 2005. Justice moves slowly but fortunately he was in prison for the probation violation. Based on his history I firmly believe he would have killed me and his supervising probation officer if given the opportunity. I had no contact with the offender since his arrest in 2005 and during court he mentioned me by name! The offender took absolutely no responsibility or accountability for his actions and prison is the place he needs to remain for the rest of his life.

    The probation search just mentioned provided information on the offender resulting in his arrest. Additionally, an employment application was found belonging to a resident who lived at the home who attempted to become a surveillance officer with the probation department. When conducting a probation/parole search take nothing for granted, maintain situational awareness, and it is imperative that searches are never done haphazardly, without prior planning, and without briefing everyone involved in the search. This is the part of the job where you are functioning as a law enforcement officer and minimizing your role as a counselor. Yet, it is still important to be professional, polite, and respectful as the search may not uncover any contraband or illegal/non-compliant activities. The offender may not be taken into custody and you will still be responsible for supervising the offender. Even if the search results in the offender being arrested he may end up back on your caseload. If you are disrespectful to the offender, family members, or property then you can assume that the offender will view you much differently after the search. Even when conducting a search you should attempt to keep a positive rapport with the offender.

Search Operational Plan

The most important element in conducting a safe search is proper prior planning. I have participated in searches that were not planned well, had a weak lead officer, and were very disorganized. In such cases each officer is acting independently and not as part of a cohesive search team. Officers fail to stay focused and become distracted when another officer finds something of interest. This can lead to serious safety violations or contraband not being found. Searches should never be conducted in this manner. This led me to the development of a **Search Operational Plan** which is included toward the end of this chapter. The purpose of the Search Operational Plan is to plan the search with as much detail as possible so that each officer knows their role and to have a contingency plan to handle potential emergencies that may arise.

A properly executed search must have a strong lead

officer that functions as the team leader and is responsible for the search. The lead officer/team leader generally is the officer who supervises the offender and determines the need for the search based upon reasonable suspicion. Reasonable suspicion is information and/or observations that would induce an ordinarily prudent and cautious person under the circumstances to believe criminal activity is occurring. According to the court case *Maryland v Buie*, 494 U.S. 324 (1990), the court stated:

> *"A reasonable suspicion is a reasonable belief based on specific facts together with rational inferences from those facts. It is more than a mere inchoate and unparticularized hunch."*

If the supervising officer does not have experience conducting probation/parole searches or being a lead officer/team leader he must find an officer experienced with searches to function as the team leader. The supervising officer must then function as the co-team leader with the goal of learning as much as possible from the team leader. It is only through experience that officers will gain the necessary skills and confidence to function as a qualified and skilled lead officer/team leader. Departments should also consider the implementation of a specialized search team that is responsible for conducting probation/parole searches. This team can either be a part-time or full time team that is well trained and experienced in probation/parole searches.

The lead officer/team leader is responsible to:

- Have a legitimate reason to conduct the search, i.e. reasonable suspicion
- Have approval to conduct the search and ensure that department policy is followed
- Utilize the Search Operational Plan
- Assemble a competent search team

Officer Survival for Probation and Parole Officers

- Ensure that all members of the search team have safety equipment on their person such as firearm, spare magazines, Taser, OC spray, baton, handcuffs, body armor, badges, gloves, ID jackets, and radio (Safety equipment will vary depending on what is issued by the department)
- Assign each member of the search team their assignment
- Ensure that a fully supplied search kit is brought to the search
- Brief *both* police and community corrections officers involved in the search
- Conduct interviews with the probationer, parolee, or other individuals
- Ensure that all contraband is processed through the chain of custody and impounded
- Write the search report or incident report at the conclusion of the search
- Testify in court if necessary

The lead officer/team leader is the glue that ensures the search is conducted safely, efficiently, effectively, and according to department policy. Utilizing a Search Operational Plan will assist with coordination and implementation of an effective search. The Search Operational Plan is composed of two parts. Part A is to be completed by the lead officer and Part B is to be completed by the recorder. The *recorder* is the officer assigned during a probation/parole search to assist the searchers with recording all items found by documenting the time and specific location where the items were located. The recorder is to be very specific with detailing what was found, the exact locations of found contraband, and writing specific times to ensure accurate documentation. The *searchers* are officers assigned to the search team who are responsible for locating contraband or evidence of new criminal activity.

Part A contains the following: (Completed by the lead officer)

- Date of search, reasonable suspicion justification of the search, and who approved the search
- Offender information and demographics to include: Name, alias, address, vehicle information, current photo, photos of tattoos/scars, height, weight, gang affiliation, history of violence, and history of drugs
- List of involved probation/parole officers to include: lead officer (team leader), recorder, searchers, and supervisor
- List of involved police officers
- Risk analysis and intelligence to include: concerns, geographic barriers, point of primary entry, fortification, secondary point of entry, potential occupants, health concerns, animals, weapons, and area threats
- Information assessment including the reliability of the information that you provided in the plan. This is based on information received from confidential informants, concerned citizen, victim, relative/family member, police, probation officers, treatment providers, etc.
- Location diagram
- Photographs of:
  - Offender (should be within the last 6 months),
  - Aerial photos of search area,
  - Map printout of the search area
- Search checklist to ensure that you have brought all required items to the search such as: search kit, copy of terms and conditions of probation/parole, copy of criminal history, offender face sheet, copy of relevant department policies, and first aid kit. It is important that any contents of the search kit used during the search are replaced after the completion of the search so that the kit will be ready for the next search.

Part B contains the following: (Completed by the recorder)

- Staging area location along with search start and end times

- Documentation of persons who are handcuffed to include name, time handcuffed, and safety checks of secured persons
- Arrest information if offender is arrested to include arresting agency, indication if a new crime has been committed, agency transporting offender, and location offender transported
- Medical plan to include:

    - Location of nearest Level I trauma center,
    - Closest non-trauma hospital,
    - Whether EMS or fire department responded, and
    - Names of individual(s) transported to the hospital along with injuries received or medical condition.
    - If the search is in a rural location where the closest hospital is a long distance and medical/EMS has an extended response time then consider having the phone number and contact information for a medical helicopter in case anyone needs to be transported. This will especially be important for trauma wounds such as a gunshot or knife injury.

Residential Information

When conducting a search of a residence it is not only prudent but necessary to have as much information on the residence and occupants as possible. This information will assist with the planning of the search and help determine the number of officers necessary to safely and effectively conduct the search. Residential information should include the following information:

- Address of location
- Name of property owner
- Names of individuals who the offender lives with to include dates of birth and social security number

when possible. Also note the relationship of these individuals to offender
- Layout of the residence to include a diagram (Figure 1)
- Map to the residence
- Aerial photo(s) of neighborhood from Google Earth, Google Maps, MapQuest or other mapping service. Aerial photos provide a birds-eye view of the neighborhood, allows you the ability to zoom in for more detailed information, and provides you with familiarization of the area. Keep in mind that some aerial photos may be outdated and no longer accurate.

When looking at aerial photos you want to pay attention to what is in the photograph, if there are any potential problems or hazards that you can identify, what is your plan of approach, and what is your emergency "get out" plan in case something goes wrong.

Do not underestimate the value of this information. It does take some extra time to put together but it may provide very useful information.

Depending on what is being searched (house, vehicle) and the size of the structure each search team will consist of the following:

Search Team	Number of Personnel
Lead Officer/Team Leader	1
Co-Team Leader	1 (Used only when Lead Officer is being trained on searches)
Recorder	1
Searchers	Between 2 – 6+ 2 for vehicle; 6+ for a house or structure
Supervisor	1

Officer Survival for Probation and Parole Officers

The number of personnel utilized can be modified depending of the circumstances of the search. It is preferable to have more officers than not enough to assist with the search.

Residential Diagram

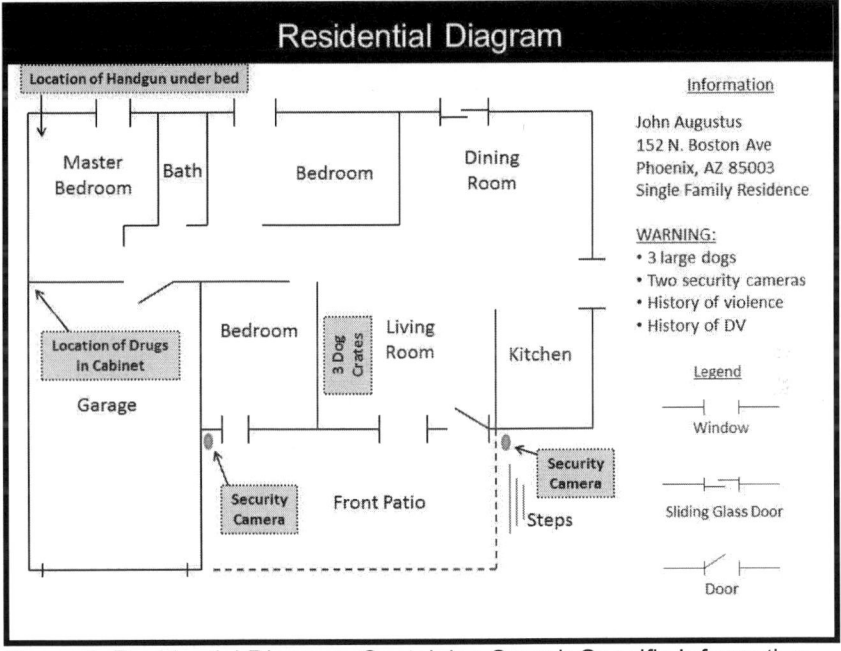

```
Location of Handgun under bed                          Information

Master    Bath    Bedroom      Dining                  John Augustus
Bedroom                        Room                    152 N. Boston Ave
                                                       Phoenix, AZ 85003
                                                       Single Family Residence

                                                       WARNING:
                                                       • 3 large dogs
                                                       • Two security cameras
                                                       • History of violence
            Bedroom   3 Dog   Living                   • History of DV
Location of Drugs     Crates  Room    Kitchen
in Cabinet                                             Legend
Garage                                                 ─┤  ├─
                                                         Window
                                        Security
                              Security  Camera         ─┤═├─
                              Camera                    Sliding Glass Door
                      Front Patio       Steps
                                                       ─┤╱ ├─
                                                         Door
```

Figure 1: Residential Diagram; Containing Search Specific Information

Residential diagrams should be drawn as accurately as possible for future reference. If the house or structure is multi-level then a diagram is to be completed for each level. When conducting a warrantless search it would be appropriate to document on the diagram important information such as officer safety concerns, cameras, potential location of contraband, etc. Consider taking digital photographs of the residence to place inside the offender's case file and field book. Optimally, this information should be obtained on the first residential contact when you have another backup officer with you for additional safety. It may be easier to take photos of the residence on your first contact at the residence when the offender will not know what to expect. If you take photos at a later time after supervising the offender for a while he may think that something is up which can lead to a potential problem. Many digital cameras also have the capability of taking video. If necessary, take video if you run across anything unusual or to assist you with drawing the diagram at a later time. Each time that you go back to the residence look for possible changes to the structure or layout. Update the diagram whenever changes occur. Also, consider taking photographs of the offender's vehicle(s).

Police Assistance on Warrantless Searches

Some probation/parole departments conduct warrantless searches without the use of police assistance while other departments require the use of police. Regardless of the probation/parole search teams experience I recommend that community corrections departments should always utilize the assistance of their local police department when conducting a warrantless search. One of the main reasons for utilizing the police is so that they can clear the structure prior to the search. While this task can accomplished by probation and parole staff who are trained in building clearing the reason I recommend that the police conduct this task is because there is a high probability they will encounter individuals who are not under probation or parole supervision. The police may need to engage these individuals with force especially if they are not cooperating with legal commands. If you do not have full police authority which most probation and parole officers do not then you are placing yourself in a precarious position that more than likely will require police intervention anyway. Additionally, police officers have much more training and experience clearing a structure which is a very high-risk task. An exception to this procedure would be if you have probation/parole officers who routinely work in a specialized capacity such as part of a warrants unit who routinely work AND train in conjunction with the police especially on building clearing tactics and techniques. These officers should be considered for having authority to clear structures with other police officers. The same would apply to dedicated search teams who routinely train and conduct searches.

The role of the police during probation/parole warrantless searches includes:

- Conduct records check on the property prior to the search to see if there has been any recent police contact or activity at the residence
- Conduct records check to see if the search may compromise any undercover police operations on the residence to be searched or the surrounding area
- Clearing the structure for officer safety
- Force entry if authorized per department policy
- Scene security to include crowd control and perimeter security
- Conduct warrant checks on individuals at the search scene if indicated
- Take over search when there is evidence of a new crime; obtain search warrant if indicated
- Take over scene for a barricaded subject or hostage situation
- Transport of prisoners if necessary
- Coordinate medical assistance if necessary
- Coordinate fire department response if necessary to include a hazardous materials response, i.e. methamphetamine lab
- Coordinate a response from animal control for dangerous animals
- Coordinate with federal law enforcement agencies depending items that may be found to include terrorism related items, military grade weapons, certain types of hazardous materials, evidence of international criminal activity, etc.

As stated, one significant reason to have the police clear the structure is to handle any resistance from the offender or other individuals not on community corrections such as family members, friends, or other collateral contacts. Before the search is conducted a community corrections officer should verify that the offender is home. When the search team arrives on scene to conduct the search the offender should immediately be restrained with handcuffs and then informed that a probation/parole search is going to be completed. Some officers may feel that it is premature to handcuff and restrain the offender at this point. I believe that the offender should immediately be restrained for the following reasons:

1. It prevents the opportunity for the offender to attempt escape. This is especially true when the offender knows that contraband or other prohibited items are in the residence.
2. It prevents or mitigates the opportunity for the offender resist or become non-compliant during the search.
3. There is a very high probability that contraband will be located and the offender will be taken into custody. Keep in mind that the search is being conducted based on reasonable suspicion where there is often very valid information that the offender is in possession of contraband.

Remember that when an offender is restrained an officer will need to stay with the offender and monitor his health and welfare. The handcuffs must be regularly checked every 20-30 minutes to ensure that they are applied correctly and not so tight that it will cause any permanent injury. Every time that the handcuffs are checked for proper application and offender safety this information must be documented by the recorder.

Generally, other occupants such as family members or friends will not need to be restrained unless there are officer safety considerations. Ideally, the police will handle individuals who are not on community corrections. It is important to know if your department policy will allow you to restrain individuals who are not on probation or parole. If not then police assistance is required. Any family members or friends who want to leave should be allowed to go unless there is a specific and legal requirement for them to stay or be detained. Know the limits of your legal authority. Typically, friends of the offender will want to leave and this should be encouraged so that the friend and offender do not try to distract officers or inhibit the search. Offenders who have children may request that a family member or friend remove the children from the residence while the search is being conducted.

Once the offender is secured and all of the occupants are either removed from the premises or gathered in one location the offender should be separated from all family and friends so that he can be interviewed. At this point the lead officer, who is typically the supervising officer of the offender, should inform the offender that information has been obtained which is resulting in a search of the premises. The search team should simultaneously begin their search of the property while you begin to interview the offender. This is a time for the lead officer/team leader to use good interviewing skills in an attempt to have the offender provide you with information that you do not currently have. Start out by telling the offender that you have received reliable information about contraband that the offender possesses. Ask the offender the following general question: "*Where is the contraband located?*" Notice that you are not asking "if" there is any contraband but asking "where" the contraband is located. Even if you do not specifically know the location of the contraband you want the offender to believe that you have more information than you do. The goal is to get the offender to provide you information that you may or may not already have relating to the prohibited items. You may bluff the offender into believing that you are aware of all his contraband when you may only know of one item. It is also important to never specifically state what type of contraband that you are looking for because the offender may possess multiple prohibited items that you do not know about. If he starts talking about the prohibited items he may provide you with much more contraband than you anticipated or knew about. If you say you are looking for a pound of marijuana but the offender also has a firearm, stolen checks, and drug paraphernalia he may give up the marijuana so that you stop the search and do not find the gun and stolen checks. Even if the offender provides you with a location of contraband you should still conduct a thorough search of the property.

When you inform the offender that you received information about contraband the offender will invariably want to know who provided this information. It is critical that you protect the confidentiality of the source that provided the information. Typically, such information is commonly provided by family, friends, or an ex-spouse. The motivation for these individuals giving you the information may be revenge, they are scared of the offender, or they genuinely want the offender to get help. Regardless of the reason you should never inform the offender who provided you the information because the offender then may retaliate against that person. Such retaliation could lead to injury or death of the source. Always protect the confidentiality of your source.

When you interview the offender and state that you know he is in possession of contraband the offender will generally deny the allegation. He will state that the source lied or that he knows who the source is and that the person is trying to send them back to jail or prison. Regardless, it is important for you to give the impression that you know more than you do. If the offender wants to deny any wrongdoing it does not matter because the search team will be looking for the contraband anyway. If the offender wants to deny any contraband you can state that officers are currently going through all of his property as we speak. Then ask the offender: *"Do you want officers to go through all of your personal belongings?"* Some offenders especially if they have done long prison sentences are very protective of their property and highly dislike that someone else is going through their belongings. This may provide enough motivation for an offender to tell you where the contraband is located.

Generally, the person conducting the interview should be the supervising officer who already has an established rapport with the offender. When interviewing the offender it is good to have no more than two officers involved in this process. When trying to obtain information on a topic that is sensitive in nature or embarrassing to an offender, privacy is important. Move the offender to a quiet area where you can interview him without having a group of onlookers. This is especially important when interviewing sex offenders who do not want to confess where their pornography is located in front of a bunch of officers. While the offender's actions for being on probation or parole may be despicable you need to be professional when attempting to gain information. For example, if you are supervising a sex offender who is on probation for sexual misconduct with a child and you have obtained information that he is in possession of a large quantity of child pornography the offender is not going to admit to anything if a large group of officers are around especially if any of the officers are female.

Search Techniques

Prior to commencing the start of the search the team leader should review with officers what areas of the property can legally be searched and what areas cannot be searched. Generally, common areas and the offender's property can be searched. Examples include the following:

- If the offender is a juvenile living with her parents then the areas that can be searched include the offender's room and common areas such as the kitchen, living room, and dining room. The parent's room would be off limits during a search.
- If the offender is renting a room in a house then only the offender's room and common areas can be searched.

- If the offender owns their own house then all of the property can be searched.

Areas that are off limits and cannot be searched must be communicated to all officers participating in the search. During the walk-through the team leader should also note any potential safety concerns and relay this information to the search team. To avoid allegations of theft, damage, or impropriety it is a good idea to conduct a walk-through of the property and photograph and/or video the area to be searched. This will provide evidence of the condition of the property prior to the search. Also, prior to beginning the search the team leader must ensure that all search participants are using appropriate personal protective equipment (PPE) such as gloves to prevent contamination of personnel. Utilization of gloves will protect officers from bloodborne pathogens which are infectious, disease causing microorganisms that may be found or transported in biological fluids.

The two most common places that community corrections officers search will be an offender's residence and vehicle. Residences can include: single story home, multiple level home, apartment, condominium, manufactured home, prefabricated home, duplex, town home, etc. Vehicles can include: cars, trucks, motorcycles, recreational vehicles, camper, bus, trailer, all-terrain vehicles, farm vehicles, etc. There are multiple techniques and patterns that officers can utilize when conducting a search but regardless of the method the key is to ensure that the search is both thorough and detailed so that contraband is not overlooked. Some of the more common types of search patterns and techniques include: grid, strip, spiral, zone, and sector. Because community corrections officer are more likely to conduct a probation/parole search in a residential structure that is normally small in size the focus will be on the use of a grid search pattern. A typical apartment may only be 850 square feet while a single family home averages about 2,200 square feet. The main reason for using the grid search pattern

Officer Survival for Probation and Parole Officers

(Figure 2) is because it works well indoors within a residence, it is a thorough search technique, and it is effective.

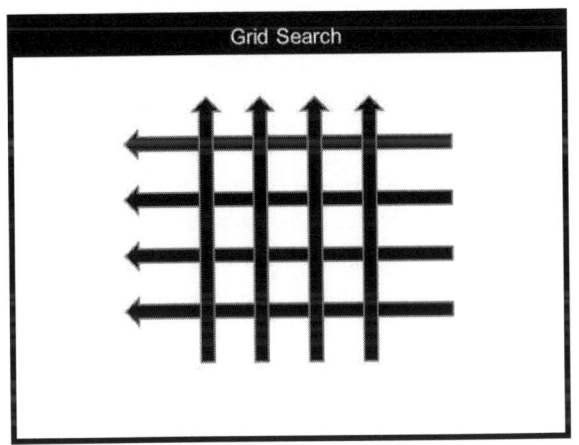

Utilizing a grid search pattern allows the area to be thoroughly searched twice by overlapping the same search region. This is especially beneficial when two officers are searching the same area for contraband or evidence of a new crime.

Figure 2: Grid Search

When searching a residence the team leader should make the determination on which search patterns and techniques to utilize. Figure 3 shows a common single family home consisting of 3 bedrooms, 1 bathroom, two car garage, living room, dining room, and a kitchen. The amount of community corrections officers needed to complete the search will depend on the size of the house, how much property the house contains, the availability of officers, and if there are any time constraints requiring that the search be completed within a specific period of time. Using the house below and assuming that it is a 2,200 square foot house with typical furniture and belongs the best scenario would be to have 2 searchers for each room of the house except the bathroom which can be effectively searched by one officer. It is understood that more times than not it is difficult to gather a team of enough staff to end up with the best case scenario especially if a search team needs to be put together in short order. Like most other tasks we do the best with what we have and putting together a search team is no different. If you are not able to gather the optimal amount of officers then the search will take a longer period of time. If the weather is excessively hot or cold this will have a negative impact on the officers conducting the search. It is the job of the team leader to know the condition of his or her team.

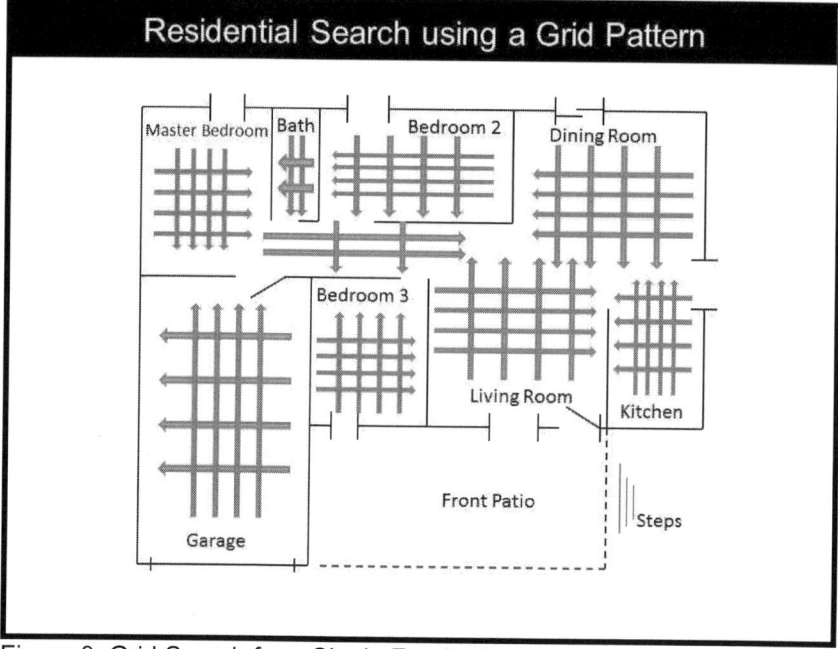

Figure 3: Grid Search for a Single Family Residence

Officer Survival for Probation and Parole Officers

Search team configuration for the house in figure 3 would consist of the following personnel:

Search Team	Number of Personnel
Lead Officer/Team Leader	1
Recorder	1
Master Bedroom	2 Searchers
Bedroom 2	2 Searchers
Bedroom 3	2 Searchers
Garage	2 Searchers
Living Room	2 Searchers
Dining Room	2 Searchers
Kitchen	2 Searchers
Bathroom	1 Searcher
Optimal Number of Personnel	*17*

As previously stated this would be the best case scenario. Realistically, there are very few departments that can put together a search team consisting of 17 officers unless there were very unique circumstances specifically requiring such manpower and enough time to gather that many officers. Some departments are so small that it would be impossible to put together this size of a search team. Now, let's look at a more realistic example of a residential search using the house in Figure 4. This time we will divide the house into three distinct sectors and assign officers to search their area of responsibility.

Search Team	Area of Responsibility	Number of Personnel
Lead Officer/Team Leader	Search Scene	1
Recorder	Documentation	1
Sector 1 – Search Team 1	Master Bedroom, Bath, Garage	2
Sector 2 – Search Team 2	Bedrooms 2 and 3	2
Sector 3 – Search Team 3	Dining Room, Living Room, Kitchen	2
Number of Personnel		8

With fewer officers to conduct the search it will take a longer period of time to complete the search. Also, because officers now have a larger area of responsibility there is a chance that fatigue will set in and lead to items being missed. If it is excessively hot or cold these elements may cause the searches to rush in order to get done. If a search team gets done with their area of responsibility these officers can be reassigned to assist with another search team.

When conducting a residential search there are times the environment will be very unsanitary and unclean. There may be old cat or dog urine and feces in the residence that give off a horrid stench. The kitchen may have old food sitting on the counters with dirty dishes all over the place. Used diapers may be piling on the floor. These are not uncommon occurrences. Yet, they are also not excuses to conduct a poor search. Remember, there is a specific reason that led to the search. If the reason was not an important one then the search would not be approved or conducted. Despite whatever challenges that you may encounter you must conduct a professional and thorough search. Fight the urge to rush or become complacent when the environment is unclean or the weather is very hot or cold. When necessary the team leader may need to have officers take a break. When this occurs it is important that the search area is not compromised by unauthorized persons.

Residential Search: Three Sectors

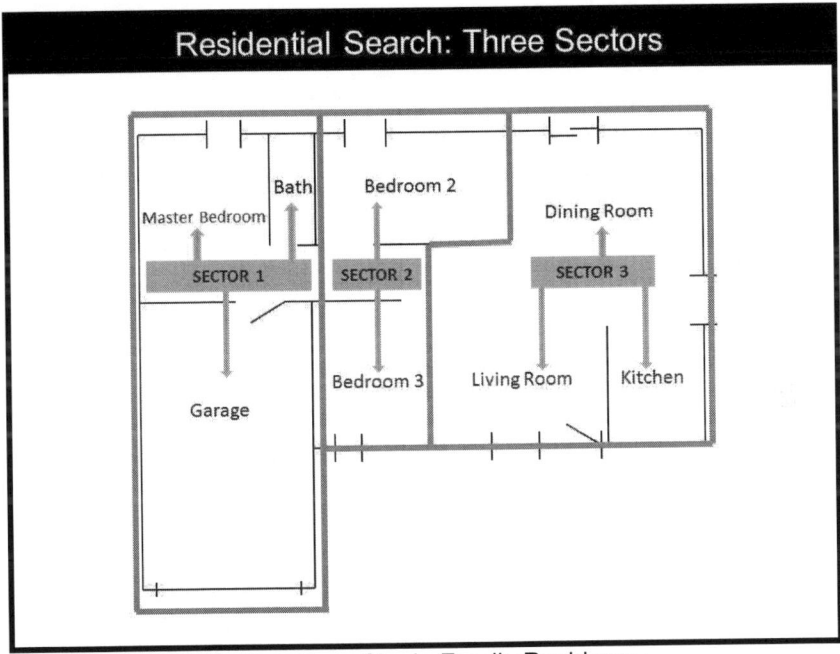

```
Master Bedroom | Bath | Bedroom 2 | Dining Room
   SECTOR 1    |  SECTOR 2  |   SECTOR 3
   Garage      | Bedroom 3 | Living Room | Kitchen
```

Figure 4: Search Sectors for a Single Family Residence

When conducting a search officer safety is the number one priority. Even when the residence is cleared and occupants are either secured or contained there always remains the possibility of dangers lurking within the property. Some of these dangers may be unintentional while others may be intentional and deadly. Some offenders may have contraband such as weapons, drugs, or excessive amounts of money that they will go to extreme lengths to protect and from being found by you or anyone else. Be aware of improvised explosive devices, booby traps, covert audio and video recording devices that may record your actions and transmit them to another location, etc. Additionally, used hypodermic needles may be in plain sight or hidden in search areas such as drawers, under beds, hidden in the kitchen or bathroom and a host of other places that can be dangerous to officers.

When conducting a search keep the following tips in mind:

- Before you begin searching your area of responsibility first scan the environment to observe what you will be searching, where you will begin the search, and to see if anything looks out of the ordinary.
- Always look for hazards and officer safety issues. Any issues that are found should immediately be communicated to the team leader and your search partner.
- Always wear gloves to protect your hands.
- Use a flashlight for areas that are not properly illuminated.
- Always look before searching an area or item. NEVER blindly reach or grab an item that you have not first observed.
- Use a mirror when necessary to search areas that may not be readily visible.
- If you come across an item that looks like a bomb or an improvised explosive device then immediate stop what you are doing, do not touch the object, leave the area, and notify the team leader and police so that the area can be evacuated. Let the police question the offender to see if it can be determined what the object is and whether or not it is dangerous.

It is important that all evidence and contraband is collected, preserved, inventoried, packaged, transported and submitted properly. It is important to establish a chain of custody. While evidence collection is not the most fun aspect of a search it is extremely valuable. Remember, if there is evidence of a new crime the probation/parole search is to be immediately stopped and the scene turned over to the police for processing and possible submittal of a subpoena for a search warrant.

As stated previously it is important that all searches are conducted in a systemic and organized manner so that no contraband is overlooked and missed during the search. Regardless of which search technique that you choose to use it is important to think outside of the box and look for items that may be concealed in potential hiding places. This will require searchers to look up, under, in, and around objects to include the floor, walls, and ceiling. Some offenders hide items in "plain sight" yet cleverly disguised in common everyday items that contain secret compartments. There does not seem to be a limit to the ingenuity of offenders and even companies that produces products to hide objects.

Vehicle Searches

Vehicles are commonly searched and like a residence can contain a host of hiding places. Even though most vehicles that will be searched are small in size compared to a residence it is important that officers take their time and utilize a systemic approach to look for contraband or other prohibited items. Following, while not exhaustive, are some examples of hiding places in vehicles:

- Drugs hidden in hollowed out car batteries
- Seat cushions that have stash compartments
- Sun visors that have hidden compartment or function as a holster for firearms
- Armrest with hidden compartment
- Headrest with hidden compartment
- Airbag hidden compartment by removing the airbag
- Knives and money hidden under dash mats
- Spare tires that have drugs hidden into the tire
- Motorcycle floorboards that contain hidden compartments large enough to store a firearm
- Hidden compartments within and behind dashboards
- Hidden compartments within door panels
- Center consoles that have a hidden compartment
- Gas tanks modified to hold contraband

- Car trunks with multiple hiding places and installed false compartments
- Vehicle ceilings that are modified to hold contraband
- Pickup truck bed walls can be modified to hold contraband
- False air vents
- Door panels can be used to hide weapons and contraband

Officer Survival for Probation and Parole Officers

Search Operational Plan

> **Part A: To be completed by Lead Officer/Team Leader**
>
> **Copies of "Part A" of this plan are to be provided to all search personnel. The lead officer is to conduct a thorough briefing with probation/parole officers and police officers to define each person's role and responsibility during the search.**

Date of Search: _____

State "Reasonable Suspicion" justification for conducting search and items of interest: _____

_____

_____

_____

_____

Locations that are **NOT** authorized to be searched (i.e., parent's bedroom of a juvenile): _____

_____

Scott Kirshner

Search approved by Supervisor: _____ Yes, _____ No

Supervisor who approved search: _____

Supervisor Phone #: _____

Supervisor Badge #: _____

Staging Location: _____

Offender Information:

Name: _____

Alias: _____

Home #: _____ Cell #: _____

Address: _____

Search Address (If different from above): _____

Location Description (circle):

    Residential   Apartment   Business   Industrial   Office

    Building   School   Vehicle

    Other, specify: _____

Legal owner of property: _____

Vehicle Info – Year, Make, Model, License/State, Color:

    #1: _____

    #2: _____

Officer Survival for Probation and Parole Officers

Photo(s): Insert multiple photos if offenders look has drastically changed.

```
┌─────────────────────┐   ┌─────────────────────┐
│                     │   │                     │
│ Insert Offender     │   │ Insert Offender     │
│ Photo #1            │   │ Photo #2            │
│                     │   │                     │
└─────────────────────┘   └─────────────────────┘
```

Date of Photo: _____   Date of Photo: _____

Offender Information, cont:

Age: _____   DOB: _____

Height: _____   Weight: _____

Hair: _____   Eyes: _____   Ethnicity: _____

Scars/Tattoos: _____

Tattoo/Scar Photos:

```
┌─────────────────────┐   ┌─────────────────────┐
│                     │   │                     │
│ Insert Tattoo/Scar  │   │ Insert Tattoo/Scar  │
│ Photo #1            │   │ Photo #2            │
│                     │   │                     │
└─────────────────────┘   └─────────────────────┘
```

Scott Kirshner

Offense(s) that offender is on probation/parole (attach copy of criminal history):

1. _____

2. _____

3. _____

4. _____

Gang Affiliation: _____ Yes, _____ No

Gang Name: _____

History of Violence: _____ Yes, _____ No

History of Drugs: _____ Yes, _____ No

Drug(s) of Choice: _____

_____

Probation/Parole Officers Involved:

Officer Name	Responsibility	Badge #	Call Sign

1. _____ Lead Officer/Team Leader _____

2. _____ Recorder _____

3. _____ Searchers _____

4. _____ Searchers _____

5. _____ Searchers _____

6. _____ Searchers _____

7. _____ Searchers _____

Officer Survival for Probation and Parole Officers

8. _____ Searchers _____

9. _____ Supervisor _____

10. _____

Police Agency Personnel:

Name   *Badge #*   *Department*

1. _____
2. _____
3. _____
4. _____
5. _____
6. _____
7. _____
8. _____
9. _____
10. _____

Risk Analysis & Intelligence

Concerns and/or type of activity that is expected to be encountered at search location:

_____
_____
_____

COMPOSITION – Wood, brick, concrete, steel, glass. Is the structure single level or multi-level?

_____
_____
_____

GEOGRAPHIC BARRIERS - Describe the structures perimeter. What barriers could create an obstacle for probation/parole or police personnel, i.e. shrubbery, ditches, fences, pools, etc.?

_____
_____
_____

POINT OF PRIMARY ENTRY - Describe the probable point of entry. Indicate location in structure, type of door, lock mechanisms, location of hinges, direction of swing, presence of screen door/security door, possible counter surveillance, possible booby traps, etc.

_____
_____
_____

FORTIFICATION - Provide any intelligence that may indicate that the location is fortified, drop bar, bars on windows, etc.

_____
_____

SECONDARY POINT OF ENTRY - If the primary point of entry were obstructed, identify and detail a secondary location for entry.

_____
_____

Officer Survival for Probation and Parole Officers

<u>CHILDREN / ELDERLY / HANDICAPPED</u> - Describe any children, elderly or handicapped persons who are likely to be present at the time of search.

_____
_____
_____

<u>HEALTH CONCERNS</u> - Describe any special health concerns relative to any person that may be present at the time of search.

_____
_____
_____

<u>ANIMALS</u> - Describe any animals that may be present and likely to obstruct personnel movement or present any potential hazard to personnel. Indicate if inside, outside, chained, free, trained, specifically dangerous, etc.

_____
_____
_____

<u>WEAPONS</u> - Describe any weapons to include: firearms, edged weapons, or any explosive device or hazardous material that may be present at the time of entry. Provide the probable location of these weapons within the structure.

_____
_____
_____

AREA THREATS - Describe any person(s) within close proximity to the objective that may pose a threat to probation/parole/police/tactical personnel.

_____

_____

INFORMATION ASSESSMENT - Describe the reliability of this information that you have provided.

- Identify sources as confidential informant, concerned citizen, victim, relative/family member, probation/parole officer, police officer, other (specify).

- Indicate the reliability of the sources information based on past performance.

_____

_____

_____

_____

_____

_____

_____

LOCATION DIAGRAMS - On additional pages, provide diagrams of the location structure. Include doors, windows, interior walls, stairways, etc. Provide separate diagrams for each floor of a multi-level structure. Include driveway access, location of utilities, location of weapons and or hazardous materials, location of any furniture that may obstruct movement, known booby traps, and any other pertinent information.

Officer Survival for Probation and Parole Officers

<u>PHOTOGRAPHS</u> - Provide photographs of:

- Offender: Include head shot, tattoos, scars, and distinguishing features.

- Aerial Photos of Scene (i.e. Google Earth, Google Maps, MapQuest). Aerial photos should include:
    - City block
    - Complete street
    - Close up of structure

- Map printout of Scene

Search Checklist

Items to be brought to the search:

_____ Search Kit to include:
- Digital camera extra batteries and memory card
- Gloves
- Markers, pens, and tape
- Flashlight
- Evidence Bags
- Evidence Forms

_____ Terms and Conditions

_____ Criminal History (i.e. violence, resisting arrest)

_____ Offender Face Sheet

_____ Search & Seizure/Evidence Collection Policy

_____ First Aid Kit

Safety is the number one priority when conducting a search. Communication with all participants is essential.

> **Part B: To be completed by The Recorder**
> **This information is to provide a documented record of the search and to assist with writing the incident report.**

Call probation/parole dispatch to provide notification that a search will be taking place. Provide address of location, police agency involved, and call signs for all officers involved.

Do not forget to clear everyone when search is complete.

Staging Area Location: _____

Arrival Time at Staging Area: _____

Search Start Time: _____

Search End Time: _____

Search turned over to Police: _____ Yes, _____ No

    Time: _____

Persons Handcuffed:

1) Name _____ Time Handcuffed: _____

Handcuffed by: _____

30-Minute Handcuff Safety Check Time(s): _____

2) Name _____ Time Handcuffed: _____

Handcuffed by: _____

30-Minute Handcuff Safety Check Time(s): _____

Officer Survival for Probation and Parole Officers

3) Name _____ Time Handcuffed: _____

Handcuffed by: _____

30-Minute Handcuff Safety Check Time(s): _____

4) Name _____ Time Handcuffed: _____

Handcuffed by: _____

30-Minute Handcuff Safety Check Time(s): _____

Arrest:

Was Offender Arrested: _____ Yes, _____ No

Arresting Agency: _____

New Crime: ____ Yes, _____ No, Police DR#: _____

If Yes, New Charge(s):

    1. _____

    2. _____

    3. _____

    4. _____

    5. _____

Agency Transporting Offender: _____

Location Offender Transported: _____

Time Offender Transported: _____

Notes: _____

_____

_____

_____

_____

_____

_____

_____

_____

_____

_____

Medical Plan:

Closest *Level I Trauma Center*:

    Name: _____

    Address: _____

    Emergency Department Phone: _____

Closest Hospital (Non Trauma Center):

    Name: _____

    Address: _____

    Emergency Department Phone: _____

Officer Survival for Probation and Parole Officers

Any Injuries sustained at search: _____ Yes, _____ No

EMS/Fire Response Required: _____ Yes, _____ No

Anyone transported to hospital: _____ Yes, _____ No

    Injured Person #1: _____

    Name: _____

    Injury: _____

    Injured Person #2: _____

    Name: _____

    Injury: _____

    Injured Person #3: _____

    Name: _____

    Injury: _____

Officer Safety Considerations - SEARCHES

Following are considerations that all officers should be cognizant of when conducting a probation or parole search.

Search Considerations:
Does the lead officer have "Reasonable Suspicion" to conduct the search?
Does the lead officer have legal authorization to conduct the search?
Is conducting the search within department policy guidelines?
Does the lead officer have supervisory permission to conduct the search?
Is the "Search Operational Plan" completely filled out?
Has the lead officer put together a search team?
Does the lead officer have enough officers to safely conduct a search?
Is the Lead Officer prepared to brief police and community corrections officers?
Does each police officer and community corrections officer involved in the search have a copy of the "Search Operational Plan"?
The residence will need to be "cleared" for officer safety purposes. Is this going to be conducted by the police or community corrections staff?
Is the offender's vehicle(s) going to be searched?
Does each member of the search team understand specifically why the search is being conducted and what officers are looking for during the search?
Does each member of the search team have safety equipment on their person? [Verify]
Is each member of the search team dressed appropriately for a search?
Does each member of the search team have personal protective equipment such as gloves?
Is each member of the search team in the proper mind-set to conduct a search?
Is each member of the search team in Condition Yellow?
Is each member of the search team committed to maintaining situational awareness?

Will a search team member(s) conduct visual surveillance on the residence prior to the search?
Does each member of the search team know his/her search roles and responsibilities?
Does each member of the search team know the procedure if there is evidence of a new crime?
Does each member of the search team know the protocol for handling emergencies?
Is there a procedure in place for handling onlookers or crowds that may develop?
Is there a procedure in place for handling unrestrained dogs or potentially dangerous pets?

ure
Chapter 8: Self-Aid / Buddy-Aid

Your ability to provide self-aid may be the difference between life and death

It is Friday at 4:45PM on a beautiful sunny afternoon and you have one last unscheduled residential contact to complete before calling it a day. This should be a fast and easy contact as all you need to do is drop off a job search form and a list of companies that hire felons for an offender who recently lost his job due to the economy. The offender left you a message on your voicemail Monday morning requesting this information. Your plan is to quickly drop off the paperwork on your way home. You have OC spray and your work cell phone on your person. Your mind is on getting home to eat dinner and then going out with some friends to relax and unwind after a long week consisting of reports, endless phone calls, a busy office day, training, and five new case assignments. In other words: A typical work week!

The offender is 25 year old Kenneth "Ken" Baker who is on community supervision for theft of means of transportation and unlawful flight from law enforcement. Ken stole a car from a local shopping center parking lot. He then proceeded to take police on a high speed car chase before being apprehended after he crashed the car.

Ken successfully completed one year of juvenile probation when he was 15 years old. He was caught drinking alcohol at a party with a blood alcohol content of .24. While on juvenile probation he completed substance abuse treatment and community service.

Ken is a likable guy with charisma. He has been on your caseload for 8 months and has never had any problems. He reports on time, completed his community service, completed cognitive skills treatment, and is current on restitution payments from the damage to the vehicle he stole. Ken is an easy client to supervise as he never causes problems and does what he is supposed to do as far as his community supervision requirements are concerned.

Ken lives with his girlfriend in her house at the end of a dead end street. The house is located in a lower middle class neighborhood that is known for criminal activity. As you approach the neighborhood you remind yourself to be in Condition Yellow, scan for threats, and to park your vehicle in a tactically advantageous location. As you approach the residence you do not notice anything unusual. You wait about 20 seconds before knocking on the front door to see if you can see, hear, or smell anything out of the ordinary. Everything appears normal so you ring the doorbell. Ken answers the door and looks surprised to see you and inquires about what brings you by. You inform Ken that you received his voicemail Monday about him losing his job and that you brought a list of companies that hire felons. Ken states that he won't need the list anymore. You ask if he got a new job. Ken states that he won't be needing a job and asks you to come in for a minute. You ask if anyone else is home and Ken states that he is alone. Upon entering the residence you notice that it is unkempt which is not normal. In the corner of the living room are four black trash backs that appear to be full. You ask Ken why he won't need a job and what is going on. Ken states that his girlfriend is kicking him out and that he needs to be gone by tonight before 6:00PM when she arrives home from work. He points to the trash bags and states that they hold all of his clothes and belongings. Ken seems very agitated and starts ranting about what a bitch his girlfriend is for kicking him out. Ken starts rambling on he knows that his girlfriend cheated on him and that she probably wants to move a new guy into the house. You are standing about 3 feet from the front door and observe 4 empty cans of beer on the kitchen table. You see Ken is agitated and decide to leave. You tell Ken that you were just dropping off the paperwork to give to him and that you need to meet with your supervisor in 10 minutes. Ken, who is standing about 18 feet from you near the dining room, pulls out a large pistol from his waistband and says you are not going anywhere. You instinctively raise your hands and begin to use your verbal skills when, without warning, Ken fires the gun at you numerous times striking you in the thigh, chest, and a very minor graze to your left arm. At this point everything seems to be happening in slow motion. You heard the gun go "pop" but it was not very loud. You see Ken fumbling with the gun and he is saying something but you do not hear what he is saying. You realize the pistol has jammed so you turn to exit the front door. You see bright red blood spurting out of your thigh but feel no pain. As you attempt to get to your car you realize that your leg is not working correctly and that you can't make it to your vehicle which is parked about two houses down the street. You take cover behind a large pickup truck in front of Ken's front yard that offers you protection. Just then Ken is standing by the front door and yells that he has a rifle and will kill anyone that approaches the house.

Less than 45 seconds has passed since you were shot and taken cover behind the trucks engine block. As you sit behind cover you realize that you are losing a lot of blood from your thigh. Bright red blood is spurting from your femoral artery. Additionally, you begin to feel an incredible amount of pain in your leg and your chest. You grab your work cell phone and call 9-1-1 to say you are a probation officer and you have just been shot numerous times. You provide the address and state that the offender has a rifle and says he will shoot anyone who comes to the house. As you are talking to the 9-1-1 dispatcher you use your other hand to apply direct pressure to your leg but it is not stopping the bleeding. Now it is 90 seconds since you have been shot and your leg is continuing to spurt bright red blood at an alarming rate. Additionally, you are having difficulty breathing. You look at your chest and realize that the bullet has punctured your lung.

Officer Survival for Probation and Parole Officers

You think to yourself this was supposed to be a quick contact!

A "routine" residential contact that was supposed to be quick and easy turns brutally violent. You have been shot three times from a handgun. Even though you are in an urban environment with an average police response time of 5 minutes for a priority call you know that police and paramedics will be delayed in getting to you to provide medical care because the offender/shooter said he will fire his weapon at anyone who approaches. You are in a life or death situation where seconds can literally be the difference between living and dying. If you do not have the skills and equipment to provide self-aid you are going to die from exsanguination (severe blood loss) within minutes.

Why is this important to you? A total of 13 probation and parole officers have been violently killed in the line of duty. Of these officers: 9 (69.2%) where killed with firearms (handgun, rifle, or shotgun) and 2 (15.4%) where killed with an edged weapon for a total of 11 officers (84.6%). These officers were killed in the field 92% of the time. Firearms and edged weapons attacks can result in significant bleeding as a result of the injury. This is important to you because time will be of the essence with severe hemorrhaging and you must have the knowledge, skills, and abilities to rapidly stop such bleeding.

13 Officers Killed in the Line of Duty

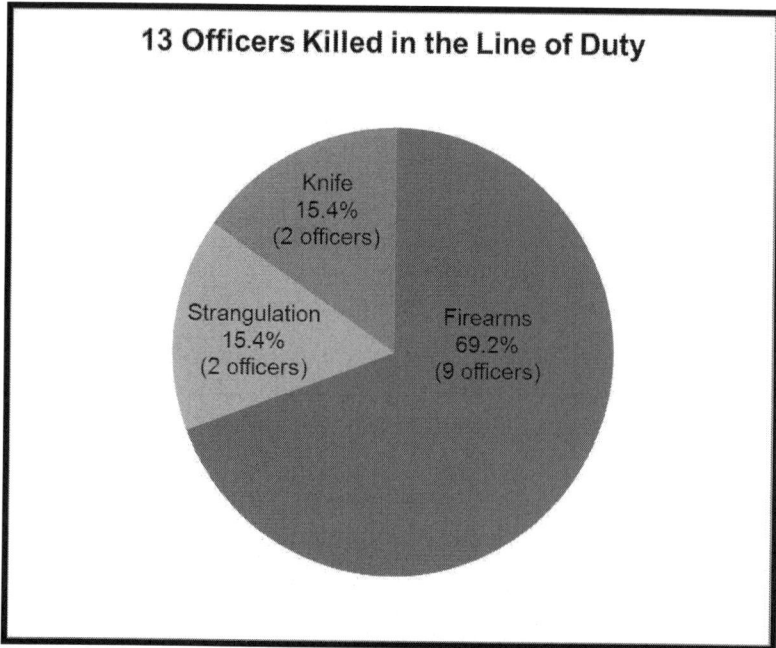

- Knife 15.4% (2 officers)
- Strangulation 15.4% (2 officers)
- Firearms 69.2% (9 officers)

Figure 1: Types of weapons used in community corrections officer deaths

Consider the following questions:

- Do you know what to do for self-aid?
- Do you carry an Individual First Aid Kit (IFAK) on your person?
- Do you know how to stop profuse arterial bleeding?
- Do you carry a tourniquet on your person?
- Do you know how to improvise an effective tourniquet?
- Do you know how to treat an open "sucking" chest wound?
- Do you have the mindset to stay in the fight despite receiving severe injuries?

Officer Survival for Probation and Parole Officers

Having the skill to perform self-aid or buddy-aid is critical. You cannot assume, even when working in an urban environment, that medical care will be able to reach your location to provide aid. In an active shooter incident law enforcement officers will move past you to hunt down the shooter. Fire department and medical personnel, who have the ability to provide lifesaving care, will be required to stage some distance away from the scene. You may be in a situation where you are being held down by gunfire which prohibits first responders from getting to you. Or, you may be the subject of a hostage situation and barricaded with the offender where you have sustained potentially life threatening injuries. Again, never assume that first responders will be capable of helping you. It is incumbent upon you to be able to provide self-aid or buddy-aid to your partner until a higher level of care will be able to provide medical assistance.

Medical care continues to improve and is constantly changing to keep up with advancements in medical research, practice, and experience. Many medical improvements, especially relating to trauma, come from the military and are then assimilated into civilian medical care. Different levels of pre-hospital medical care include:

Civilian
- Basic first aid/ Cardiopulmonary resuscitation (CPR)
- Emergency Medical Technician (EMT) - Basic Trauma Life support (BTLS)
- Paramedic - Advanced Trauma Life Support (ATLS)

Military
- Combat Lifesaver
- Combat Medics
- Tactical Combat Casualty Care (TCCC)

Law Enforcement
- Basic first aid/ Cardiopulmonary resuscitation (CPR)
- Emergency Medical Technician (EMT) - basic trauma life support (BTLS)
- Paramedic - advanced trauma life support (ATLS)
- Tactical Emergency Medical Services (TEMS) [Part of a tactical team]

There are a variety of levels and certifications of care depending on what type of environment that you work. Most probation and parole officers receive basic first aid and CPR training. Rarely taught to community corrections officers is providing self-aid and buddy-aid in a tactical environment especially when being shot at by an offender or other individual. And while this situation may be rare for community corrections officers it is potentially life threatening when it does occur. It is a situation that cannot be ignored in training. Always train for the worst case scenario; not the best case scenario! This chapter is not a rehash on what you have learned in your first aid training but discusses what you can do to save your life or the life of a fellow officer in a tactical environment. To begin it is important to understand that the role of a community corrections officer is significantly different than that of a military service member or a police officer. The main difference is that community corrections officers are not bound by the completion of a mission. Additionally, community corrections officers are not obligated to conduct contacts that are potentially dangerous.

Probation or parole officers are frequently told there is no contact that is so important that an officer should voluntarily place themselves in harm's way. On the other hand police officers and members of the military typically do not have such a luxury. They are not afforded the opportunity to leave. They have a mission that must be completed. The mission takes priority. If a probation officer had any indication that a contact with an offender would escalate into a potentially dangerous situation such as a gunfight the officer would avoid the contact. When a call comes in for "shots fired" at a residence police officers don't have the ability to tell dispatch they are going to sit this call out because it is too dangerous. When members of the military receive a mission objective they don't get to say it is too dangerous I'm not going. Probation officers and parole officers, for the most part, are fortunate that they are not mandated by their job duties to voluntarily place themselves in a dangerous environment. In fact, most are encouraged not place themselves in a dangerous situation and to remove themselves from situations that are escalating. The only exception to this may be specialized teams who are tasked with apprehending absconders or those who work on a joint task force with other law enforcement agencies. Yet, community corrections officers may find themselves in an incident where they are seriously injured and may need to provide self-aid or buddy-aid to a partner.

More than likely you have been trained in basic first aid and cardiopulmonary resuscitation. But such training rarely, if ever, discusses what actions you may need to take if the threat is still active and you, or a partner, are injured requiring medical attention. Do you know what to do when you end up in an incident where you have received injuries requiring medical attention but there is still an active threat to your safety and first responders are unable to reach you based upon the events of the situation? The military has developed Tactical Combat Causality Care (TCCC) which was originally developed for special operations command to instruct medics and personnel on how to respond to injured soldiers on the battlefield in an austere environment with the goal of completing the mission. The implementation of TCCC has been a major factor in U.S. forces having the highest casualty survival rate in history. It should be noted that research needs to be conducted to see how TCCC protocols based upon a military combat environment translates to injuries that law enforcement officers receive while performing police duties. Law enforcement, i.e. police, has begun to incorporate many aspects of TCCC into Tactical Emergency Medical Services (TEMS) to apply to a law enforcement environment. Not all police departments have adopted TEMS but many are moving down this path. In a military and law enforcement environment casualty care is often secondary to completing the mission. Remember, community corrections officers do not willingly or knowingly place themselves in harm's way and are not tasked with a mission to complete. So, when a community corrections officer finds themselves injured they are not obligated to continue with a mission to complete. If there is any mission for community corrections officers it is to extricate yourself from the danger and obtain appropriate medical care. Yet, some situations may require that you still need to engage the threat because the threat is still capable of causing you further harm. Also, you may be required to perform self-aid for life threatening injuries to yourself or perform buddy-aid for a partner especially if medical care is unable to reach your location. Has your department provided such training? If not, this chapter will provide you with basic information that will assist you with a medical emergency in a less than ideal environment.

> **The information provided in this chapter is NOT a substitute for receiving hands on training. Additionally, you should seek advice from a medical professional trained in tactical medicine who will be able to determine the needs for your department.**

Realistically, most community corrections officers work alone even though we know working with a partner is significantly safer. You must have the ability to perform self-aid when working alone and buddy-aid when working with a partner.

Officer Survival for Probation and Parole Officers

Based in data from the military preventable causes of combat death include[xxx]:

61% Hemorrhage from extremity wounds
33% Tension pneumothorax
6% Airway obstruction

Considering that 61% of preventable deaths are from extremity wound hemorrhaging it shows that a main priority is to control severe bleeding effectively and early especially when help may be delayed. <u>This is a skill that all community corrections officers must have the ability to perform.</u>

A tension pneumothorax is life threatening condition where air progressively builds up in the chest cavity typically due to a lung laceration such as from a gunshot wound or from being stabbed in the chest. Air pressure collapses the lung and pushes it on the heart. The heart becomes compressed and is not able to pump blood well which can lead to death if not treated. The treatment consists of a needle thoracostomy, also known as a needle decompression, which can be done in the field but is above the skill level of community corrections officers. A tension pneumothorax can be minimized or prevented by treating an open "sucking" chest wound with the use of an occlusive dressing. This is a skill that community corrections officers can apply. An open chest wound can be caused by the chest wall being penetrated by a bullet, knife, or other object. When a person with an open chest wound breathes, air goes in and out of the wound and may cause a "sucking" sound. Due to the distinct sound an open chest wound is often called a "sucking chest wound."

The ability to rapidly and effectively treat severe bleeding from an extremity wound and an open chest wound can increase survival rates by a significant amount. Considering this information, it is important that officers carry a first aid kit on their person so that they have the ability to treat such wounds. Oftentimes such a first aid kit is referred to as an

Individual First Aid Kit (IFAK). Contents of an IFAK will be discussed later in this chapter. Let's review some of the basics of Tactical Combat Casualty Care (TCCC) and see how the military model can be applied to community corrections officers. Note: One aspect that significantly impacts a community corrections officer is whether the officer is armed with a firearm or not. Those officers who are not armed will be significantly more restricted in their ability to neutralize an offender who is armed and shooting at you.

Three objectives of TCCC are:

1. Save preventable deaths by providing lifesaving care to the injured
2. Prevent additional casualties
3. Complete the mission

Community Corrections Application:

Priority is to save yourself and your partner. Remember, you have no "mission" that needs to be accomplished relating to offender contact. Depending on the circumstances that you are faced with your mission becomes:

- Prevent injury when possible by the use of avoidance or tactical disengagement/tactical retreat
- Stop the threat when necessary which may include the use of force up to and including lethal force
- Treat any sustained injuries to yourself
- Assist with treating injuries to your partner
- Assist with treating other innocent parties when possible
- Assist with providing aid to the offender if possible and only if it does not place you in jeopardy

Factors that influence your ability to provide care:

- Offender is firing rounds at you and/or your partner
- Lack of first aid equipment such as an IFAK

Officer Survival for Probation and Parole Officers

- Evacuation time

Community Corrections Application:

1. Your ability to provide self-aid or buddy-aid will be significantly hampered if an offender is actively shooting at you or your partner.
2. If you do not have an IFAK on your person you will need to improvise such items as a tourniquet, field dressing, or occlusive dressing.
3. If you or your partner is pinned down by gunfire then evacuation to an appropriate medical facility may be delayed.

Three Phases of Tactical Combat Casualty Care:

- **Care Under Fire:** The initial medical care provided to a casualty when operators remain under effective fire by a hostile opposition force.

   Community Corrections Application for *Care Under Fire*:

   Care rendered by yourself or your partner at the scene of the injury while still under fire from the offender or other hostile threat. The only medical equipment is what you have on your person.

- **Tactical Field Care:** The initial care provided by medical providers after effective hostile fire has ended, often in austere conditions.

   Community Corrections Application for *Tactical Field Care*:

   Care rendered by yourself or your partner but you are no longer under fire or threat. Again, the only medical equipment is what you have on your person. Community corrections officers will generally not have a medical provider with them to render aid.

- **Tactical Casualty Evacuation Care (TACEVAC):** The care provided during transport to a trauma hospital and which most closely resembles conventional civilian EMS operations.

    Community Corrections Application for *Tactical Casualty Evacuation Care*:

    Care rendered by first responder rescue personnel such as fire department, paramedics, and emergency medical technicians. Typically either an ambulance or helicopter will be used to transport you to an appropriate medical facility. Depending on the circumstances such as your proximity to a hospital you may be transported in a police vehicle, your department vehicle, or personal vehicle.

Basic Management Plan for Care Under Fire

Care Under Fire provides you with information on how to respond when a threat is still active and you or a partner have sustained an injury. It has to be reiterated that if you are not an armed officer your options during a Care Under Fire situation become very limited in your ability to stop the threat. Following are guidelines from TCCC modified for community corrections:

1. Return fire and take cover.

    Officers who are armed must do what they can to get to cover and return fire to stop the threat. As long as there is an active threat that person has the ability to cause significant injury or death to you, your partner, and innocent civilians.

    Officers who are _not_ armed must get to cover as soon as possible. If the threat continues to move to

Officer Survival for Probation and Parole Officers

your location your options are very limited. Consider weapons of opportunity that are in your immediate environment. If you have OC spray then possibly spray the area to impair the offender's vision and breathing while you move to a better form of cover. In the absence of cover, movement is your best option.

2. Direct your injured partner to remain engaged as a combatant against the offender/threat.

    If you become injured you must remain engaged against the threat unless the injury prevents such action. Never give up and never quit.

    If you are working with a partner that is injured then direct him/her to remain engaged against the threat unless their injury prevents such action.

3. Direct an injured partner to move to cover and apply self-aid if able.

    If you are working with a partner that is injured then direct him/her to move to cover to provide protection from the threat. Direct your partner to apply self-aid unless their injury prevents such action.

4. Try to keep your partner from sustaining additional wounds.

5. An injured partner should be extricated from burning vehicles or buildings and moved to places of relative safety. Do what is necessary to stop the burning process.

    Situations that may apply to community corrections include driving in a vehicle where your partner is shot which causes the vehicle to crash. The accident may start a vehicle fire which will require immediate extrication. Another example may be a methamphetamine lab that explodes or catches on fire which requires immediate evacuation from the structure.

6. Airway management is generally best deferred until the Tactical Field Care phase.

    The primary goal is to get the casualty to cover as quickly as possible and to prevent additional injuries from an active threat. Airway management should be deferred until the Tactical Field Care phase when the injured officer is safe from hostile fire.

7. Stop life-threatening external hemorrhage if tactically feasible:

    - Direct casualty to control hemorrhage by self-aid if able
    - Use a tourniquet for hemorrhage that is appropriate for tourniquet application, i.e. extremities
    - Apply the tourniquet proximal to the bleeding site, over clothing, tighten, and move the casualty to cover

The use of tourniquets has been controversial in civilian pre-hospital care settings but has been the recommended management for all life threatening hemorrhage by the military. The benefits of tourniquet use over other methods include:

- In a Care Under Fire incident it will be difficult to apply direct pressure and compression when an offender or other threat is shooting at you which can also delay your ability to move to cover. Remember, you are still being engaged from an active threat.
- Tourniquets can be applied by the injured officer (self-aid) thereby reducing the chance of your partner

Officer Survival for Probation and Parole Officers

getting injured as he attempts to get to your location to provide buddy aid.
- There are few complications with tourniquet use relating to ischemic (lack of blood supply) damage especially if in place for less than two hours.

Utilizing TCCC principles emphasizes extremity hemorrhage control over airway management for Care Under Fire. Tourniquet application to control life threatening extremity hemorrhage is the only procedure used while there is an active threat. The priorities for community corrections officers when in a Care Under Fire incident are:

- Stopping the offender from firing at you which is most effectively accomplished if you are armed
- Moving to a position of safety behind appropriate cover
- Treating severe lift-threatening bleeding

In a Care Under Fire incident you are in the "hot zone" and must maintain your situational awareness to know where the threat is at all times. Do what you can to stop the threat from injuring you which is accomplished much more easily if you are an armed officer utilizing cover. Community corrections officers who are not armed are at a significant disadvantage when faced with an armed assailant because you are limited in your response options. Regardless of whether you are armed or not it is important to scan the environment for cover. Scanning will also aid in avoiding tunnel vision so that you do not get overly focused or "missile locked" on obtaining cover to the point that you lose sight of the threat. In the absence of cover your best tactic is to keep moving as it is much more difficult to hit a dynamic moving target as opposed to a static target.

Contrary to popular misconceptions officers who receive non-lethal penetrating wounds are often not incapacitated. If you are injured while under fire you should attempt to remain engaged, take cover, provide self-aid to control severe hemorrhage and re-engage to stop the threat. If you are injured to the point that you cannot move you may need to "play" dead and possibly the threat will move on. Playing dead may be your last option in the absence of cover and without the ability to move. When safe to do so you must address severe bleeding. If you are working with a partner who is injured you may need to determine the status of the officers injuries. This should be done from a point of cover or concealment if there is still an active threat. If the officer is not treating himself you may need to relay information on what to do such as apply direct pressure to a wound or tourniquet to severe bleeding. It is also a good idea to provide encouragement so that the officer does not give up. It is important to communicate with your partner when tactically appropriate. The following box illustrates a common saying often used in TCCC:

> *Good medicine can sometimes be bad tactics;*
>
> *Bad tactics can get everyone killed.*
>
> *Doing the right thing at the right time is critical.*
>
> *Doing the right thing at the wrong time can get you killed.*

Your ability to provide pre-hospital care may be the most important factor in determining your survival or the survival of your partner. Some incidents may require that you make both medical and tactical decisions very fast especially if an offender is attempting to kill you. There is no "time-out" just because you or your partner receives an injury. The lifesaving tactics discussed in this chapter will not turn you into a paramedic but will give you the skills to provide time critical treatment. Your goal is to perform self-aid or buddy-aid to keep alive long enough to reach the hospital for more advanced medical care. It is bad enough have an offender shoot at you or attack you with a knife but this experience rapidly progresses from bad to worse if you become injured. In this situation you must maintain the combat mindset discussed earlier and never give up. Being shot, stabbed, or wounded does not mean that you are helpless, out of the fight, or dead.

Do not lie down and die. Never give up.

Basic Plan for Tactical Field Care

Tactical Field Care is care rendered by yourself or another officer once you are no longer in the line of fire and there is not an active threat. This is the time when you can conduct an appropriate assessment and more thoroughly treat injuries based upon your skill level and safety gear that you have on your person. Keep in mind that the military has combat medics available to provide aid and some law enforcement agencies have tactical emergency medical services (TEMS) personnel assigned to SWAT units. Community corrections officers will not have this type of medical backup readily available. The medical equipment you have will consist of the first aid kit you carry or whatever you are able to improvise based on your clothing or what is available in the immediate environment. For example, if you do not have a commercially made tourniquet you may have to improvise one from a belt or other item of clothing. Death from exsanguination (severe blood loss) due to an extremity injury is preventable but requires quick and effective action to stop the bleeding. It would be a travesty to lose a community corrections officer because he bled to death due to a severe extremity wound. Your goal at this stage is to stay alive by treating life-threatening injuries until paramedic units arrive and can transport you and/or your partner to an appropriate medical facility. If you work in a remote area that requires a long travel time by ground ambulance to a hospital then first responders should immediately put an air ambulance helicopter on standby. If your injuries are non-life threatening the helicopter can always be cancelled.

Being shot or severely injured will cause your body to have both psychological and physiological responses that can negatively impact your ability to respond to the situation. It is critical that you maintain focus to control these responses so that you can cognitively process what actions to take to keep yourself or your partner alive. This is especially true in a care under fire incident. Remember to use the breathing exercises taught earlier in this book. It is important to breathe and not hold your breath during periods of extreme stress.

In a **Tactical Field Care** situation you are no longer under effective hostile fire. You now have the opportunity to perform self-aid or buddy-aid when working with a partner. Keep in mind that the situation can change and you end up back in a Care Under Fire situation. Because events can change it is important to maintain situational awareness of your environment. Following are guidelines from TCCC modified for community corrections:

1. If your partner has an altered mental status and is armed with a firearm you should disarm your partner immediately.

    An altered mental status can be the result of shock, hypoxia, or brain injury. Officers with an altered mental status may lose the ability to cognitively process information and become incapable of using proper judgment about threats. These officers should be immediately disarmed and their weapon rendered safe.

2. Airway Management – Airway intervention does not need to be addressed if the officer is conscious and breathing well on her own.

    a. Unconscious officer without airway obstruction:
      - Chin lift or jaw thrust maneuver
      - Nasopharyngeal airway (NPA) - generally well tolerated if consciousness

is regained. Training should be received prior to using a NPA.
- Place in recovery position

b. Casualty with airway obstruction or impending airway obstruction:
- Chin lift or jaw thrust maneuver
- Nasopharyngeal airway
- Allow casualty to assume any position that best protects the airway, to include sitting up
- Place unconscious casualty in recovery position

For both situations a. and b. listed above officers would benefit to receive training on the proper procedure to insert a nasopharyngeal airway which is a tube designed to be inserted into the nasal passageway to secure an open airway. As in a Care Under Fire incident, cervical spine immobilization is generally not required for penetrating injuries and assumes a lower priority than caring for massive hemorrhage or airway obstruction. Cervical spine immobilization should be considered for blunt trauma injuries. If the previous airway management techniques are not effective then the casualty will need treatment from a responder trained with a higher level of care and who can perform an intubation or cricothyroidotomy. Intubation is the placement of a flexible plastic tube into the trachea (windpipe) to maintain an open airway so that the patient can be properly ventilated. A cricothyroidotomy is an emergency surgical procedure in which a hole is cut through a membrane in the patient's neck into the windpipe in order to allow air into the lungs. **Such techniques should never be attempted by untrained individuals.**

Utilization of the recovery position helps a semiconscious or unconscious person breathe and permits fluids such as blood, mucous, or vomit to drain from the nose and throat so they are not breathed in. This position should not be used if the officer has a back or neck injury.

3. Breathing

    a. Treat all open "sucking" chest wounds (open pneumothorax) with an occlusive dressing and secure it in place over the wound.

    b. If a tension pneumothorax develops the officer will need a needle chest decompression performed by a paramedic or other medical provider. A tension pneumothorax is a life threatening development that is preventable if higher level medical care can get to the officer in a timely manner.

4. Bleeding

    a. Use a tourniquet to control life threatening hemorrhage that is amenable to tourniquet application.

    b. For hemorrhaging that is not amenable to tourniquet application use a hemostatic agent such as Combat Gauze applied with direct pressure for a minimum of three minutes. A hemostatic agent is a substance that stops bleeding. The most common form of hemostatic agents used in a field setting are dressing, powder, and granules.

    c. Control other significant bleeding that has not previously been addressed.

Individual First Aid Kit (IFAK)

Law enforcement officers carry a firearm because the need may arise when they will have to use their weapon against a violent offender. They wear body armor just in case they are shot. They also wear seat belts in case they are in an automobile accident. Officers take precautions to minimize the risks of bad things that may occur. Statistically most officers never fire their duty weapon or get shot. Unfortunately too many officers are killed in vehicular accidents. The point being that bad things can and do happen to officers. And whether they are statistically relevant or not officers should take precautions for those times when you become the statistic. Carrying an Individual First Aid Kit (IFAK) is one of those items you hope to never have to use but should the need occur the kit can literally save your life, your partner, or a civilian.

> **An Individual First Aid Kit (IFAK) is designed to enable community corrections officers to treat potentially life-threatening traumatic injuries typically associated with gunshot and stab wounds.**

There are literally dozens of commercially available IFAK's on the market that go by a variety of different names such as: Individual Patrol Officer Kit (IPOK™), Patrol Trauma Pak, Operator IFAK, Basic Life Support Tactical Operator Response Kit (BLS TORK™), Advanced Patrol Officer's Trauma Kit, Patrol Officer's Pocket Trauma Kit, Police Academy Personal Trauma Kit, Tactical First Response Kit, etc. The list goes on and there are many choices to choose from when it comes to your medical kit. Some are good quality while others are lacking. When it comes to your IFAK I cannot stress enough the importance of only carrying quality components. Remember, the kit you carry may save your life one day so don't skimp. Before we discuss IFAK components lets discuss what an IFAK is not.

An IFAK is not a "boo-boo" kit designed to treat minor injuries such as cuts, scrapes, blisters, hang nails, sore muscles, or a bloody nose. It is not a place for an assortment of Band-Aids or over the counter medications for pain, allergies, cramps, or headaches. If you are required to take prescription medication throughout the day or as needed those medications would not be included in your IFAK. While the items mentioned do not belong in your IFAK you should have a separate kit to keep such items that will probably be utilized with some regularity. This separate kit can be kept in your work desk, gear bag, or vehicle. Your IFAK is reserved specifically for the treatment of life-threatening injuries.

IFAK Considerations

Choosing an IFAK is an important decision because the time that you need to use the kit will be under the "worst case scenario" when either your life or another person's life is at risk. You will be impacted from both psychological and physiological reactions to stress that were discussed previously. To make matters worse is that 'time is of the essence' when treating a life-threatening injury such as a severe hemorrhage. Having a quality kit along with the knowledge of how to use each component will give you piece of mind should you ever need to treat yourself or another person.

When choosing an IFAK you can buy one that is a commercially available pre-made IFAK or you can purchase items individually and create a kit to your own specifications.

Officer Survival for Probation and Parole Officers

Following are some considerations when choosing or building an IFAK:

Cost:	Basic kits can be very inexpensive but tend to lack needed items. Comprehensive kits will cost more and provide higher quality components.
Quality & Effectiveness	There are many companies that make products that can be placed in an IFAK but not all are equally effective. I recommend only using the highest quality most effective items. For example, there is no sense in having a tourniquet that is small and compact yet will not stop a major hemorrhage.
Size	The more comprehensive your IFAK the larger it will be. Smaller kits tend to lack important components. You will need to find a balance that fits your needs. Sometimes this is easier said than done.
Portability	Whatever IFAK you choose you must commit to carrying it with you at all times as it serves you no good in your desk or vehicle.
Maintenance	Any items that are used will need to be immediately replaced. Some components may have expiration dates.

Training It is important to train with each component of your kit so that you are completely familiar with its use and functionality. This may require that you purchase duplicate items so that you can train and become proficient with each component. Also, some items such as a Nasopharyngeal Airway (NPA) may require that you attend formal training or certification in its use.

As with wearing body armor officers easily come up with many excuses not to carry an IFAK. Excuses such as: it is too big, too cumbersome, I will never need it, no one else carries one, it is too expensive, I will wait for paramedics, I hate the sight of blood, etc. Such excuses will fail to serve you well during a crisis. There is no better substitute for having a high quality IFAK during an emergency requiring immediate and effective treatment. Ultimately you have to decide what components to put in your kit and must accept the consequences if you choose not to have a comprehensive IFAK or if you choose not to carry a kit at all.

IFAK Components

As previously stated there are many commercially available IFAK's. Some are small and compact but lack necessary items such as a quality tourniquet, an occlusive dressing, or hemostatic agent. A comprehensive kit is larger and more expensive but will effectively treat major traumatic injuries from a gunshot wound or a severe cut from an edged weapon. At a minimum an IFAK must be able to effectively and quickly address severe hemorrhage to an extremity which is the leading causes of death.

Following are components that I believe should be an integral part of an IFAK:

Tourniquet

It is possible to bleed to death from an injury to a major artery such as the femoral artery in 3-5 minutes. A high quality tourniquet is essential. I recommend the following tourniquets:

1. Combat Application Tourniquet (C-A-T) [Primary choice]

2. SOF Tactical Tourniquet (SOFTT) [Secondary choice]

Pressure Dressing

Pressure dressings must have the ability to actually exert pressure on the wound to assist with stopping the bleeding. They can also function as an improvised tourniquet, wrap, or sling to immobilize an appendage. I recommend the following pressure dressings:

1. Emergency Trauma Dressing, 4 or 6 inch by North American Rescue [Primary choice]

2. Israeli Bandage (Israeli Battle Dressing), 4 or 6 inch [Secondary choice]

Hemostatic Agent

Hemostatic agents are used on bleeding that is not amenable to tourniquet application. There are many different types and brands of hemostatic agents currently available. New and more effective agents are currently being researched.

I recommend the following hemostatic agent:

1. QuikClot Combat Gauze [Primary choice]

Chest Seal

Rapid treatment of an open pneumothorax (sucking chest wound) by forming a seal with help the downed officer breathe easier.

I recommend the following chest seals:

1. Hyfin Vented Chest Seal [Primary choice]

2. Asherman Chest Seal [Secondary choice]

3. Bolin Chest Seal [Tertiary choice]

Nasopharyngeal Airway (NPA)

To be used on an unconscious or semi-conscious individual. Use of an NPA typically requires formal training and should not be used without such training.

I recommend the following NPA:

Nasopharyngeal Airway (28 Fr.) with Surgilube by Rusch [Primary choice]

Gloves

Gloves are essential to protect from bloodborne pathogens.

I recommend the following personal protective gloves:

Black Talon Nitrile Gloves [Primary choice]

Keep in mind that the above list is subject to change based on new products that are developed or current products that are improved. It is important to conduct some research to find which components will suit your needs best and then train with your IFAK so that you are familiar with each item that you carry. You can also purchase a pre-made commercially available IFAK and modify it to your needs.

Proper Use of IFAK Components

Tourniquet

Recommended Tourniquet: Combat Application Tourniquet (C-A-T). The C-A-T is a one-handed windlass tourniquet that can completely occlude arterial blood flow in both an upper or lower extremity.

Tourniquets are used to control <u>severe</u> external hemorrhage from an extremity due to a traumatic injury such as a gunshot wound, knife wound, explosive device, or amputation. Major bleeding occurs when an artery is cut or damaged which can result in death within 3-5 minutes. Your ability to stop major arterial bleeding is critical even when working in an urban environment and emergency services are available and capable of providing aid in a relatively short period of time. Assuming that paramedics are able to treat you within 5-6 minutes still means that you may have lost a substantial amount of blood leaving you in critical condition. The average adult contains approximately 5 liters of blood so it is important to keep every precious drop of blood in your body. An arterial bleed is evidenced by bright red blood that spurts out while a venous bleed is dark in color and flows out but does not spurt. Arteries carry oxygenated blood throughout the body while veins carry deoxygenated blood back to the lungs to pick up oxygen. The major artery in the arm is the brachial artery and the major artery in the leg is the femoral artery.

There was a time when utilization of a tourniquet was the last possible option which was highly discouraged and the belief was that the limb would be lost although a life would be saved. Much research has been done which clearly indicates that this is not the case and that tourniquets can be used in a safe manner over a prolonged period of time (6+

hours) without limb damage. There is a well-documented case of tourniquet application that was applied for 16 continuous hours without loss of the limb. According to a study on tourniquet use on combat casualties it states, *"Of tourniquets evaluated in this work, the CAT is the best prehospital tourniquet...*[xxxi]*"*

Remember that in a Care Under Fire situation you will only address severe extremity bleeding and that tourniquet application is your first choice of control for such life-threatening bleeding. Do not attempt direct pressure, pressure dressing, or any other type of hemorrhage control. Go directly to a tourniquet to control life-threatening bleeding. Survival rates are improved when tourniquets are applied before the patient goes into shock. Tourniquets should **not** be used for wounds with minor bleeding. Non-life-threatening bleeding should be ignored until the Tactical Field Care phase.

Tourniquets are to be applied approximately 2-3 inches above the wound and never placed directly on the wound. Tourniquets should not be placed directly over the knee or elbow. The tourniquet can be placed over clothing if necessary but it is best if clothing is removed. Do not place a tourniquet over a cargo pocket that contains bulky items. Once applied the distal pulse should be check to verify that the tourniquet is tight enough. If you still can feel a pulse then tighten the tourniquet more. A second tourniquet can be applied directly above the first tourniquet to control bleeding.

Common mistakes with tourniquet application include:

- Failure to apply a tourniquet when it is needed
- Waiting too long to apply the tourniquet
- Failure to tighten it enough to eliminate the distal pulse

- Utilizing a tourniquet for minimal bleeding that does not require a tourniquet
- Applying the tourniquet too high on the limb
- Removing the tourniquet prematurely (generally you will have a medical professional remove the tourniquet at a medical facility)

When utilizing a tourniquet pain and discomfort is to be expected. It is important to understand that pain and discomfort does not indicate that the tourniquet was incorrectly applied and it does not mean that it should be removed. Utilization of a tourniquet is necessary to save your life or the life of your partner.

Hemostatic Agent

Recommended Hemostatic Agent is the QuikClot Combat Gauze. This product does not produce heat as some of the older hemostatic agents. QuikClot Combat Gauze is highly effective in stopping bleeding, is safe, has no known contraindications, and has a three year self-life. This product is simple and easy to use with the added benefit that the product instructions are written directly on the package. You must apply direct pressure for a minimum of three minutes when using Combat Gauze.

Pressure Dressing

Recommended Pressure Dressing is the Emergency Trauma Dressing (ETD), 4 or 6 inch by North American Rescue. The ETD is a sterile dressing used for applying direct pressure. The North American Rescue website has a video of proper use of this pressure dressing which is viewable at:
http://www.narescue.com/portal.aspx?CN=3628A28F222B&BC=DAD06AB67C9C

Chest Seal

Recommended is the Hyfin Vented Chest Seal. This seal is a 6"x6" occlusive dressing used for the treatment of penetrating injuries to the chest. Treatment of an open "sucking" chest wound (open pneumothorax) consists of covering the wound during expiration (breathing out) with an occlusive dressing. An occlusive dressing should extend a minimum of two inches past the edge of the wound to provide the best seal possible. There are many commercially available products that have very functional adhesive properties to seal the wound. Following are some of the more popular chest seals on the market: Hyfin, Asherman, Bolin, and Halo. The wound should be sealed on all four sides and the officer should then be placed in a sitting position if there are no other injuries. Application of an occlusive dressing should improve the officers breathing. The officer should then be monitored for the development of a tension pneumothorax which can result in increasingly difficulty breathing. If a tension pneumothorax develops the injured officer will need a needle decompression which needs to be performed by a person with appropriate medical training.

If there is a knife in the chest or other part of the body do not remove it. Leave in in place and attempt to secure it with dressings so that the knife does not move and cause further injury.

The North American Rescue website has a video of proper use of this chest seal which is viewable at:

http://www.narescue.com/Portal.aspx?CN=1BB57448570E

Nasopharyngeal Airway (NPA)

While insertion of a Nasopharyngeal Airway is not a difficult skill it is also best that you receive professional hands on training in its application. It is also important to know that there are some contraindications for using a NPA which will be covered in training.

Summary

Training for the worst case scenario is a must. Officers need the knowledge, skills, and abilities to know what to do if they receive an injury but there is still an active threat who is actively engaged in trying to hurt or kill you. A severe hemorrhage can lead to death within a matter of minutes. Your ability to provide self-care and buddy care for a partner may be what keeps you or your partner alive until a higher level of medical care can assist. Unarmed officers are severely limited in their ability to stop an active threat in a care under fire incident. Departments that currently do not issue firearms to officers really need to re-evaluate their stance on this issue. Officers must also have training that goes into more depth than basic first aid and CPR. Basic first aid training is really training geared toward the best case scenario while care under fire training is the training for the worst case scenario. Officers must not only have the skills to treat severe bleeding and chest wounds but they must also carry a quality Individual First Aid Kit on their person.

Practical Exercises

Following are a list of practical exercises to expose you to some of the concepts in this chapter. Each scenario can be modified in any way that meets your needs or the needs of your department. These exercises should be performed under proper medical and tactical guidance. I cannot stress enough the importance of receiving proper medical training on first aid, CPR, CCR, AED, and use of a tourniquet, nasopharyngeal airway, chest seal, and hemostatic agents.

Never perform medical care that is above your level of training as you are placing the patient in danger and can potentially be held liable for your actions.

Remember the mantra: **Do no harm.**

> **NOTICE: THE INFORMATION PRESENTED IN THIS CHAPTER SHOULD NOT BE CONSIDERED MEDICAL TRAINING OR ADVICE AND IT DOES NOT PROVIDE ANY LEVEL OF CERTIFICATION.**
>
> **TO RECEIVE SUCH TRAINING CONSULT WITH A PROFESSIONAL MEDICAL ORGANIZATION THAT OFFERS TRAINING AND CERTIFICATION IN THESE SKILLS. THE AUTHOR ASSUMES NO LIABILITY FOR ACTIONS OR CARE THAT YOU PROVIDE WHICH MAY BE ABOVE YOUR LEVEL OF TRAINING.**

Officer Survival for Probation and Parole Officers

Practical Exercise 1: Evaluation Sheet
[UNARMED OFFICERS]

Scenario:

In this scenario you are the "cover" officer for your partner who is the "primary" officer. You and your partner practice the "contact/cover" principle.

The primary officer, who is your partner, is conducting a residential contact at the home of an offender. The home is a typical single story residence located in an urban environment. The primary officer is having the offender sign a document on the kitchen table. The offender is sitting down and the primary officer is standing. The offender signs the document then stands up to hand the document to the officer. As the officer reaches for the document with his right hand the offender pulls out a knife and slashes the officer in his right bicep. The primary officer's arm is spurting bright red blood and he is not able to move his arm.

As the cover officer what action do you take?

Primary Officer Gear:
OC Spray, Handcuffs, Tactical Flashlight, Individual First Aid Kit (IFAK), Department Issued Radio and cell phone, personal cell phone

Cover Officer Gear:
OC Spray, Handcuffs, Tactical Flashlight, Individual First Aid Kit (IFAK), Department Issued Radio and cell phone, personal cell phone

Performance Activities for Cover Officer:	Complete	Incomplete
- Takes appropriate action to stop the threat?		
- Presses the emergency button on the radio?		
- Moves primary officer away from the offender to a safe location?		
- Performs an accurate patient assessment?		
- Does not cause further injury to primary officer?		

	Yes	No
- Rapidly identifies a brachial artery hemorrhage and utilizes a tourniquet?		
- Correctly applied tourniquet?		
- Tourniquet properly placed above wound?		
- Tourniquet applied until bleeding controlled?		
- Application time for applying tourniquet: _____		
- Secured tourniquet securely and annotated time of application:		

Officer Survival for Probation and Parole Officers

Practical Exercise 2: Evaluation Sheet
[ARMED OFFICERS]

Scenario:

In this scenario you are the "cover" officer for your partner who is the "primary" officer. You and your partner practice the "contact/cover" principle.

The primary officer, who is your partner, is conducting a residential contact at the home of an offender. The home is a typical single story residence located in an urban environment. The primary officer is having the offender sign a document on the kitchen table. The offender is sitting down and the primary officer is standing. The offender signs the document then stands up to hand the document to the officer. As the officer reaches for the document with his right hand the offender pulls out a six shot revolver shooting the officer in the chest 5 times and once in the thigh. The officer was wearing body armor so the five rounds to the chest did not penetrate the body armor. The primary officer falls to the ground and his leg is spurting bright red blood.

As the cover officer what action do you take?

Primary Officer Gear:
Firearm, 2 Spare Magazines, Expandable Baton, OC Spray, Handcuffs, Tactical Flashlight, Body Armor, Individual First Aid Kit (IFAK), Department Issued Radio

Cover Officer Gear:
Firearm, 2 Spare Magazines, Expandable Baton, OC Spray, Handcuffs, Tactical Flashlight, Body Armor, Individual First Aid Kit (IFAK), Department Issued Radio

Performance Activities for Cover Officer:	Complete	Incomplete
- Takes appropriate action to stop the threat?		
- Presses the emergency button on the radio?		
- Performs an accurate patient assessment?		
- Does not cause further injury to primary officer?		

Scott Kirshner

		Yes	No
-	Rapidly identifies a femoral artery hemorrhage and utilizes a tourniquet?		
-	Correctly applies tourniquet?		
-	Tourniquet properly placed above wound?		
-	Tourniquet applied until bleeding controlled?		
-	Application time for applying tourniquet: _____		
-	Secured tourniquet securely and annotated time of application:		

Officer Survival for Probation and Parole Officers

Practical Exercise 3: Evaluation Sheet
[ARMED OFFICERS]

Scenario:

In this scenario you are the "cover" officer for your partner who is the "primary" officer. You and your partner practice the "contact/cover" principle.

The primary officer, who is your partner, is conducting an offender contact at the offender's place of employment. You have a working relationship with the employer because he hires numerous offenders who have felony convictions. The employer was a former offender who spent 10 years in prison for armed robbery but has turned his life around. When you arrive the boss states that the offender is in the break room.

Unknowingly you and your partner enter the break room as the offender is selling a bag of methamphetamine to another employee. The offender turns around and sees your partner. The offender, without saying a word, pulls out a semi-automatic pistol and shoots the primary officer once in the side of the chest and then runs out the door to escape. The employee who was buying the drugs goes to the ground and is compliant. The primary officer immediately collapses to the ground and is gasping for air.

As the cover officer what action do you take?

Primary Officer Gear:

Firearm, 2 Spare Magazines, Expandable Baton, OC Spray, Handcuffs, Tactical Flashlight, Body Armor, Individual First Aid Kit (IFAK), Department Issued Radio

Cover Officer Gear:

Firearm, 2 Spare Magazines, Expandable Baton, OC Spray, Handcuffs, Tactical Flashlight, Body Armor, Individual First Aid Kit (IFAK), Department Issued Radio

Performance Activities for Cover Officer:	Complete	Incomplete
- Takes appropriate action to stop the threat?		
- Presses the emergency button on the radio?		
- Performs an accurate patient assessment?		
- Does not cause further injury to primary officer?		
	Yes	No
- Rapidly identifies an open chest wound and utilizes a chest seal?		
- Correctly applies chest seal?		
- Positions the officer either in a sitting position or on his side with the injured side next to the ground?		
- Treats for shock?		

Officer Survival for Probation and Parole Officers

Practical Exercise 4: Evaluation Sheet
[ARMED OFFICER]

Scenario:

In this scenario you are an armed officer conducting office day in the probation/parole office. You are alone in your office and finishing some paperwork before going to lunch with some co-workers. It is 11:49AM when you hear multiple gunshots in the office from what appears to be a rifle. Seconds later you hear loud blood curling screams. You hear four gunshots from a pistol and then hear another officer yell, "*I got the shooter. The shooter is down.*" Your firearm is out of your holster as you cautiously walk to the location of the shooter who is obviously deceased. It is now 11:51 and the incident is over.

You see an offender that is shot once in the chest. She is a female about 32 years old, thin build, conscious, but having difficulty breathing. Another officer says 9-1-1 has been called and police, fire, and EMS are responding.

What action do you take?

Officer Gear:

Firearm, 2 Spare Magazines, Expandable Baton, OC Spray, Handcuffs, Tactical Flashlight, Body Armor, Individual First Aid Kit (IFAK), Department Issued Radio

Performance Activities:	Complete	Incomplete	N/A
- Takes appropriate action to stop the threat?			
- Presses the emergency button on the radio?			
- Performs an accurate patient assessment?			
	Yes	No	
- Rapidly identifies an open chest wound and utilizes a chest seal?			
- Correctly applies chest seal?			
- Positions the offender either in a sitting position or on her side with the injured side next to the ground?			
- Treats for shock?			

Scott Kirshner

Practical Exercise 5: Evaluation Sheet
[UNARMED OFFICER]

Scenario:

In this scenario you are an unarmed officer working in a federal courthouse. Today is your office day to see offenders on your caseload.

A probationer, who went through the court screening process, is waiting in the lobby to see his PO. This offender is calmly sitting by the door that PO's use to call back their offenders. A PO, who you are friends with, goes to the lobby to call his offender. As he opens the door this offender stabs him two times in the upper thigh with a very strong and sharp polymer plastic knife with a 6 inch long blade. This incident occurs in less than one second. After your friend and fellow officer is stabbed the offender drops the knife, runs out of the lobby, and leaves the building.

You are standing right behind the officer who got stabbed because you were going to call your offender back to your office. The officer who got stabbed falls to the floor in pain as he is grabbing his upper thigh which is bleeding. The injury is too high on the thigh to use a tourniquet.

What action do you take?

Officer Gear:

Firearm, 2 Spare Magazines, Expandable Baton, OC Spray, Handcuffs, Tactical Flashlight, Body Armor, Individual First Aid Kit (IFAK), Department Issued Radio

Performance Activities:	Complete	Incomplete	N/A
- Takes appropriate action to stop the threat?			
- Presses the emergency button on the radio?			
- Performs an accurate patient assessment?			

Officer Survival for Probation and Parole Officers

	Yes	No	
- Exposed the injury by cutting away the officer's clothes?			
- Opened the sterile Combat Gauze package?			
- Placed the Combat Gauze directly into the wound where the bleeding was the heaviest?			
- Held pressure for **3** minutes?			
- Reassess the wound to ensure that bleeding has stopped – leaves the Combat Gauze in place if bleeding is controlled.			
- Applied a sterile pressure dressing over the bandage to security it in place?			

Scott Kirshner

Practical Exercise 6: Evaluation Sheet
[UNARMED OFFICER]

Scenario:

In this scenario you are an armed officer conducting a random visit to a sex offender treatment group class with 15 offenders. Two offenders you supervise attend this group twice a week and you are there only to observe and not participate in any manner. You are sitting toward the back of the room to create some space between you and the group class. What you do not know is that before you entered the group another offender went to the restroom. This is an offender you supervised years ago who was sentenced to prison for 5 years on a probation violation for having contact with children at a school. This offender harbors resentment for you because you held him accountable which resulted in a prison sentence. This offender sneaks behind you and as you turn around you are hit in the forehead with a chair. You have a large cut on your forehead that is significantly bleeding. You are dizzy but do not lose consciousness and blood is pouring onto your face obscuring your vision.

What action do you take?

Officer Gear:

OC Spray, Handcuffs, Body Armor, Individual First Aid Kit (IFAK)

Performance Activities:	Complete	Incomplete	N/A
- Takes appropriate action to stop the threat?			
- Presses the emergency button on the radio?			
- Performs an accurate patient assessment?			
	Yes	No	
- Opened the sterile Combat Gauze package?			
- Placed the Combat Gauze directly into the wound where the bleeding was the heaviest?			
- Held pressure for **3** minutes?			
- Reassess the wound to ensure that bleeding has stopped – leaves the Combat Gauze in place if bleeding is controlled.			
- Applied a sterile pressure dressing over the bandage to security it in place?			

About The Author

Scott Kirshner, M.Ed., has held many positions within the criminal justice system and has extensive experience in officer safety and survival. He has been a Correctional Officer, Probation Officer, Supervisory Probation Officer, and a Parole Administrator. Throughout his career he was an officer survival instructor and was integral in the development and implementation of officer safety curriculum for two large agencies. He served as a Certified Firearms Instructor, Lead Defensive Tactics instructor, and has a black belt in three martial arts. He taught classes on: Use of Force, Tactical Mindset, Applied Defensive Tactics, Low-light Shooting, Force-on-Force, Judgmental Shooting, Verbal De-escalation, Safety Policies, and other courses. He has consulted and provided training for probation and court departments on staff safety. Mr. Kirshner has worked with numerous municipal, county, state, and federal law enforcement agencies relating to probation and parole. He has trained with the FBI SWAT Team – Phoenix Division, Phoenix Police Department, SureFire Institute, Pro-Active Training Institute, Pima County Sheriff's Department, and many other government and private agencies on topics to include: officer survival, active shooter intervention, force-on-force training, shoot house instructor, terrorism, weapons of mass destruction, building searches, school violence, workplace violence, flashbang operator, tactical scouting, and others. He has also received specialized training on the topics of: Sex Offenders, Domestic Violence Offenders, Mental Health Offenders, Critical Incident Stress Debriefing, Motivational Interviewing, Risk and Needs Assessments, Public Information Officer training, numerous leadership schools, Faculty Skills Development, Advanced Faculty

Skills Development, and Curriculum & Lesson Plan Development.

Mr. Kirshner has received Supervisor of the Year, Exceptional Service Award, Director's Team Award, Trainer Excellence Award, Letters of Commendation, and was nominated for Officer of the Year on two occasions. He has a Master's of Education Degree in Counseling and a Bachelor of Science in Business Management. He is currently the Curriculum and Training Coordinator for one of the largest court systems in the United States.

The author can be contacted at: officersurvival@cox.net

You can also visit the **Officer Survival for Probation and Parole Officers** Facebook page at:

https://www.facebook.com/CommitToWin

References

Chapter 1

[i] Data from the Bureau of Justice Statistics, December 2010, NCJ231681
http://bjs.ojp.usdoj.gov/content/pub/pdf/cpus09.pdf
[ii] Estimates were rounded to the nearest 100 and include some offenders held in a prison or jail but who remained under the jurisdiction of a probation or parole agency.
[iii] Source: Bureau of Justice Statistics Correctional Surveys
[iv] Data from the Bureau of Justice Statistics, December 2010, NCJ231674
http://bjs.ojp.usdoj.gov/content/pub/pdf/ppus09.pdf
[v] Data from the Bureau of Justice Statistics, December 2010, NCJ231674
http://bjs.ojp.usdoj.gov/content/pub/pdf/ppus09.pdf
[vi] Data from the Office of Juvenile Justice and Delinquency Prevention
http://www.ojjdp.gov/ojstatbb/probation/qa07102.asp
[vii] Some information used with permission from the Officer Down Memorial Page: www.odmp.org/
[viii] It is unclear if Officer McReynolds was making a residential contact so he is not included in this section, therefore the percentage will not total to 100%.
[ix] http://www.csc-scc.gc.ca/text/pblct/ci-report05-06/report-eng.pdf

Chapter 2

[x] Howe, Paul (2011). Leadership and Training for the Fight: Using Special Operations Principles to Succeed in Law Enforcement, Business, and War.
[xi] 1990, Worker Safety in Probation and Parole
[xii] 1999, U.S. Probation and Pretrial Statistics
[xiii] 1999, U.S. Probation and Pretrial Statistics

[xiv] Uniform Crime Report, Law Enforcement Officers Killed and Assaulted, 2011

[xv] The remaining three officers were killed with a vehicle that was used as a weapon

[xvi] Law Enforcement Officers Feloniously Killed, 2000-2009, Note: due to rounding percentages the total may not add up to 100.0

[xvii] Law Enforcement Officers Feloniously Killed: Age Group of Victim Officer, 2000-2009

[xviii] Law Enforcement Officers Feloniously Killed: Years of Service of Victim Officer, 2000-2009

[xix] http://www2.fbi.gov/ucr/killed/2009/data/figure_05.html

Chapter 3

[xx] Remsberg, Charles (1986). The Tactical Edge: Surviving High-Risk Patrol

[xxi] Department of the Army FM 1-02 (September 2004). Operational Terms and Graphics.

[xxii] Artwohl, Alexis and Christensen, Loren (1997). Deadly Force Encounters: What Cops Need to Know to Mentally and Physically Prepare for and Survive a Gunfight.

[xxiii] Siddle, Bruce (1995). Sharpening The Warrior's Edge: The Psychology & Science of Training.

Chapter 4

[xxiv] The X26 is a trademark of TASER International, Inc., and TASER® and ADVANCED TASER® are trademarks of TASER International, Inc., registered in the U.S. All rights reserved.

[xxv] Miller, William and Rollnick, Stephen (2002). Motivational Interviewing: Preparing People for Change, 2nd Edition.

[xxvi] Graham v. Connor, 490 U.S. 386, 396-97 (1989)

Chapter 5

[xxvii] http://www.readyhoustontx.gov/videos.html

Chapter 6

[xxviii] The calculation is: 20 minutes ÷ 43,200 minutes = 4.6296 x 100 = .046. Rounded up = .05.
[xxix] Staff Safety Training Program, Federal Judicial Center, Staff Safety Curriculum Planning Committee, 1986

Chapter 8

[xxx] Bellamy RF. "The Causes of Death in Conventional Land Warfare: Implications for Combat Casualty Care Research." Mil Med 1984
[xxxi] Kragh JF. "Practical Use of Emergency Tourniquets to Stop Bleeding in Major Limb Trauma." The Journal of TRAUMA Injury, Infection, and Critical Care, February Supplement 2008

Made in the USA
San Bernardino, CA
26 December 2014